VOICE THERAPY FOR CHILDREN

The Elementary School Years

MOYA L. ANDREWS
Indiana University

This book was developed
under the advisory editorship of
Donnell F. Johns,
Director of Clinical Research,
Division of Plastic Surgery,
The University of Texas Health Science Center at Dallas

Longman
New York & London

Executive Editor: Gordon T.R. Anderson
Production Editor: Pamela Nelson
Text Design: Nina Tallarico
Cover Design: Laura Ierardi
Text Art: Nina Tallarico
Photos: Clifton Hess
Production Supervisor: Eduardo Castillo
Compositor: Graphicraft

Voice Therapy for Children

Longman Inc.
95 Church Street
White Plains, N.Y. 10601

Associated companies:
Longman Group Ltd., London
Longman Cheshire Pty., Melbourne
Longman Paul Pty., Auckland
Copp Clark Pitman, Toronto
Copp Clark Publishing Inc., Boston

Library of Congress Cataloging in Publication Data
Andrews, Moya L.
  Voice therapy for children.

  Bibliography: p.
  1. Voice disorders in children—Treatment. I. Title.
[DNLM: 1. Voice—in infancy & childhood. 2. Voice Training—in infancy & childhood. WV 500 A568v]
RF511.C45A53 1986   616.85′506   85-24085
ISBN 0-582-28476-7

85 86 87 88 9 8 7 6 5 4 3 2 1

Contents

Preface

Inappropriate vocal behavior may negatively affect an individual's performance in many areas of life. Such a handicap, however, may not be fully understood by the afflicted person or by teachers and concerned relatives. It is not usual in our society for listeners to acknowledge explicitly that their general reactions to a person may be related to the sound of his or her voice. For example, a teacher may not say directly, "The fact that your voice is unusual affects your grades on oral reports" even if this is indeed the case. The penalty is exacted, but the explanation is withheld because of politeness or lack of understanding. Any handicap, however subtle, that restricts options and limits the achievement of full potential, warrants attention.

Elementary school children would seem to be ideal candidates for voice therapy. During these years children appear to enjoy experimenting with different ways of expressing themselves. They are usually eager for genuine attention from adults. Frequently, inappropriate habits are not yet ingrained and unacceptable compensations have not been overlearned. My own clinical observations lead me to conclude that it seems sensible to treat children with voice problems as early as possible. The school environment frequently offers an ideal setting for intervention. However, school-aged children respond well in any therapeutic environment if the treatment program is tailored to fit their developmental stage, lifestyle, interests, and needs.

This book focuses specifically on remediation programs for school-aged children. The aim in restricting the material to a defined age range is to allow for an indepth exploration of relevant theoretical information in order to apply it directly to program planning. It is not suggested that the disorders themselves are specific to the age group.

In Part I of the book I review theoretical information and extract some basic principles that underlie my approaches to treatment. In Part II, I demonstrate how the theory is applied in practice. I describe individual children I have taught and outline illustrative program plans. The reader should be aware that these are sample programs that were effective when they were used by one clinician. They are not presented as model programs.

Most clinicians seem to select from an array of theories, informational sources, and practical experiences and to develop a personal style. Throughout our professional life we are constantly modifying our approaches in response to new information. Our philosophy, priorities, and repertoire of techniques are shaped by many influences: Some are dramatic and easily documented, and others are subtle and difficult to recall.

When I speculate concerning the influences that shaped my current approaches to voice therapy with children I am awed by the complexity of the task. The source of many valuable ideas are unfortunately obscure. A discerning reader, however, will be able to identify the strong influence exerted by D. Kenneth Wilson whose landmark work on voice problems of children first described this area of specialty. Similarly the work of Frank Wilson and Kenneth Burk increased my understanding of children's special needs in voice therapy.

Daniel Boone's rationale and description of symptomatic voice therapy, and Arnold Aronson's extensive contributions to the clinical literature, particularly in the areas of neurogenic and psychogenic disorders, have provided valuable resources on which I have repeatedly drawn. Joy Wilt's ability to describe emotional states and reactions in a manner that children understand (see her book, *Handling Our Ups and Downs: A Children's Book About Emotion*), inspired me to use a similar approach in voice therapy programs. My awareness of the need to consider interpersonal skills relevant to vocal re-education, expanded significantly as a result of exposure to the works of psychologists such as Richard Dodge and his colleagues, and Joseph DeVito and Carol Tavris.

It is my hope that some of the intervention approaches presented in this book will encourage both students in training and experienced clinicians to engage in spirited discussions and clinical research related to the area of voice therapy for children.

I am indebted to many people who have stimulated my interest in voice and whose voices vibrate in my memory. In particular, my first mentors, Florence Pugh, Daphne Roemermann, and Sadie Foster with whom I worked when I was a young student in Queensland, Australia. Later, as a graduate student in the United States, I benefited from the wise voices of such splendid professors as John Snidecor, Theodore Hanley, Edward Mysak, and Ronald Baken.

Opportunities to work with many very special children, and to observe imaginative and skillful clinicians, have added immeasurably to my own professional development. My thinking concerning voice therapy has been enlarged as a result of the contacts I have enjoyed with gifted graduate students and stimulating colleagues at Indiana University, Bloomington, at the Indiana University Medical Center, Indianapolis, and in the Monroe County Community School Corporation. In particular I have benefited greatly from my collaboration with Anne Chamberlin Summers over the past decade. She read this entire manuscript and contributed to it significantly. In addition, I am grateful to Karen Forrest, and Laura Brewer (B.S. in Pharmacy) who read and advised me on sections of the manuscript. Gordon T. R. Anderson at Longman supported this project from its inception, and Pamela Nelson provided insightful professional assistance. Clifton Hess supplied the photographs in the book. Shirleen Goodlett, Glenda Washburn and Roberta Berry provided exemplary secretarial assistance.

The voices of my parents, family, and friends, transmitting caring and support, were especially important to me throughout this entire project. Those special voices that we all carry with us across space and time remind us of the unique role voices play in our human experience. Finally, my son Alistair both knowingly and unknowingly provided extensive material for this book. His informed perspective on many of the examples was invaluable. To him I owe a special debt of thanks.

Moya L. Andrews

PART I
THEORY

While children and adults may exhibit similar kinds of voice disorders, therapy programs for children necessarily differ from those for adults. A child's treatment strategy must mesh with the developmental stage of a particular child and must be relevant to that child's world. Part I of this book details various theories on treating children with voice disorders, identifying basic assumptions and discussing in depth the various diagnostic and therapeutic processes. This section also discusses how to apply relevant theoretical information toward designing appropriate evaluation and treatment protocols. Both students of voice therapy and working clinicians can use this section to help bridge the gap between theory and everyday clinical practice with children.

chapter 1
Voice Therapy for Children: A Clinical Perspective

Our voices are always changing. Predictable voice changes are related to age and sex and occur during the maturation process. In addition to the normal vocal changes that occur throughout the life cycle, short-term and intermittent changes result from varied conditions and situations. For example, your voice may sound different first thing in the morning than it does at night. It may change in response to the weather, the seasons of the year, the amount and kind of use, overall fatigue, and your feelings. A tremendous variety in vocal behavior falls within the normal range.

The voice is also a very important part of the self-concept, and our identity is projected through our voice. Through vocal expression we reveal ourselves to other people and sometimes come to a better understanding of our own thoughts and feelings. A dramatic example of how important voices are is seen in the reactions of patients who have had laryngectomies because of cancer of the larynx. They awaken from surgery feeling as if part of their personality has been lost when the larynx was removed. They report that their inability to make any sound at all is terrifying and diminishes their whole sense of self.

We have all felt a bit of this loss and frustration when we have suffered from acute laryngitis and have "lost our voice" for short periods of time. A short-term voice loss makes us aware of how much we depend on our voices during the course of a, day. We need our voice to get what we want, to release feelings, to reach out to others, and to experience ourselves in relation to our world. Without our voice we feel out of control, and we are painfully aware that other people react differently to us.

Each individual develops idiosyncratic ways of using his (or her) voice to express himself, to initiate and maintain contact with others, to satisfy his needs, and to control his world. Some people do a better job of this than others, and we are all refining our skills throughout life. Voice models influence our early vocal behavior a great deal. At first we imitate the voices of our parents and family members; later, the peer group assumes greater significance. Trial and error and the pattern of reinforcement operating in the home and school environment also have an effect. If children get what they want when they talk loudly or use a whining tone or keep talking incessantly, they learn to perpetuate those vocal strategies. If their needs are frustrated, they sometimes try harder using the same technique (i.e., talking more loudly), or they may switch and try a different strategy. Families usually have identifiable vocal styles of interacting, as do school classes and most social groups. As children grow older and are exposed to a greater variety of groups and models, most of them learn to adjust their vocal style spontaneously according to the communication context. There are contextual and interpersonal constraints and rules that they learn and internalize.

DEVIANT VOCAL BEHAVIOR

We do not know why some children with normal mechanisms habituate unproductive vocal behaviors, even when those strategies are repeatedly unsuccessful. Imitation of poor vocal models and faulty learning undoubtedly contribute in some cases. Other deviant patterns of voice production are the result of either short-term or permanent changes in the vocal mechanism. When the voice problem is related to anatomical or physiological deviations of the vocal tract, the child frequently attempts to compensate. In some cases, this results in an overlay of additional deviant or even harmful vocal behaviors. Thus the problem becomes more complex and more difficult to evaluate. Unless a voice problem is the direct result of an obvious or severe organic abnormality of the mechanism, and we have specific medical information about the extent of the abnormality, it is perplexing to try to establish a direct cause–effect relationship concerning the etiology of a voice problem. Usually many factors are operating simultaneously in precipitating and maintaining problems.

An example from our own experience may help illustrate this. We have all had periods in our lives when we kept talking even though our voices were not functioning normally. We may have been suffering from a cold or allergic reaction that caused swelling of our vocal folds and impeded their smooth vibratory pattern during phonation. At such times we probably used more effort to adduct our swollen folds, coughed and cleared our throat frequently to get rid of the feeling of mucus on our folds, and strained to make ourselves heard. On some occasions we may also have automatically continued these compensatory behaviors long after the original infection or allergic reaction had subsided. Eventually we could even have caused new irritation or swelling of the folds by continuing to overadduct, strain, talk too loudly, cough, and clear our throat. In other words, we may have eventually abused the voice mechanism by perpetuating behaviors that were no longer appropriate. If this occurred infrequently during our lives, or if we quickly became aware of what we were doing and adapted our behavior, no long-term consequences were felt. If we were especially susceptible to upper respiratory tract infections, however, or suffered frequently from allergic reactions affecting the vocal tract, we may have set up a pattern of behavior that put us at risk for vocal problems. Children who are prone to allergic reactions (Frazier, 1978, says that one in four children are allergic) or childen who suffer from frequent infections are especially susceptible to vocal abuse secondary to their primary problem. The intermittent nature of the primary problem and the gradual habituation of the abusive behaviors across time tend to confound the clinical task of early diagnosis and treatment.

THE COMPLEXITY OF THE CLINICIAN'S TASK

The example just cited reminds us of one way in which the adoption of a pattern of compensatory behaviors may lead to a long-term vocal problem that was precipitated by a short-term or intermittent change in the vocal mechanism. This is just one example illustrating the complexity and interrelationship of vocal behaviors. Other symptom patterns are discussed in Chapter 5, which deals with assessment. At this point, however, it is clear that deviant vocal behavior cannot be considered in isolation. Children with voice disorders are using their voices in a particular way; and this response pattern may be the result of the interplay of anatomical, physiological, social, emotional, or environmental factors. These children are operating in a context, and that context needs always to be considered. An analysis of the success a child achieves by the use of his or her voice to satisfy basic needs and drives is as important as the analysis of the specific vocal behaviors produced. The child who is not meeting basic needs because of the use of unproductive vocal behaviors can be motivated to change and adapt. One of the challenges of voice therapy with children is the task of analyzing each child's vocal interactions and assessing how well they are working. When children can be helped to understand why certain vocal strategies work for them and others do not, motivation to change is enhanced.

Although we have noted that the voice-disordered child must be considered in context, and that this child's vocal behavior is shaped by many factors, we have not yet discussed the specific task of focusing on the actual sound of the voice. The evaluation of an individual child's voice is difficult because of the transitory nature of voice patterns. In addition, the voice is the fleeting end product of a series of complex physiological events. The larynx, or sound source, is not visible, and the voice itself is only one aspect of the total message transmitted to a listener. A clinician, listening to the voice of a child, first has to concentrate on separating the vocal patterns from the semantic content of the utterance, then to attend to the individual parameters of the sound—pitch, loudness, quality, and timing. Later in this book we discuss specific diagnostic procedures that are useful in evaluating these individual parameters. Since evaluation is a comparative task, it is helpful to remember that the more children's voices we have listened to, the easier it is for us to have a reliable set of auditory references available as we compare each new voice. This storehouse of experience helps provide an auditory context within which we can make judgments concerning what is an appropriate voice with respect to age and sex.

We have discussed the complexity of both normal and deviant vocal behavior and the way in which the human voice is a bridge between the individual and the world. We are aware that the child with a voice problem experiences difficulties not only in using his or her mechanisms effectively but in relating to others within his or her world. When we think about developing voice therapy programs to help children, we are often overwhelmed by the task. Part of the reason for our feelings of insecurity in working with these children may be related to the lack of published materials dealing with techniques for diagnosis and treatment specifically designed for use with children. The material in this book can help in this regard.

Many clinicians believe that they need special qualities or skills to treat voice problems, yet we know that speech pathologists' skills are not disorder specific. All speech pathologists who understand basic anatomy and physiology and basic principles of programming have the potential to develop effective voice therapy programs for children. Clinicians who have the listening and discrimination skills to evaluate articulation disorders are certainly capable of applying the same skills in voice evaluations. Practice and experience are all that is needed to refine these skills.

A myth that needs to be addressed is that voice disorders are esoteric problems that can be treated only in a medical center. An extension of this idea is that a clinician in a school setting may possibly do harm to a child with a voice problem. Since a child spends most of the day at school, however, the school speech pathologist is in a unique position to coordinate the voice therapy program. The clinician will, of course, insist on a complete medical report and will frequently work as part of a team that includes otolaryngologists, psychologists, and so on. The team approach ensures that the clinician understands the exact nature of the problem and the type and extent of medical treatment provided or projected. But the school clinician is usually able to provide the kind of continuity of treatment and team support that supplements what is available in medical settings. The school environment provides special opportunities for the clinician to shape a child's vocal behavior in direct response to that child's everyday world.

Many of our fears and insecurities concerning voice disorders stem from our eagerness to do our best with these children. Since they represent varied symptom patterns, we are sometimes anxious if we encounter a child who seems different from those we have worked with before. Yet this variety can become an asset. It helps us to look at each child as a unique individual. There is certainly nothing mysterious about voice-disordered children. Each is different; but then so is every child we teach.

HOW VOICE THERAPY WITH CHILDREN DIFFERS FROM THERAPY WITH ADULTS

An adult who enrolls in a voice therapy program is usually aware of the nature of the problem and can describe some of the ways that listeners respond to the voice disorder. Although in some cases the disruption in overall communicative effectiveness may not be understood fully, the adult usually presents with at least a partial understanding of the need for, and possible benefits of, intervention. Thus, in the initial phase of an adult voice therapy program, it is usually not necessary for a clinician to create an awareness of the problem or to demonstrate the need for therapy. The awareness phase of therapy can focus on developing a more complete understanding of the specific characteristics of the disorder and identifying the behaviors to be modified.

On the other hand, children, particularly those of elementary school age, are frequently unaware that their voices are significantly different from those of their peers. It is not unusual for voice-disordered children to be unable to analyze the complex speech signal. Thus they may not even understand that meaning and feelings are communicated, not only through the semantic context of words, but also through the voice used to express those words. Unless listeners' reactions to their voices have been extremely pointed, or they have been teased by their peers, children also may not be aware of negative reactions. Therefore, in the beginning of a voice therapy program designed for elementary school children, the clinician must frequently spend considerable time teaching the children about vocal communication in general, and specifically about the characteristics of their own vocal behavior. This creation of an awareness of the problem and definition of the possible benefits of therapy is frequently challenging and time-consuming. If it is completed successfully, motivation can be enhanced, and momentum through subsequent therapy stages can be increased. It is critical to present the expected outcome of therapy in a way that is relevant to the child's current needs and daily life. Whereas an adult may be able to project that an improvement in voice may lead to increased satisfaction in personal or occupational relationships, a child may not automatically make this connection. Such an abstract generalization of the benefits of changing vocal behavior may seem unimportant to a child. The child's reality is in the present; future benefits or detriments may seem remote from everyday needs. For many children, and probably for most young children, cause–effect relationships need to be explicitly tied to situations that are concrete, current, and meaningful. For example, a young boy may be encouraged to change unproductive vocal behaviors if he can see that a different vocal strategy is more effective in getting what he wants from his parents, siblings, or playground peer group. Therefore, he may first need to be helped to identify what it is that he wants and needs; for instance, he wants to be liked, he wants to be able to persuade others, he wants other people to listen to what he is saying. If he first learns to analyze what he wants to achieve, and how he can help or hinder his chances of success by the way he uses his voice in specific situations, he may then be helped to develop a personal rationale for change.

Therefore, one important difference between voice therapy for adults and children is the assumptions that we, as clinicians, hold as we approach therapy. Although we can reasonably assume that an adult client recognizes a problem exists, we cannot safely assume that a child understands this. Although we can assume that most adults automatically know that an improvement in their voice is related to improvement in other areas of their life, this is not necessarily the case with children. Thus there is a very real difference in the way clinicians approach the task of planning the initial phase of a therapy program for children as opposed to that for adults. It is probably realistic to say that in all cases, the awareness phase of a therapy program for children will take a longer period of time to accomplish. The relevance of the therapy goals and procedures to the everyday life of the child need to be stated more explicitly and tied to specific situations that are meaningful.

An integral part of the awareness phase of any voice therapy program is the introduction and explanation of descriptive terminology. Again, there are differences in what can be assumed by a clinician. Adults, unless they are intellectually handicapped, will generally have the prerequisite linguistic development to understand the meanings of most terms used in voice therapy. Specialized terminology can also be easily grasped by an adult when a clinician explains or demonstrates. Children in the early elementary school grades, however, may not have the linguistic development necessary to equip them to understand and use all the terms appropriately. Further discussion of the importance of gearing the language used in voice therapy to the developmental level of the child is found in Chapter 2. But it is important to emphasize here that there are significant differences between the way we communicate with children and adults during voice therapy. We frequently need to teach important linguistic concepts to children during the early stages of the therapy program.

An additional concern when we plan voice therapy programs for children is the importance of the role of the family and other significant adults. Rarely in the case of an adult client do we need to ensure that parents and teachers are actively involved in the therapy process. With the child client, the family's understanding and cooperation are essential. If, for example, the parent does not believe that a problem exists, or refuses to cooperate in obtaining a medical examination, the clinician is faced with the additional task of attempting to change the parent's attitude if the child is to be helped. The enlistment of support from parents and teachers, and the ongoing need for communication between the clinician and these significant adults, is an important aspect of voice therapy for children.

Another reason why contact with the child's family is important during the design and implementation of voice therapy programs for children is the part played by voice models. In arriving at an understanding of the factors precipitating or maintaining a child's voice problem, the clinician needs to hear how the parents use their voices. An adult client can tell us if people say he or she sounds "just like" a parent or other family member. The sound of a child's voice, or the child's style of vocal interaction, is frequently similar to that of a significant person in the environment, but the child may not be aware of this. The clinician working with children assumes a far larger role in the data-gathering process. Direct observation and analysis of the context in which the child operates at home and at school become tasks for the clinician. The child is not usually able to be the reliable informant that the adult client may be. During both diagnosis and therapy the clinician works closely with the child's family and with school personnel. In most cases the team approach is more critical to the success of therapy with children than it is with adults.

The charting of therapy progress is another area to consider when we are discussing effective voice therapy for children. Task sequences need to be designed and described in a way that fits the developmental stage of the child. Specific concrete examples of the steps to be accomplished in achieving long-term goals need to be clearly laid out. The use of visual aids assumes great importance when a clinician discusses a child's progress. The adult may "know" when he or she is improving. The child needs frequent and tangible evidence of progress across time. Examples of charts and summaries that can help children see the steps to be accomplished can be found in later chapters. It is important to remember how specifically and concretely the behaviors need to be defined for children as they progress through the therapy program. The clinician must reduce complexity and abstractness of tasks so that children can focus on observable and discrete behaviors.

Children are different from adults. They are developing and changing as we work with them. Their development is much more dramatic and dynamic than adult development. Our therapy programs need to be designed with this fact in mind. Although the disorders exhibited by children and adults are similar with respect to symptom patterns, treatment approaches for children are different. They need to be designed so that they mesh with the child's developmental stage. Therapy tasks need to be relevant to the child's world, translated into the child's language, and tied to specific concrete events and situations.

JUSTIFICATION FOR INTERVENTION: COST-BENEFITS

Incidence studies show that approximately 6–9% of elementary school children have voice disorders and yet only about 1% of children on clinicians' caseloads are voice cases (Wilson, 1979). The discrepancy between the incidence percentages and the treatment percentages is puzzling. One possible reason for this discrepancy, often discussed by clinicians, is the difficulty in ensuring that a child is examined by a physician before enrollment in therapy. The recommendation that all voice cases be given a medical examination is certainly sensible and necessary. We know that vocal problems are sometimes symptoms of complex physical or emotional disorders. For example, a hoarse voice is sometimes associated with malnutrition or other health problems that increase susceptibility to upper respiratory tract infections. The possibility that the clinician's detection of vocal problems can, on occasion, result in a child's receiving attention for a major health problem alerts us to the need for accurate voice diagnosis and appropriate medical referrals. The benefits of early identification of children with voice problems are obvious, but there are practical difficulties. Medical examinations cost money. They are not available as part of school services and necessitate that the child's family schedule an examination with a physician. Of course, when a child's voice problem is severe or incapacitating, the question of the need for the medical

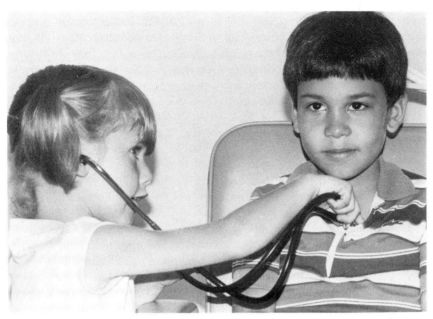

Role-playing a physician's examination is an excellent way to prepare children for a visit to the doctor.

examination is rarely debatable. Clinicians can be skillful in seeking out agencies and service clubs that may help. School personnel may also assist in helping to offset the expense incurred by families of limited means who are motivated to seek help for their child. The most provoking problems are likely to occur when a family does not perceive the need or does not consider the problem severe enough to warrant the medical expense. In such cases, or when the problem is a subtle one, a clinician is placed in an uncertain position. At such times clinicians ask themselves such questions as "How handicapping is the voice problem?" "Should I wait and see if it improves as the child gets older?" "How much time can I afford to spend counseling this family in order to persuade them to get help for their child?"

If the child in question has difficulties in addition to the voice problem, there is considerable temptation to assume that the vocal problem may indeed be the least pressing. In a hierarchy of priorities for treatment, there may seem to be other areas that need help first. If the child is presenting vocal problems only, and is a high achiever in all other areas of performance, the temptation may be to assume that the vocal symptoms will be compensated for by other strengths.

Understandably, these reasons for failing to proceed with time-consuming and frustrating attempts to gain parent cooperation may seem attractive to a busy clinician. When a clinician has many children to serve, and many parents to counsel, it may not appear to be cost efficient to persevere. Clinical experience suggests, however, that short-term costs may not be the only factor to consider. Chronic voice disorders rarely disappear without treatment. Unlike some developmental disorders of articulation, maturation alone does not seem significantly to affect vocal symptoms. The most striking example of a common and persistent vocal problem is that of vocal abuse. A cluster of identifiable vocal symptoms is associated with this. We are all familiar with the behavior of the child who uses too much effort to talk or talks too much. Such a child habituates a hyperfunctional pattern that in time may result in additive lesions on the vocal folds. Even if, as has sometimes been suggested, the lesions themselves disappear at puberty, the hyperfunctional vocal pattern may continue. Excessive effort and tension during vocalization, inappropriate interpersonal skills, and inefficient respiratory support during speech are liabilities that some children carry with them into high school and adult life.

Habituated maladaptive vocal behavior and styles of vocal interaction do not seem always to disappear spontaneously. Some adults with voice disorders reveal a history of vocal abuse dating back to their elementary school years. Behaviors that have been habituated and overlearned across time are the most difficult to ameliorate. Thus the lack of early intervention may result in costly long-term consequences. The costs will be borne by the child and affect the individual's personal and professional development. They may also impinge on school personnel. Each year the same child may be referred for testing. A series of classroom teachers may inquire about what is wrong with the child's voice. The music teacher may complain about and eventually exclude the child from the choir. A child who is a habitually loud or incessant talker may exhibit disruptive behavior throughout his or her school career. In extreme cases such children are stigmatized as nuisances. A ripple effect occurs, and the fallout eventually obscures the root cause of the problem. Initially, some of these children may have been trying too hard, and so their efforts to communicate were misdirected and inefficient. Some vocal abusers seem especially eager to communicate. Unfortunately, this kind of child can easily become trapped in inappropriate habits that arose from an eagerness to talk and a need to be heard.

As we assess the cost effectiveness of voice programs, we may find ourselves listening to a child's voice problem and asking the question, "To whom does this difference make a difference?" (Burk, 1979). We might ask an additional question, "Could this child's voice be a liability in life?" Of course, we can neither see into the future nor be sure about the validity of our predictions. But it is interesting to consider how many successful politicians we have heard who had abnormal-sounding voices.

Could a hyperfunctional voice user become President of the United States? Or would such a candidate be perceived by the electorate as under strain, tense, or anxious? It is possible that none of the children we teach will aspire to such a high office. But many will certainly become professional voice users, for voice use is an important part of a great variety of occupations. Lawyers, ministers, physicians, salesmen, executives, teachers—all these and others depend on their voices. In taking a long-term view of the benefits of effective voice therapy, it is surely important to ensure that children's future options are not restricted. A voice that draws attention to itself and results in negative listener reactions is a significant, although at times insidious, lifetime handicap.

There is also the importance of the effect of vocal models to be considered. In occupations such as teaching, for example, a person with a voice problem may serve as a model for many, many children during an active career. It also may be reasonable to assume that the majority of voice-disordered children who do not receive treatment may grow up to be voice-disordered parents.

THE PREVENTION OF VOICE DISORDERS IN CHILDREN

While it is well documented in the literature that a significant number of school-age children have voice disorders (Baynes, 1966; Senturia & Wilson, 1968; Shearer, 1972; Silverman & Zimmer, 1972; Warr-Leeper *et al.*, 1979; Wilson, 1979), it also is clear that many of these children do not actually receive voice therapy. Some of the reasons for this discrepancy between incidence and treatment has been discussed already. Some clinicians do not feel as comfortable with voice cases as they do with other kinds of cases because of the nature of their training (Shearer, 1972). There are also problems involved in convincing parents of the importance of seeking help (Baynes, 1966; Cook *et al.*, 1979; Wilson, 1979) and difficulties involved in obtaining medical examinations. Teachers' awareness of differences in vocal behavior among children also varies significantly, and contributes to the quite small number of children referred by them for evaluation and treatment (Diehl & Stinnett, 1959; Wilson, 1979). In addition, as Mowrer (1978) and Nilson and Schneiderman (1983) suggest, children who have voice problems that do not seem dramatically to affect their academic performance in the classroom setting may not be considered by their teachers to be eligible for services under P.L. 94–142. As noted in the previous section, the effect of hoarseness and other vocal symptoms is often insidious rather than dramatic, but can certainly limit the achievement of full potential.

Education of classroom teachers through personal and public discussion, and through in-service programs, needs to be vigorously pursued. For not only are classroom teachers important in identifying children with difficulties and as models of vocal behavior, but they are a population that is at risk for voice problems. Deal, McClain, and Sudderth (1976) showed that in-service training and direct instruction enhanced teachers' abilities to identify hoarseness and vocal abuse in children. It is likely that teachers who participate in programs of this kind benefit additionally from an increased awareness of vocal hygiene as it applies to their own vocal practices.

Nilson and Schneiderman (1983) reported on a successful educational program to prevent vocal abuse and misuse developed and presented to second and third graders in a public elementary school. The program taught basic information concerning the vocal mechanism, discrimination of voice qualities, and identification of abusive and compensatory behaviors. Teachers were asked to remain in their classrooms during the times the program was implemented. Teachers were also tested subsequently, and their awareness of the parameters of voice was compared with that of teachers who had not participated in the program. Results showed a significant difference between teachers who participated and those who did not, thus demonstrating the efficacy of the approach. The teacher participants were positive about the program, supported carryover activities, and were receptive to future programs. This report and others dealing with similar activities (Cook *et al.*, 1979; Deal, McClain, & Sudderth, 1976; Blonigen, 1978) emphasize the importance of educating school personnel in the basic principles of vocal hygiene.

One specialist group of teachers who are knowledgeable and concerned about vocal behavior, and who provide an additional resource for speech–language pathologists in the schools, is the music teachers. In a program conducted during the 1982–1983 school year in the Monroe County schools in Bloomington, Indiana, it was found that a speech–language pathologist and a music specialist working as a team were considerably more effective in identifying children with vocal abuse, in educating classroom teachers about these problems, and in conferring with parents than when they approached the tasks individually. The advantages of this team approach are that the child's vocal pattern can be described in terms of both speaking and singing and that the two professionals can coordinate a more comprehensive program of intervention. Additional benefits are that vocal screenings and vocal hygiene lessons can be combined with music lessons and choir activities, and increased communication and heightened awareness occurs among all school personnel. In some schools in Monroe County the interest in working as a team in the area of vocal abuse has resulted in requests that the music teacher and the speech–language pathologist be scheduled to work in the same schools on the same days. In one school, the speech–language pathologist regularly conducts, during choir rehearsal periods, a voice therapy group for children with vocal abuse who are excluded from choir.

The American Speech and Hearing Association statement (1974), and other statements in recent years, encourages speech–language pathologists to engage in activities to prevent communication disorders in children. Flynn (1983) has presented some specific ideas showing how a philosophy concerning the necessity for prevention can be translated into positive strategies. She mentions that activities should be designed to reflect Katz, McDonald, and Stuckey's (1972) three levels of preventive activity. Let us consider these three levels and the ways in which speech–language pathologists can initiate activities related to the area of voice. We will review many of Flynn's (1983) suggestions.

The *tertiary level* of preventive activity includes all activities carried out to alleviate existing disorders. We have already seen that much still remains to be accomplished at this level. Specifically, training programs in universities and colleges need to strengthen the preparation provided for students in the area of vocal rehabilitation. Students in training need to be exposed to a greater variety of clinical training experiences with voice cases. More research needs to be completed to increase our understanding of normal and disordered vocal behavior. Testing procedures need to be improved and standardized. Our aim should be to improve our therapeutic skills in the area of voice disorders of children so that we narrow the gap between the incidence and treatment figures.

The *secondary level* involves activities related to early detection. If problems are detected in their early stages, it is reasonable to assume that remediation is quicker and easier. Activities that help teachers and school personnel recognize the early symptoms of vocal problems are significant at this level. Programs that improve collaboration with other specialists (e.g., classroom teachers, otolaryngologists, music teachers) are helpful in this regard.

Nevertheless, it is at the *primary level* of prevention that most work still needs to be done. A focus on primary (before the fact) preventive activity is obviously the most positive and economical approach. The general public, school personnel, parents, and children need to be exposed to information that will heighten awareness of the importance of good vocal hygiene and preventive strategies for voice conservation. Populations who are at risk for vocal problems (e.g., professional voice users, people who suffer from allergic conditions affecting the vocal tract, individuals with a family history of voice problems, cheerleaders) need information that will alert them to their susceptibility. We need to disseminate information in a variety of ways. Materials need to be prepared (articles, pamphlets, films), and programs need to be presented (at in-service training sessions for teachers, during classroom science lessons, at science fairs, at career days, during health lessons, and as part of disability-awareness activities). Specifically, we need to educate ourselves, the general public, and the children we teach by explicitly discussing the importance of vocal health and ways in which vocal health can be jeopardized. Environmental considerations of noise level and pollution; the effects of stress on the vocal mechanism; the structure of the mechanism itself; and common illnesses, injuries, and accidents that affect the voice are other issues that need to be addressed. The creative clinician will find many opportunities to develop and disseminate information relating to the prevention of voice disorders in children.

SUSCEPTIBILITY: CONDITIONS OF THE UPPER RESPIRATORY TRACT

We have noted that alterations in the vocal tract that occur as the result of medical conditions can heighten a child's susceptibility. Conditions that occur repeatedly, or that result in compensations that are habituated across time, are especially significant in precipitating voice problems. Children who experience frequent allergic reactions or upper respiratory tract infections are particularly at risk, especially if their life style includes many activities that are vocally demanding. Normal reflexive activities, such as coughing and sneezing, if they occur repeatedly because of congestion or irritation, may also become habituated and result in abuse to the vocal mechanism. With this in mind, let us consider some of the medical conditions that occur frequently in elementary school children and contribute to susceptibility.

Upper Respiratory Tract Structures

Before turning our attention to the specific conditions that may occur, it may be useful to review some general information concerning the upper respiratory tract.

The entire pathway from the lungs, bronchi, trachea, through the larynx, pharynx, oral cavity, and nasal cavity is continuous and lined throughout with moist mucous membrane. In addition, the pathway to the middle ear, the eustachian tube, is also connected to the respiratory tract, since the eustachian tube opening is located in the nasopharynx. Because of the continuity between structures, and the interrelationship that exists, upper respiratory tract conditions tend to spread readily and affect changes throughout the entire pathway.

Infection   The suffix *itis* means redness, heat, swelling. Words ending in this suffix are frequently used to describe changes in the upper respiratory tract. It is not uncommon for an individual to contract, for example, an infection that attacks the nasal cavities, and to experience rhin*itis* or sinus*itis*. If there is a discharge that causes a postnasal drip, the infection and irritation of the tissues may spread and result in pharyng*itis* or laryng*itis* and maybe even bronch*itis*. Vigorous nose blowing may also force an infection to spread into the eustachian tube and middle ear cavity, resulting in ot*itis* media. The sequence or progression of an infection varies, of course, but the location of the discomfort rarely is confined to one area of the continuous respiratory tract. Swelling of the tissues and an excess of secretions usually accompanies infections. The tonsils, located between the faucial arches on either side of the mouth cavity, and the adenoids in the nasopharynx are frequently affected. These structures are made up of lymphatic tissue, and as part of the body's defense mechanism, they play a role in helping prevent bacteria from invading the system. At times they become enlarged, and when they are infected, we can often see the redness, increased size, and even white flecks of pus on the tonsils when we inspect the mouth cavity of an individual who has tonsill*itis* or adenoid-*itis*. When the adenoids are very swollen, they may even press on the eustachian tube opening, causing that opening to be blocked. This prevents free circulation of air into the middle ear. In such cases, or if there is congestion blocking the tube, we say that it is no longer "patent," or open. Enlarged adenoids may also block the nasopharynx to such an extent that the individual has difficulty breathing through the nose and has to resort to relying completely on mouth breathing until the swelling subsides.

It is pertinent to note at this point that there are three kinds of infection; viral, bacterial, and fungal. Frequently, children experience a sore throat as the first symptom of diseases caused by all kinds of infection. A sore throat may be a symptom of a serious bacterial infection, such as bacterium beta hemolytic streptococcus ("strep"). If a sore throat is associated with a high fever, headache, and swollen glands in the neck, it may be due to a strep infection. A diagnosis of strep is based on a throat culture. This is accomplished by a swab of the throat that is smeared on a special laboratory dish and incubated overnight. In addition to the throat culture, an examination by a physician is essential for an accurate diagnosis. If a diagnosis of strep or some other bacterium is made, the patient can be treated with antibiotic therapy. This can be administered in injection form or taken orally. If taken orally, it is critical that the patient not stop taking the medication when the symptoms disappear. Medication must be continued as prescribed for the entire period (usually 10 days) advised by the physician. The physician usually takes another culture at the completion of the full course of antibiotics to ensure that the infection has cleared completely.

Sore throats or other symptoms of the upper respiratory tract that are not caused by a bacterial infection are usually the result of viral infections. Whereas the symptoms of bacterial infections tend to appear suddenly, the symptoms of viral infections usually start slowly. There is often a feverish feeling, loss of appetite, headache, dry cough, and runny nose associated with the onset of a viral infection. One virus that causes frequent sore throats in children and is common during the summertime is herpangina. A child's temperature may soar, and the patient may complain of a reduced energy level and very painful raised sores at the back of the mouth. Symptoms usually disappear by the fourth day.

Although such symptoms as sore throats are very common (the most common cause is viral infection), it is important to be vigilant when children complain of such symptoms. A sore throat may reflect something as mild as a common cold or as serious as leukemia, tuberculosis, or infectious mononucleosis. Consequently, any one of the following warning signs warrants a prompt call to a physician: (1) a severe sore throat or one that causes the child to have difficulty swallowing; (2) a sore throat that has persisted longer than a week; (3) a temperature of over 102 degrees Fahrenheit for children under eight and 100 degrees for older children or difficulty in breathing; (4) soreness accompanied by coughing or hoarseness; (5) episodes of similar soreness that have recurred several times in recent weeks; (6) a past history of rheumatic fever. Although all of the above conditions do not necessarily mean that the child has a serious illness, they do suggest that the condition merits medical attention.

We have discussed some of the symptoms and implications of sore throats in detail in order to provide a framework of reference that may be useful for a speech–language pathologist. During the process of evaluation of children with atypical voices, the clinician needs to consider the length of time children have had problems and the possibility of recurrent infections. Through discussions with the classroom teacher and with parents, the clinician may discover indications that suggest that the child's vocal symptoms may be related to his or her general state of health. As noted, a malnourished child, or one with chronic physical problems, may experience recurrent upper respiratory infections that are secondary to a more serious health problem. If a clinician suspects that this may be the case, vigorous attempts should be made to persuade the parents to obtain medical help.

Allergies   Approximately 35 million Americans are allergic or hypersensitive to something, and the tendency to be allergic seems to run in families. If both parents have allergies, there is a 75% chance that a child is likely to develop them; if only one parent is allergic, there is a 50% chance that a child will be allergic (Frazier, 1978). Allergies are the result of an unusual immune response. When bacteria, viruses, or other harmful foreign substances enter the body, it responds by producing antibodies, which are proteins in the blood to neutralize invaders. When an individual is allergic, the immune system produces antibodies against inappropriate substances. These substances, or allergens, may be inhaled (e.g., pollen or dust), ingested (e.g., foods or drugs), or contacted through the skin (e.g., detergents or poison ivy).

Allergens that affect the upper respiratory tract are most frequently inhaled. Allergic rhinitis afflicts more people than any other kind of allergic reaction and is typically caused by airborne allergens. It may be seasonal; for example, reactions caused by pollens. Or it may be year-round; for example, reactions caused by such allergens as house dust or animal dander. Mold, a frequent offender, may be present year-round but particularly worrisome to the affected individual at specific times (e.g., during the fall when damp leaves are being raked or when the basement is damp after heavy rain and the individual is indoors). When a specific allergen is inhaled, antibodies immediately go into action. Histamine is released, dilating blood vessels and causing swelling of the mucous membranes of the nasal passages and surrounding tissues. Symptoms may range from congestion (e.g., a stuffy nose), breathing difficulties, watery eyes, itching, and irritation of the lining of the entire respiratory tract.

In rare cases a violent production of histamine in response to an allergen can cause a critical condition called anaphylaxix. This may include hives, swelling of the mucous membranes of the throat and respiratory tract, bronchial spasm, nausea, sudden pallor, and a rapid drop in blood pressure. The condition may affect people who are highly allergic to insect stings, some drugs (such as penicillin), and, very rarely, foods. Most allergies, however, are more annoying than life threatening. They can be counteracted by pinpointing the offending substance, either by trial and error and observation or by consultation and testing by a physician. Once identified, it is sometimes possible for an individual to avoid situations in which the substance is present. Also, air conditioners and filter systems can help screen out pollens, mold spores, and dust. Since all airborne substances cannot be completely avoided, physicians usually prescribe antihistamines to lessen symptoms such as sneezing, nasal discharge, and irritation of the lining of the upper respiratory tract. Nasal spray steroids such as Nasalide or Vancenase are also used to relieve allergic inflammation of the mucous membranes. If standard medication does not help, a doctor may recommend a series of desensitization injections.

Occasionally, irritation and congestion of the upper respiratory tract may be caused by an allergen initially but may lead to a secondary bacterial or viral infection. In other words, the primary allergic condition may increase susceptibility for a secondary infection. Long-term or chronic allergic congestion and irritation of the upper respiratory tract may heighten susceptibility for other secondary problems, such as vocal abuse and misuse. Children whose vocal tracts are altered for long periods of time by the presence of swelling and excess secretions may develop compensatory behaviors, such as habitual throat clearing and coughing.

Frazier (1978) provides a listing of some warning signs that may alert a clinician. As mentioned, family history is particularly significant. Other signs that may be significant are the presence of a rash on a newborn's body, or colic. While there may be other reasons for colic, Frazier believes that the chances are good that a colicky baby is also an allergic one. Excessive sweating (and night sweats) are allergy clues in older children. Other signs of allergy in children are

Pallor	Snoring at night
Dark circles under eyes	A tendency to croup
Unexpected fever	Constant throat clearing due to
Drooling	postnasal drip
"Allergic salute" (a dis-	Watering of the eyes
tinctive wiping of the nose)	A general feeling of malaise

Some allergic children show fluctuations in weight. Frazier attributes this to the retention of fluids during severe allergy bouts. Since allergy is a disease that may at times be serious, it is important that an allergic child receive medical assessment as early as possible; the earlier the medical intervention, the better the chance that the condition can be controlled successfully. Physicians use the phrase "the allergic march" to describe the rather common progression of childhood allergy through the stages of colic to eczema to asthma. This progression may be arrested if medical attention is obtained. The voice clinician needs to be aware of the warning signs, take careful medical histories, and recognize the part that allergy may play in increasing children's susceptibility to vocal problems. Hansel (1975) provides a comprehensive questionnaire (pp. 23–30) that is useful for the clinician to use during interviews with parents.

Asthma   Asthma is a bronchial condition that affects some 9 million children and adults in the United States. It is characterized by wheezing, coughing, and difficulty in exhaling because of an obstruction, such as an accumulation of heavy mucus, in the airways. Symptoms may be triggered by allergens, viral infections, exercise, stress, cold air, and a variety of irritants. (Cystic fibrosis is a disease with symptoms similar to those of asthma, and a physician may order a sweat test if this is suspected.) Physicians sometimes use pulmonary function studies to test single-breath vital capacity and maximal voluntary ventilation. From the results of these tests, the doctor can determine whether the child has an obstructive disease of the airways (e.g., asthma), whether the problem is located in the upper or lower part of the bronchi, or whether there is restriction caused by problems such as lung tumor or fluid in the chest area.

Today asthma can usually be controlled by the use of medication in the form of tablets, sprays, and inhalants. Antihistamines are seldom prescribed for asthma patients because they tend to dry out the mucus plugs in the bronchi, making them difficult to dislodge. When infection is present, however, antibiotics are frequently given. Epinephrine (adrenalin) is given by injection in a physician's office or hospital to treat severe systemic allergic reactions or severe asthma. It works by relaxing the smooth muscles that the allergen–antibody battle has constricted, and thus opens the airways (Frazier, 1978). Epinephrine is also used in conjunction with the corticosteroid drugs in aerosol therapy or inhalation therapy with steam vaporizers or nebulizers. Corticosteroids are powerful drugs that decrease swelling and inflammation. Most doctors use them very cautiously and only when the asthma does not respond to routine procedures. Two of the newer drugs are *cromolyn sodium*, used to reduce the frequency and severity of attacks, and *beclomethasone dipropionate*, an antiinflammatory steroid in aerosol form that is replacing oral steroids in the treament of severe asthma and allergic rhinitis. Unlike oral or injected steroids, which can have serious side effects—particularly in children, whose growth may be retarded —the inhaled drug appears to be effective and much safer to use. In recent years there has been a trend to increase use of inhalant medications in order to reduce dangers to the respiratory tract. Drugs such as Proventil, originally available only for oral use, can now be used as inhalants with resultant minimal systemic side effects.

Bronchodilator aerosols or nebulizers are used frequently and are effective and fast acting. They have the advantage of being small and easy to carry in the child's pocket. Nevertheless, parents and clinicians need to be reminded that even though some of these products may be purchased over the counter, they can be dangerous if children overdose through excessive use. Sometimes, for example, a child who is frightened of having an asthma attack will use a nebulizer unnecessarily. Continued use may make asthma attacks worse and can lead to respiratory complications. A clinician who observes an asthmatic child frequently using inhalants during school hours would be wise to check with the child's family concerning the physician's instructions for dosage, since such medications can become addictive and are potentially dangerous. Symptoms of overdosage include dizziness, flushing, weakness, nausea, excitability, and rapid heartbeat.

Some Reflexive Behaviors

We have reviewed some conditions that can affect the continuous pathway between the nose, mouth, and lungs. When we inhale, the air is filtered by the cilia, or hairs, in the nose and warmed and moistened by the mucous membrane lining the entire passageway down to the lungs. When we exhale, the air travels from the lungs through the bronchi into the trachea (windpipe) and through the valvelike larynx, to be emitted finally through the mouth and nose. The respiratory tract is protected by various reflexive mechanisms, and the primary biological function of the larynx is to act as a protective valve to prevent foreign bodies from entering the lower airway.

One protective reflex is that sudden glottal closure that occurs when an individual is suddenly plunged into water. This immersion reflex, as it is sometimes described, protects the airway from the entry of water into the lungs. We have all felt the movement of this laryngeal reflex when we have suddenly been jolted downward in an elevator. We are also aware of the sudden closure reflex activated when it is necessary to build up subglottal air pressure preliminary to sudden exertion associated with lifting, pushing, or pulling. When force needs to be exerted, the laryngeal valve closes abruptly in order to stabilize the thorax to facilitate the necessary action.

Biological functions of the larynx are of interest to the voice clinician for more than one reason. For example, a diagnostician may check to see if a child who is not phonating can use the larynx for nonspeech functions. A child with aphonia associated with emotional difficulties will usually exhibit appropriate responses during nonspeech activities. In some children with severe central nervous system impairment, however, reflexive behavior may be affected. In addition, the frequency of occurrence of certain reflexes, such as coughing and sneezing, may be helpful in indicating health problems. Coughing and sneezing help rid the respiratory tract of irritating or potentially dangerous substances. When nerve cells in the nose sense an irritating substance, they send a message to the medulla. This part of the brain controls breathing and swallowing. A series of involuntary spasmodic reactions is set into motion. There is a quick, deep inhalation, and the abdominal muscles contract and push against the diaphragm. Then there is a sudden explosive exhalation propelling air through nose and mouth at a rapid speed in order to expel the irritant. This process is repeated until the irritant is eliminated.

Hansel (1975) says that coughing is the most frequent respiratory manifestation of allergy, and yet the allergic causation is frequently unrecognized unless it is associated with bronchial asthma. There are several kinds of allergic coughs. The first is the hacking, nonproductive cough that characteristically begins when the child goes to bed and continues throughout the night. It may be accompanied by an itching sensation in the throat or chest. A second type is associated with mild nasal stuffiness, postnasal discharge, and frequent attempts to "clear" the throat. The third kind of cough accompanies allergic or asthmatic bronchitis. There is mucus in the respiratory tree, but the lumen is not sufficiently occluded to cause the wheezing that is typically associated with asthma. This cough is often a forerunner of an asthma attack. It may also be associated with purulent sinusitis and then subsides when the sinuses have been treated. In addition, there is the cough associated with bronchiectasis complicating allergic respiratory disease. This cough is productive, and the secretions expelled during coughing will be more purulent or thick, foul smelling and discolored, than the transparent, more fluid secretions seen in uncomplicated cases. Allergic coughs do not respond to sedative cough mixtures or cough suppressants. Such patients are usually given ephedrine or some other bronchodilator (Hansel, 1975). Expectorants are given during asthma attacks to help the child cough up and get rid of the excess mucus (Frazier, 1978). When prescribing medication, physicians try to determine such things as whether the cough is productive or nonproductive, the characteristics of any mucus produced during productive coughing, whether the cough is present in association with colds, elevations in temperature, and whether it is paroxysmal or seasonal or both (Hansel, 1975). Since coughing is sometimes also a habituated response associated with vocal abuse, voice clinicians need to ascertain the possible relationship between physical condition and repetitive coughing. A careful medical history and physician's report should be obtained before the clinician embarks on any voice therapy with children exhibiting chronic coughing behaviors.

THE RELEVANCE OF RESPIRATORY DIFFICULTIES TO VOICE DISORDERS

During interviews with parents, it is important that the speech–language pathologist ask questions geared specifically to obtain information concerning a child's history of medical conditions of the respiratory tract and treatment procedures that may have affected the airway. The airway may be obstructed by foreign bodies, excessive mucus, swollen tissues, or congenital deformity. Today, many critically ill children survive a variety of serious illnesses that formerly would have proved fatal because physicians can provide prolonged assistance to breathing. Ventilation is initiated through an endotracheal tube, and because of greater use of this treatment for longer periods of time, there has also been an increase in laryngeal injury. The injury may be temporary and reversible (as is often seen in premature infants treated for respiratory distress in intensive-care units), but the potential for an iatrogenic stenosis of the airway does exist (Henry, Pashley, & Fan, 1983). Injury of the vocal folds and of the subglottal airway can occur, and Noyce (1983) reported that injuries that occur during intubation of the infants may be due to the shape of the infant subglottis. He studied 45 neonatal and infant larynges and found that the subglottal area varied significantly in shape from the vocal cords down to the lower border of the cricoid cartilage. The subglottal area below the vocal cords is elliptical in shape, but this shape changes until it is circular at the lower border of the cricoid cartilage. The size and shape of the endotracheal tube inserted into the airway is therefore an important consideration for physicians dealing with infants. Subglottal injuries can lead to a serious narrowing or stenosis of the airway. Pashley, Henry, and Fan (1983) noted that anterior cricoidotomy has been successfully used as a surgical method of decompression of the laryngeal subglottis in infants and children with a failure of endotracheal intubation resulting from subglottal injury. When children cannot be intubated successfully, the therapeutic alternative is tracheotomy. This procedure involves the insertion of a tracheostomy tube to allow the patient to be ventilated through a stoma in the anterior neck. This procedure is frequently used in cases where there is progressive glottal injury as a result of intubation or severe edema due to viral croup, or in cases where anterior cricoidotomy is not appropriate.

Another condition that frequently is treated either by nasotracheal intubation or tracheotomy is acute epiglottitis. In this condition, airway obstruction occurs as a result of enlargement of the epiglottis. Hengerer and DiTirro (1983) retrospectively studied 113 cases of acute epiglottitis in children treated between 1965 and 1980. Patients seen before 1975 were usually managed with tracheotomy and intravenous antibiotics; those seen after 1975 were usually managed with nasotracheal intubation plus antibiotics and steroids. Tracheotomized patients averaged 6.5 days of hospitalization and 5 days cannulated; intubated patients spent 4.5 days in the hospital with 2.5 days intubated. Both procedures were found to be equally safe in managing the airway.

Simon, Fowler, and Handler (1983) studied the communication development of 77 children aged 2 months to 7 years with long-term tracheostomies. All were aphonic and consequently deprived of speech experience for extended periods while tracheostomized. Twenty-three were studied post-decannulation. They found that children with long-term tracheostomies can develop speech and language skills commensurate with intellectual functioning despite extended periods of deprivation of babbling. Monitoring and follow-up are important in ensuring identification of later problems in vocal quality and breath support. Direct speech–language therapy for the linguistically mature child, including use of alternative communication modalities, was crucial in decreasing frustration and maximizing skill. The role of the speech–language pathologist in relation to the tracheostomized child has been specifically described by Simon and Handler (1981).

During the history-taking portion of the voice evaluation, the clinician should be alert for indications such as respiratory distress suffered following birth, periods of time in intensive-care units, and surgical and medical procedures that could have affected the laryngeal or tracheal structures. If information given by parents suggests that the child may have been intubated during infancy or childhood, it is helpful to request a medical report providing details of any possible residual effects on the phonatory system.

As more and more children survive serious illnesses as a result of improved neonatal and pediatric medical care, the clinician's responsibility to obtain the medical history assumes greater importance. We also may be seeing more children with permanent tracheotomies. Most frequently, the tracheotomy is a temporary condition, but occasionally, if an airway obstruction persists (as in the case of malformation of structures or chronic illness), a child may be forced to continue to breathe through a tracheostomy tube. Sometimes the tracheotomy will be kept open in order to suction mucus and secretions from the airway at periodic intervals. In these instances the opening may be closed most of the time, and the child will be able to phonate normally when it is closed. When the child is forced to breathe through the trach tube all of the time, because of a long-term problem, medical and educational management is more complex. In such cases the speech–language pathologist will need accurate information concerning the child's potential for voice usage. If the larynx is normal, the child may be taught to phonate by using a finger to occlude the stoma during exhalation so that phonation may occur. If the child exhibits malformation of the laryngeal structures, or other conditions that prohibit normal phonation, consultation with the child's physician and a team approach to treatment is necessary. In such cases the use of an artificial larynx or sign language may be appropriate alternatives to oral communication.

Schoen, Gill, and Wallace (1983) described a program in southeast Los Angeles for normal school-age children with tracheostomies. These children attended regular public schools and participated in most (excluding sand and water) activities. Speech–language clinicians worked with teachers, specially trained nurses, and parents. Special in-service training sessions were conducted to teach tracheostomy care. The description of this program development, and the protocols that were established, provides excellent guidelines for the speech–language clinician faced with the problem of helping a child with a permanent tracheostomy.

The majority of the children we evaluate, however, will suffer from less dramatic medical conditions that may nevertheless be relevant to their vocal symptoms. Children who suffer from allergies and asthma may have periodic partial occlusion of the airway that affects their airflow during phonation. In such instances the clinician should seek medical information concerning the conditions, the type of medication prescribed, and the possible effect of the condition on phonatory behavior. The effects of excessive mucus, vocal-fold edema, intermittent or persistent irritation that may increase reflexive coughing and sneezing, and dryness of structures related to specific medications taken may be important considerations. Goldstein and Abramson (1983) reported on airway obstruction in the lung that was due to allergy. This is an uncommon pediatric problem where an abnormally viscid mucoid plug, mimicking a foreign body, obstructs the endobronchial airway and must be removed surgically. Frequently, but not necessarily, the patient has a history of asthma. After bronchoscopic removal of the obstruction, a complete allergy evaluation is necessary.

Kero *et al.* (1983) reported on the treatment of children who had inhaled foreign bodies in the tracheobronchial tree. In the management of foreign bodies bronchoscopy is the method of choice, but sometimes postural drainage, tracheostomy, and other surgical treatments are needed. Many children experience edema and trauma to the larynx subsequent to the bronchoscopy. There may be quite a long asymptomatic period of months or even years between time of inhalation of a foreign body and development of symptoms. Spasmodic coughing and choking are the most frequent symptoms and inspiratory strider may be present. Symptoms may subside or recur intermittently. Such examples remind us that if we observe children who appear to have respiratory difficulties that persist, or who have trouble phonating when they are engaged in physical exertion that requires additional air expenditure, or who have problems regulating a smooth, even exhalation, we should ensure that a medical referral is made.

Voice symptoms may be residuals of earlier trauma sustained by the laryngeal mechanism, or may be indications of more comprehensive medical conditions. The clinician will frequently encounter children whose past medical history and present medical management will be critical to a comprehensive evaluation of the voice disorder. An understanding of the significance of medical conditions and treatments affecting respiratory and phonatory function is therefore important for the speech–language clinician who must seek and interpret medical information.

Additionally, persistent or recurrent alterations in the respiratory or phonatory structures, or both, may predispose a child to adopt compensatory behaviors that, if habituated, may be abusive or distracting. When a clinician considers such behaviors as throat clearing, coughing, excessive tension during phonation, and the like, it is helpful if he or she is knowledgeable concerning underlying conditions that may predispose, precipitate, or maintain maladaptive vocal behaviors. Children who suffer from chronic infections, allergies, or asthmatic conditions may be "at risk" for developing hyperfunctional patterns of vocal behavior. When voice symptoms occur in association with such conditions, the clinician will need to make sure that medical care is part of the total management program.

VOCAL COMPETENCE: AN ASPECT OF COMMUNICATION COMPETENCE

There is no evidence that, as a group, children with voice disorders have problems with linguistic competence, and if we suspect that they may have problems in this area, tests are available to help us diagnose their specific problem. Another area of competence is more difficult to test formally: the area of communicative competence, or the knowledge of the more social aspects of interpersonal communication. Subsumed under this is the knowledge of the role vocal behavior plays in determining the form and substance of communication messages. Children must learn, for example, when to talk and when to remain silent and when certain kinds of vocalization are appropriate or inappropriate. We learn such rules of communication by observing others, by imitating others, by explicit instruction, and by trial and error. Some children have learned these rules better than others. Some children, for example, abuse thier voices continually, maybe because they have never learned to adjust their vocal volume to particular situations. Thus they talk in the quiet library at the same loudness level as they talk on the noisy playground. These children may need specific training in order to improve this aspect of their communicative competence. Specifically, they need to learn to focus on and interpret the feedback they get from listeners (e.g., words and sentences, eye movements, facial expressions) in face-to-face communication, and the purely vocal feedback available during telephone interactions.

Context

The context in which interpersonal communication takes place has at least four dimensions: physical, social, psychological and temporal (DeVito, 1980). An individual must adjust his or her voice in relation to the concrete, tangible demands of the physical environment in which he or she is operating, as shown in the following examples:

1. The physical demands of an open-air, dusty, noisy playground or football stadium differ from the restrictions of a sickroom, a library, or an art gallery.
2. The social dimension involves a recognition of, and adaptation to, the status relationships among the speakers, the rules of the games, the roles of the participants, and the general norms of the culture. Children must make adjustments in the vocal behavior required for appropriate responses to a reprimand by the principal in his office and an unfair play by a peer on the ballfield.
3. The psychological dimension consists of aspects such as the amount of emotional involvement or distance possible in a given interaction, the recognition of the degree of formality or informality, or the seriousness or humor involved. The perceived need for friendliness or guardedness in a specific communicative exchange may also be important. A boy may wish to be accepted by a peer group but may misjudge the psychological effects his group-entry behaviors have on his peers. The vocal behavior demanded by clowning with peers with the teacher out of the room contrasts sharply with a subsequent attempt to convince the teacher that "It wasn't me yelling, Miss, it was Juan." A significant change in loudness, level of formality, emotional involvement, and nonverbal behavior would be necessary if she was to be persuaded!
4. The temporal dimension includes the time of day as well as the time in history. How likely is a teacher to respond positively to a denial of a child's culpability if that same child had been active in similar skirmishes all day, or perhaps all semester? Some children are adept at interpreting the temporal aspects during communication and adjusting their behavior accordingly (e.g., "I'd better be careful and talk quietly and nicely, 'cause she's mad about all the noise today"); others are not. They operate in every interaction as if it existed in an isolated present, with no past and no future.

Of course, all four dimensions of context interact, and each is influenced by the other. If, for example, the temperature changes (a physical change) or it is the last afternoon before Christmas vacation (a temporal change), there are probably changes in the social and psychological dimensions too.

Field of Experience

The effectiveness of communication is related to the extent that the participants share the same experiences. As children develop increased affective maturity they realize that everyone does not necessarily feel the same way as they do in similar situations. With increased social awareness comes the insight that people are indeed different in the way they see the world and the way they respond to it. The amount of overlap that exists in experiences and the stage of awareness participants have achieved determines the effectiveness of the communication process. Parents sometimes have difficulty communicating with their children because children do not share the parental experience (DeVito, 1980). Children who transfer from a different school or who come from different cultural backgrounds also encounter difficulties adapting their communicative behavior. Strategies that worked in one classroom or playground environment do not always work in the new context. The child needs time to accumulate some shared experiences before he or she can predict and modify behavior and share a common experiental field. This is why the technique of role playing can be such an effective teaching tool during voice therapy.

Effect

Communication always has some effect, since for every communication act there is some consequence (DeVito, 1980). Even when an effect is not observed, it is there. As children develop, they become more adept at observing subtle clues that illuminate the effect that their communication has on others. Usually, at first, they seem to attend only to the effect of their words on their listeners. Gradually, they become aware of the paralinguistic features (e.g., loudness, voice quality, eye contact, facial expression). They also learn to interpret their own reactions to these aspects of other people's behavior. Some children may need special assistance in learning to decode the more subtle aspects of the communication process. It is possible that some children with voice disorders plateau at immature levels in their development of communicative effectiveness. They lack the observational skills to detect that their vocal strategies are not working for them, or they are powerless to modify their habituated vocal behaviors. When this occurs, frustration and tension levels increase. This exacerbates the problem, especially if the voice disorder has a hyperfunctional pattern.

Voice therapy with children often needs to include analyses of communication effectiveness. What is the child trying to achieve in specific interactions? What does he (or she) want? Does he want to be liked, to influence others, to express his feelings, to share his ideas? Once personal goals have been defined, it is easier for a child to understand the reasons for working on changing vocal behavior in therapy.

Ethics

No discussion of communication effectiveness and how an understanding of the communicative act is basic to voice therapy programming would be complete without a consideration of ethics. It is feasible that when the clinician asks, "What did you want when you screamed at the teacher, 'It wasn't me, Miss'?" that the response could well be, "I wanted to con her into blaming Juan." As well as using an unproductive and naive vocal strategy (e.g., defiant yelling), the child is demonstrating unethical behavior. There is an ethical dimension to interpersonal communication: a rightness–wrongness aspect to any act. We cannot always so easily observe the rightness–wrongness of the act itself, but we can speculate concerning intent. Interwoven into the fabric of understanding the effectiveness of communication is the basic consideration of ethical intent. This raises the question of choice. Communication is the art of making choices. When we communicate, we choose—consciously or unconsciously. DeVito (1980) notes some of the ways we choose:

To talk or not to talk.
To begin with this point or another.
To say certain words or others.
To be open or to withhold information.
To lie or not to lie.
To consider others' feelings or not.
To maintain a relationship or terminate it.
To answer questions or not to.
To assume the right to choose for another, or not.

We can learn to predict and control our behaviors only when we know ourselves. Children need to understand the nature of the choices available to them and the ways in which ethical effective interpersonal communication affects their self-esteem, friendships, family relationships, ability to love and be loved, ability to resolve conflict and attain personal goals. Such understanding provides a springboard from which they can move into dynamic, motivated behavioral change.

THE RELATIONSHIP OF VOCAL COMPETENCE TO VOICE DISORDERS

Many people in our society, both children and adults, are handicapped by inappropriate habits such as excessive talking and insensitivity to their listeners. Many individuals seem to exhibit inappropriate interpersonal communication patterns. Evidence of this is the number of self-help books on the market designed to help improve communication skills. Clinical experience suggests that many children (e.g., some children with learning disabilities, fluency problems, articulation disorders, and voice disorders) also exhibit inappropriate interpersonal communication skills. Nevertheless, we have no research evidence to tell us the extent to which immature or ineffective interpersonal communication strategies affect the development or maintenance of a voice disorder. We do not know the extent of the overlap between the group of children who have problems with interpersonal communication in general and those who have problems with interpersonal communication in the presence of a voice disorder. As we work with children day by day, we often suspect, for example, that there may be a causal relationship between immature vocal competence and a child's susceptibility to develop hyperfunctional vocal behavior. But we have no way of knowing whether children with interpersonal problems (e.g., insensitivity to the reactions of others, unsatisfied needs for attention) are more prone to develop vocal symptoms than are other children. Nor do we know the extent to which a vocal handicap, once developed, affects a child's self-esteem, acceptance in the peer group, and so on. Research is needed before any definitive statements can be made.

However, it is certainly possible that a child's communicative competence (especially the level of vocal competence acquired) does have an impact on his or her vocal behavior. Common sense and practical experience suggest that this is so.

Thus, when we observe a child with a voice problem, we need to be cognizant of what the child is trying to achieve through his or her voice use. In the absence of normative data, we must rely on subjective impression. As we watch and listen to a child we can observe whether or not the vocal strategies used seem to be helping or hindering his or her interactions with others. If the child has two problems (i.e., interpersonal problems as well as a voice problem), considering and treating both is a valid approach even if we cannot define a clear causal relationship. It may be that a child with a voice disorder needs even better interpersonal skills than other children if the problem is to be understood and the vocal mechanism protected.

SUMMARY

We have described some aspects of interpersonal behavior with special reference to the development of vocal competence. Vocal competence can be seen as underlying vocal behavior. In subsequent sections of this book we illustrate methods of teaching improved awareness and practice of appropriate vocal interactions.

chapter 2
Children's Vocal Behavior: A Developmental Perspective

Studies of the normal development of the prepubertal voice have focused primarily on the frequency characteristics. Little information is available concerning the quality, intensity, or rate characteristics of the voices of elementary school children. The variables of age and sex have been considered mainly by obtaining samples of boys' and girls' voices and accoustically analyzing the frequency characteristics with respect to cross-sectional age groups. A variety of experimental techniques have been used to elicit samples and analyze the frequency characteristics.

PITCH CHARACTERISTICS

Age Mean, median, and modal frequencies have been obtained, and composite pitch charts (see, e.g., Wilson, 1972, pp. 72–73) have been constructed. In his review of the research of age-related changes in fundamental frequency from birth on, Kent (1976) noted that the results he cited support the following generalization. There is a discernible gradual decline in fundamental frequency (f_o) from age 3 through 11 or 12 years. He concluded that fundamental frequency data may not actually reflect the developmental changes occurring as children grow. He pointed out that what appear to be age-related changes related to maturation may actually be due to the variability in vocalizations and differences in methodology. He also noted the small number of subjects studied in some of the age groups. Discrepancies in the findings reported for children in the 7- to 11-year-old groups in particular prompted Bennett (1983) to collect data on children in this age range, using a longitudinal approach. She noted that when she used group rather than individual data to obtain year-to-year comparisons of the same children, both sexes showed a generalized lowering of f_o over a three-year period.

The largest decrements occurred between the ages of 8 years 2 months and 11 years 2 months. The only exception to the general downward trend from 8 years 2 months to 11 years 2 months was the one-year period between 9 years 2 months and 10 years 2 months when neither of the group means showed any change.

Sex   There do not seem to be any fundamental frequency differences between boys' and girls' voices prior to puberty. With the exception of Hasek *et al.* (1980), who found a significant sexual distinction at ages 7, 8, 9, and 10 years, most other studies, acoustic and anatomic, cross-sectional and longitudinal, suggest that boys' and girls' voices are similar before adolescence (Bennett, 1983; Kahane, 1975; Weinberg & Bennett, 1971; Bennett & Weinberg, 1979; Fairbanks, Herbert, & Hammond, 1949; Fairbanks, Wiley, & Lassman, 1949, and Vuorenkoski *et al.*, 1978).

Puberty   Many references in the literature concern the effect of vocal mutation on the pitch characteristics of children's voices. It is not clear when mutational changes occur, especially in boys, since there is no dramatic physiological change signifying the onset of puberty. Physiologists such as Rose Frisch (1975) have described such a salient factor as the amount of body fat in relation to overall body weight, which affects the onset of the menarche in females. Variability in the onset of puberty itself (Tanner, 1969), in the length of time from its beginning to end, and in the timing of the laryngeal changes that relate to vocal mutation (Kahane, 1975; Klock, 1968) cause practical difficulties for researchers. Wilson (1972) states that a boy's voice may lower as much as an octave during the period of mutation, and a girl's voice may lower three or four semitones. Huskiness and voice breaks may also be noted. Voice breaks were noted by Fairbanks, Herbert, and Hammond (1949) and by Fairbanks, Wiley, and Lassman (1949) in both boys and girls as young as 7 or 8 years of age. None of Bennett's (1983) 10- or 11-year-old boys showed evidence of changes in their voice. Hollien and Malcik's (1967) data suggest that changes occur during 14 to 18 years of age in males. Duffy (1970) suggests that girls undergo a form of vocal mutation at the time of the menarche, though the transition from the child to the adult voice probably occurs gradually over a long time. Limited data are available, and the relationship between the onset of menstruation and voice change in girls is not completely understood. Since in this book we are concerned with elementary school children, we probably can assume that most of the changes in children's voices occur after the fifth grade and during the middle school or high school years. Ten- and 11-year-old males, as seen in studies by Bennett (1983), Curry (1940), Hollien and Malcik (1962), and Hollien, Malcik, and Hollien (1965) appear still to exhibit childlike frequency characteristics. It might be important for us to remember, however, that articles in recent health publications dealing with the onset of puberty in girls refer to the gradual lowering during the twentieth century of the age of the onset of menstruation. Frisch (1975) has noted that the diet of children in highly developed countries has changed significantly during the last century, and this may have contributed to an increased proportion of body fat, which triggers an earlier onset of puberty. Some females may begin to enter puberty as young as 8 years of age. Certainly, more information is needed before we fully understand the relationship between puberty and vocal development. Variables such as height and weight, in addition to chronological age, may need to be considered more carefully.

Experimental Tasks

As Kent (1976) noted, variability in results of studies of children's voices may be related to differences in methodology. Especially important may be the way that the vocal behavior is elicited and the kind of sample analyzed. In any discussion of the vocal behavior of young children, one needs to consider carefully the way in which the vocal response is obtained. Young children frequently do not understand an abstract vocal task, and they may also be influenced by the voice of the adult experimenter. Eguchi and Hirsh (1969) had their 7-year-old speakers repeat sentences after the investigator and derived their f_o values from spectrograms of six vowels occurring in two short sentences. Their older children read the sentences, as did the children in the study by Fairbanks, Wiley, and Lassman (1949). Vuorenkoski *et al.* (1978) and Hasek *et al.* (1980) analyzed a single isolated sustained vowel. Bennett (1983) provided a model for her subjects and asked them to say the sentence with a comfortable level of loudness. She notes that f_o values obtained from a single vowel would probably differ from those in a sentence utterance and that it is difficult to ascertain where, in their vocal range, children produce an isolated vowel. Reading tasks and imitation tasks are probably also likely to result in differences in suprasegmental patterns when compared to spontaneous utterances. When we consider that the subjects participating in the studies mentioned were between 7 and 11 years of age, we also must consider the influence of cognitive development of the younger versus the older children in responding to task instructions. As we see later in this chapter, when we discuss cognitive development, children younger than 8 years of age sometimes respond differently than older children when given instructions concerning vocal performance. For example, a 7-year-old child may not comprehend the instruction "a comfortable loudness level" as completely as a 10 year old.

Basal Pitch

As well as considering tasks to elicit voice samples of average fundamental frequency of vowels, spontaneous speech, and sentences that are read, let us look at another measurement of frequency characteristics. In some studies, and in clinical practice, we are sometimes interested in obtaining measurements of basal pitch. Basal pitch is the lowest pitch that an individual can produce (i.e., the lowest note in the pitch range). It is a useful landmark, since it can be compared with habitual or average pitch and allow an estimate to be made of how close to the bottom of the range the child's habitual pitch level actually is. The stability of measurements of basal pitch in adults was first affirmed by Pronovost (1939) and reiterated by Van Riper and Irwin (1958) and Fairbanks (1960). Cooper and Yanagihara (1971) questioned the stability when they showed that their adult subjects varied one to three semitones at different times during two days.

Austin and Leeper (1975) measured basal pitch levels of school-age children and concluded that individual levels varied as much as four semitones across days and as much as three semitones at different times during a single day. It is important to note that the oldest children in the Austin and Leeper study were 10 years, 11 months. It is possible that the difficulty of the task may have been confounded by the length and complexity of the verbal instructions used. Andrews and Madiera (1977) reported that 8-year-old subjects were less proficient at comprehending relational terms (high–low; higher–lower) when they referred to auditory events than when the same words were describing spatial relations. Instructions such as "lowest yet most comfortable pitch" involve complex abstract relationships.

Andrews and Huffman (1984) studied a comparison of two methods of eliciting basal pitch levels and found that basal pitch levels were significantly lower when children were given visual feedback. This difference was consistently observed when the children subsequently were tested on two different days and at different times of day (morning and afternoon).

We have discussed basal pitch in some detail in order to illustrate the differences in measures that can be obtained depending on elicitation method. The importance of basal pitch measurements may also be considered in terms of comparison with other measures. It is possible that a difference score obtained by subtracting the basal from the habitual level may be useful in charting the developmental changes that occur as a child matures. If indeed, as Wilson (1972) suggests, boys' voices lower an octave at puberty, the basal pitch–habitual pitch differential may be a useful way of recording such changes. It is reasonable to assume that lower notes may be added to the range prior to significant changes occurring in the average habitual pitch level during the early stages of voice mutation. The efficacy of this approach needs further study. It may provide a way of documenting subtle developmental differences that have eluded researchers in the past.

DURATION OF SUSTAINED VOCALIZATIONS

Measurements of children's ability to sustain phonation on vowels and voiced and unvoiced consonants have been reported by a number of investigators. The duration of prolonged sounds (i.e., mean phonation time) has been measured by some investigators in order to ascertain whether an individual has a sufficiently long exhalation to support connected speech. Westlake and Rutherford (1961) reported that whereas normal children could sustain a tone for 20 seconds or longer, their study of cerebral palsied children led them to hypothesize that a child needs to be able to phonate for a minimum of 10 seconds in order to speak in phrases of more than two or three words. Clinicians have also traditionally used prolongation tasks to ascertain information about continuity of voicing and to note pitch breaks or variations in voluntary control. Boone (1977) stated that the phonation of /s/ and /z/ provided information about how well an individual sustained exhalation with and without voicing. More recently, Eckel and Boone (1981) found that 95% of their adult voice patients with laryngeal pathologies demonstrated s/z ratios in excess of 1:4. They found that individuals with glottal lesions exhibit significantly shorter /z/ durations than normal patients, although /s/ durations were of normal length.

Thus the limited information available concerning the average or mean phonation time of sustained vowels and consonants produced by elementary school children assumes greater importance to us. We need additional information in order to understand more completely how the behavior of vocally handicapped children compares to the behavior of normal children of the same age.

Frey (1978) studied preschoolers' prolongations and noted the importance of standardized protocols for testing that ensure that young children understand the concept of continuity. She advocated the use of specific concrete materials, visual clues, and models. Michel and Tait (1977) reported average phonation times for elementary school children aged 5, 7 and 9 years. The results of these two studies are summarized in Table 2-1.

Launer (1971) reported on both boys' and girls' average phonation times for the three vowels /a/, /i/, and /u/ and found that there were no significant differences between the three vowels. The males' phonation times were longer for all ages (9 through 17), except for the 12 year olds where the phonation time was the same for both sexes. A summary of some of these data appears in Table 2-2.

Table 2-1 **Prolongation of /s/ and /z/ by Normal Children**

Age	N[a]	/s/		/z/		Researchers
		Mean in Secs.	S.D.	Mean in Secs.	S.D.	
3.0 yr. to 4.8 yr.	183	3.7	1.99	4.15	2.08	Frey
5.3 yr. to 6.6 yr.	162	4.56	2.12	5.31	2.94	Frey
3–6 yr.	450	4.07	2.52	4.71	2.30	Frey
5 yr.	15	8.13	3.25	9.47	2.97	Michel and Tait
7 yr.	14	9.79	2.27	13.40	3.83	Michel and Tait
9 yr.	24	15.80	7.21	17.20	6.36	Michel and Tait
5–9 yr.	53	12.06	6.33	13.95	5.95	Michel and Tait

Sources: Marsha J. Frey, "The Prolongation of /s/ and /z/ by Pre-school Children" (Master's thesis, Indiana University, 1978); and John F. Michel, University of Kansas, and Nancy A. Tait, University of Kansas Medical Center, Kansas City, "Maximum Duration of Sustained /s/ and /z/" (paper presented at ASHA, Chicago, November 3, 1977).

[a]N = sample size.

Table 2-2 **Average Durations of Sustained Vocalizations**

Age	Vocalization			Average Phonation Time in Seconds	
				Females	Males
9 yr.	/a/	/i/	/u/	8.8	11.4
10 yr.	/a/	/i/	/u/	9.4	10.4
11 yr.	/a/	/i/	/u/	11.5	12.8
12 yr.	/a/	/i/	/u/	12.2	12.8

Source: P. G. Launer, "Maximum Phonation Time in Children" (Master's thesis, State University of New York at Buffalo, 1971).

RELEVANT INFORMATION ON CHILD DEVELOPMENT

As we said earlier, it is important to remember that children, even though they may frequently exhibit the same kinds of vocal symptoms as adults, cannot be treated in exactly the same way. Children are not miniature adults, and strategies that work with adults do not necessarily translate to children. The cognitive, linguistic, social, and emotional developmental level of the child is an important consideration in all our planning of therapy. We have noted that children are not always aware of the nature of their problem of the effect of their vocal behavior on themselves and others. The abstractness of the behaviors compounds the difficulty. One of the challenges of voice therapy with children is to reduce the general level of abstractness. We can do this best when we understand the developmental stages that young children go through in acquiring concepts and skills that are relevant to voice therapy.

Cognitive Development

Some of the cognitive skills that a child needs in order to participate in voice therapy are, of course, the same as the skills needed to participate in other learning tasks (i.e., the ability to attend to stimuli, focus on relevant elements, understand instructions, remember, match auditory patterns and so on). Many associations that are made in voice therapy are especially complex, however, and children do not always make these associations the same way that adults do. For example, in an association between a target voice and the obligatory modifications in the vocal tract, the target response is a fleeting sound that is "heard"; the sequence of behavior used to produce the sound may be "felt" in various parts of the mechanism; and visual cues may be minimal. Thus the child is asked to make a connection between a vocal sound and a kinesthetic awareness of how that sound is produced. We cannot assume that children automatically focus on the salient aspects of the behavioral gestalt. Explicit statements, such as, "If I feel this, then my voice sounds like that," need to be explained, taught, and reiterated. This kind of explanation usually involves cause–effect relationships. A review of some literature concerning children's development of causative reasoning is helpful.

The early work by Piaget (1928, 1929, 1930) on causality, substantiated later by work done by Inhelder and Piaget (1964), suggests two important aspects of children's development. First, the development of a concrete operational conception of causality stems from the child's egocentric projection of his or her own point of view onto the material world, while reversible mental operations remain absent. Egocentric projection leads to the assignment of psychological or human causes to natural or mechanical phenomena (i.e., precausal thought). Second, the child develops the concept of objective causality, which involves the relationship between two phenomena in the object world, independent of their relationship to the subject. Hood and Bloom (1979) additionally discuss that a child first refers to actions by self and others as aspects of his (or her) own egocentric world. Later, his development continues to extend to both actions and intentions of self and others; it is no longer merely restricted to his egocentric world. Hood and Bloom (1979) also state that a child's causal reasoning continues to be qualitatively different from the adult's until age 7 or 8 (Piaget, 1926, 1928, 1930; Werner & Kaplan, 1963). In other words, a child's causal reasoning develops until it approaches the adult's concept of causality around 7 or 8 years of age.

It is critical that we do not merely assume that because we understand causal relationships, they are equally obvious to the children we teach. Indeed, it is probably the case that most children under age 8, and children over age 8 who have cognitive deficits, will not understand them exactly as adults do. Some common examples of statements in voice therapy that may need to be reexamined in relation to this are: "If you yell and scream, you'll get bumps on your vocal cords"; "If you talk too much, you'll hurt your throat"; "If you don't breathe deeply, you'll run out of air"; "If you talk softly, no one will hear you."

Champley (1977) studied the way that preschool children could be helped to process the instructions given during tasks to elicit vocal samples. For children in the preoperational stage of cognitive development, intellectual processing is marked by intuitive assimilation and accommodation. According to Neubauer (1965), "intuitive cognitive functioning refers to an implicit, relatively imprecise and informal type of understanding" (p. 18). In the preschool child this is marked by the relatively nonverbal character of cognitive functioning and a reliance on overt manipulation of concrete-empirical props when attempting logical operations (Neubauer, 1965). Because of this, it is necessary to provide young children with the means for processing verbal directions at a concrete level.

Imagery research offers some insights concerning the representation of abstract ideas. Reese (1970) suggests that information can be presented to children in two ways in order to foster acquisition:

1. In a meaningful linguistic content rather than in isolated terms, with some kind of spatial relation or meaningful interaction between objects.
2. With a cue for response that is concrete rather than abstract, pictorial rather than verbal. (pp. 404–414)

Writers in the areas of teaching mathematics and music (Jeffrey, 1958; McMahon, 1961) to young children have provided further pertinent insights concerning specific use of visual cues and relationships to represent abstract ideas. Welsh and Harvin (1976) suggest a developmental hierarchy of visual representations in mathematics proceeding from the most concrete representation to the most abstract.

1. Concrete, manipulable objects
2. Colored photographs
3. Black and white photographs
4. Colored pictures
5. Line drawings
6. Diagrams
7. Symbolic representations (includes written symbols)

Schiffman (1976) said that discrimination of auditory stimuli is one of the most important psychological processes involved in learning, and the one about which we know very little. It may develop as a Gestalt-like abstraction through experience or through a gradual extraction of differentiated attributes. It is clear, however, that young children's ability to process information and instructions related to vocal behavior depends to a large extent on the type of visual clue used to represent the focal attributes of the signal. The younger the child, the more necessary the visual clue is, and the more concrete that clue needs to be. While the use of the visual-clue method may provide a child with a means for a more overt manipulation of abstract ideas, some degree of verbal mediation is usually still required. The simplest form of verbal mediation is the basic model–response paradigm. The use of modeling is an integral part of speech–language–voice therapy programs. The classical psycholinguistic definition of modeling refers to an imitation of vocalizations "which occur in close temporal proximity" to a given target (Prutting & Connolly, 1976). Elicited imitation, according to Prutting and Connolly (1976), refers to "those imitations which occur when a child responds to an examiner's request to 'say what I say' and repeats a model" (p. 415). Elicited imitation has long been used in language evaluations and allows a great variety of language stimuli to be investigated (Carrow, 1974). The assumption has not been explored fully in relation to voice evaluation techniques. Nonetheless, it seems the only feasible method with very young children, since it eliminates the need for verbal and symbolic mediation and emphasizes sensory decoding and encoding of the vocal model. Imitation of vocal patterns is a practice that children engage in from early infancy. Champley (1977) found that the use of a vocal model was especially critical in vocal tasks involving pitch and loudness.

The Visi-Pitch machine allows for a target production to remain in view while the child attempts to match it.

Visual cues are important, especially for younger children, but it is also important to note that equipment that provides biofeedback and electroacoustical monitoring can be used most successfully with children. Any noninvasive instrument can be used safely in school settings; however, the portability and cost of such equipment often limits widespread acceptance in schools. One serviceable piece of equipment is the See-Scape, manufactured by C.C. Publications, Tigard, Oregon. This portable tool, which allows a child to monitor emission of air through the nose, can be purchased inexpensively. The Visi-Pitch, manufactured by Kay Elemetrics Corporation, Pinebrook, New Jersey, is also a valuable aid for diagnosis and therapy. It allows for frequency and intensity information to be displayed on an oscilloscope screen. The split screen also allows for a target production to remain in view as the child attempts to match it. The Visi-Pitch is rugged and portable, but the cost has limited its use in school settings.

Linguistic Development

Let us consider some of the simplest descriptive terms used in voice therapy. Adjectives or antonyms such as *loud*, *soft*, *high*, and *low* name poles on a continuum of perceptual judgments of frequency or intensity.

They are called *relational terms* because they describe perceived relationships. Appropriate receptive and expressive use of such terms requires at least a partial understanding of certain complex relationships. The terms also can be used in more than one sense. We do not know the ages at which normal children acquire these terms, but it is likely, for example, that children acquire *high* and *low* initially in the spatial sense and only later apply these words to auditory events. Similarly, the word *soft* is probably learned first in association with tactile stimuli.

Clark (1969b, p. 206) states that the senses of certain positive adjectives, like "good" and "long," are stored in the memory in a less complex form than the senses of their opposites. Many writers have noted that a number of antonymous adjectives are not symmetric opposites (Sapir, 1944; Lyons, 1963; Greenberg, 1966; Vendler, 1968; Clark, 1969a). The scale is named in many cases by the unmarked "positive" member of the pair of adjectives when both adjectives describe the same dimension. Also, in many pairs the positive adjective is neutralized at times. For example, "How high is it?" asks simply for information, but "How low is it?" seems to imply that the object is expected to be low. Both the unmarked and the marked adjectives can be used in a contrastive sense such as "Pete's voice is loud" and "Bill's voice is soft." In this way the terms specify the dimension, contrast with each other, and imply an assumed standard. Sapir (1944) said that even when an unqualified relational term is used, for example, "Your voice is loud," it is no less relational than when a standard is given: "Your voice is louder than mine." Sapir called it the unqualified "ungraded" term when it depends on a comparison with a norm relevant to that particular subject. Therefore, "Motorcycles are loud" implies in relation to other vehicles; "That motorcycle is loud" implies in relation to other motorcycles.

When the terms *loud* and *soft* are compared, it appears that *loud* is unmarked, and *soft*, as it is used to describe a pole on the scale of loudness, is marked. *Loud* can possess neutral qualities for use in a nominative sense, as in "How loud is the TV?" as well as in a contrastive sense, "That TV was loud." *Soft* seems to be used only in a contrastive sense. When using the terms *high* and *low* to describe tonal stimuli, *high* appears to be the unmarked term, while *low* is marked. However, it is apparent that "How high is the man's voice?" is not a neutral question. Both high and low can be marked when applied to descriptions of the postpubertal human voice, depending on the sex of the speaker.

When the comparative constructions of the terms are used ("Your voice is louder" or "Which one is highest," for example) the problems of implied standards and complex relationships are compounded. Although it may seem that young children should easily understand the simple descriptive terms used during voice therapy, it may not necessarily be so (Andrews, 1975).

Discussion of the Problem with the Child   It is interesting to observe the responses of children hearing recordings of their voices. Unless they have had a great deal of listening training, they seem to respond, not to any specific attribute of the auditory signal, but to the total sound as a symbol of self. Thus the child is likely to say "That's me, isn't it?" or "That's not me" rather than "That's my voice" or "That's not my voice." Such evidence of the strong association of self with voice reminds us that it is certainly ill advised to use any negative terms such as *wrong, bad,* or *unpleasant* to describe vocal symptoms. It is also apparent that in attempting to describe the possible effects of inappropriate vocal behavior, words such as *hurt, harm* or *damage,* which suggest bodily injury, should be avoided.

It is probably reasonable to refer to a child's voice as "different" when attempting to make him or her aware of the problem. It is important, however, that the parameter to be focused on is clearly understood. When selecting terms to be used in describing the target vocal parameter, it is probably wise for a clinician to avoid using the same terms for more than one parameter. For example, *low* is sometimes

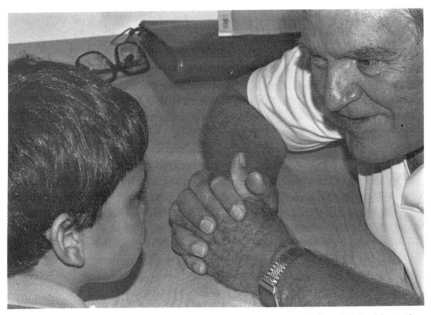

The clinician's nonverbal behavior during discussions with the child adds to the effectiveness of the communication.

used to refer to both pitch and loudness levels. It is also helpful if the words used to describe the parameter under discussion can be applied readily in changing situations. For example, *inappropriate* is a term that relies heavily on context. A voice that is inappropriately loud in the library may be perfectly appropriate or even mandatory outdoors. Even the use of the word *too* before a descriptive adjective (e.g., "too loud") also implies that the child has internalized some kind of standard for both the loudness and the situation. It is helpful if the clinician uses terms that can later mark points on a realistic continuum when finer contrasts are demanded. Clinicians can become trapped by their own terminology if this has not been considered in advance.

Attempts to Make Therapy More Concrete   It seems easiest to find suitable nonauditory representations of the intensity parameter; more variety is found in materials used to illustrate various loudness levels. Visual feedback can be provided by pictures, instruments with needles, or lights reflecting changes in intensity (e.g., the sound-level meter and the decibeloscope), and objects of various sizes. Pictures most frequently used seem to fall into one of the following categories: size difference, facial expression, or gesture showing speaker effort, or listener reaction (e.g., hands cupped around mouth or finger to lips), effect on an object (e.g., a vibrating drum or slammed door) and varied distances between speaker and listener.

McDonald and Chance (1964), referring to therapy with cerebral palsied children, advocate the use of role-playing activities in which the child pretends to be whispering a secret, giving an order like a policeman, and so on. In this way the context or interaction helps define the loudness level.

When pitch or quality are under consideration in therapy, however, fewer options are available. Pitch differences may be depicted spatially by using pictures of stairs, ladders, or, as Wilson (1972) suggests, children standing on rocks of different heights. Wilson (1972) also noted that puppets can be used. The sizes of the puppets can be related to differences in pitch levels. Quality differences may be represented pictorially with type of movement, such as pictures of palm trees moving gently or vigorously in the wind (Wilson, 1972), or by using differences in texture, such as grains and materials representing a variety of tactile sensations (Andrews, 1973).

There seems to be no way to make perceptual evaluations tangible and concrete, or to make imitation of vocal patterns as clear-cut as imitation of the placement of articulators can be made. Voice therapy can never be absolutely clear and direct in its approach because of the obviously inaccessible sound source. It is reasonable to assume, nevertheless, that procedures can be refined and realistic expectations for children developed if the complexities of the concepts and linguistic terms used in voice therapy are considered.

Affective Development

Our voices reflect our feelings, and our ability to understand the feelings of others depends, in part, on our ability to perceive significant cues in their vocal expression. Studies of parent–child interactions have shown that even infants and very young children adapt their vocal behavior in response to the vocal patterning of the adult. In a study reported by Lieberman (1975) infants modified their pitch levels to approximate the adult model. They vocalized at a lower pitch when interacting with the father and used a higher pitch when babbling in response to the mother. This study, and studies of recognition of speaker's voices by infants (see Aslin, Pisoni, & Jusczyk, 1983, p. 657) illustrates the importance of the effect of vocal models on the child's learning of vocal expression.

There is another interesting line of research that has relevance to our understanding of how children learn about the expression of their own and others' feelings. This involves the ways an individual learns to identify his or her own emotional state (Schacter, 1975). Skinner (1971) stated that children initially identify emotion in terms of external cues. This continues until the linguistic community draws their attention to the less salient cues associated with the external circumstances. If we accept the premise that the linguistic community plays an important part in shaping the child's focus on the more subtle cues, we would assume that considerable variation exists in the way children learn to attend to variations in vocal expression. There would also be the potential for some young children to identify cues inaccurately or fail to attend at all to certain cues.

It seems that young children are usually unaware of the possibility that different feelings and emotions may be felt by different individuals responding to the same external cues. They assume that everyone feels and reacts the same way they do in a given situation. Their descriptions of their feelings are concrete and specific to the external situation or event. For example, when asked to explain "happy" a young child might say, "I feel happy when it's my birthday." It is obvious that the emotion is defined specifically in terms of the situation. The emotion itself is seen as a predictable consistent part of that event. The underlying assumption that everyone feels or reacts the same way is revealed in answers to questions such as, "Does your friend feel happy then, too?" Frequently a young child will reply, "Yes, she knows it's my birthday."

It is only as children grow older that they begin to understand that it is possible for people to hide their true feelings. Ekman and Oster (1979) discussed this aspect of affective development. They said that older children acknowledge that sometimes one is unaware of another's true emotion, or might mislead another person regarding an emotion. Lazarus (1968, 1975) states that strategies might be employed not only to manipulate the external signs of the emotion but also to reduce or augment the emotional experience itself.

Some knowledge of emotions, and the ways in which they are expressed, is probably an important prerequisite to success in modifying certain kinds of vocal behavior. If we do not understand that our own behavior may be affected by our feelings, or recognize the feelings of others, it is difficult to focus on vocal behaviors that reflect a part of a general emotional response. Voice clinicians frequently need to help children increase their understanding of feelings generally, and then help them learn how feelings are reflected in specific vocal behaviors. Some information about the sequence of development of children's understanding of emotion is, therefore, relevant to voice therapy programming.

Harris, Olthof, and Terwogt (1981) investigated the existence of marked changes with age in children's knowledge of situational, personal, and strategic factors. Concepts of happiness, anger, and fear were explored. In this study, subjects in three age groups (mean age 6, 11,15) responded to questions. The responses were analyzed with respect to the use of cues to identify each emotion, the strategies of self-control, and the effects of the emotion on other psychological processes.

Results indicated that the number of children defining emotion in terms of situational cues declined with age, and the citing of mental cues increased with age. The older children, but not the youngest group, concentrated on the observed rather than the observer. These results confirmed the speculation that many of the younger children had difficulty in imagining a situation where an observer might be unaware of another person's emotion. The two older groups of subjects were also more able to realize that another person's detection of their emotion is contingent on how they behave. There was also evidence to suggest that a child's detection of emotion depends on the nature of the emotion. The revealing of the positive emotion is more likely to occur through actions, while negative emotions are more likely to be revealed through answers in which an inner state, distinct from outward expression, is implied. Both the younger and older subjects conceived of the intentional display of emotion through actions, statements, and facial expression. The older children were more sensitive to the possible conflict between inner and outer states, however, the younger children focused on the outer display of emotion only. In addition, the three age groups demonstrated different strategies when asked how they could change their emotion. Although subjects of all ages suggested changing the situation, only the two older groups proposed cognitive strategies, such as redirecting one's thoughts.

Results of this and other studies indicate a progression in the development of the conception of emotion. One pattern predominates among young children, and this pattern changes somewhere between the ages of 6 and 11 years. By 11 years of age most children have begun to move from the conceptualization that can be described as standard behavioristic (or stimulus–response) described by Skinner (1971) to what Miller *et al.* (1960) have described as subjective behaviorism. In other words, the young child focuses on publicly observable components of emotion—the eliciting situation and the overt behavioral reactions. Children age 11 and older consider not only the observable components but also the hidden mental aspect of emotion.

It would probably be helpful to the voice clinician if we summarized children's knowledge of emotion in terms of two distinct developmental stages (adapted from Harris, Olthof, & Terwogt, 1981):

Stage I: Younger than 6 years of age

$$Emotion = situation + own\ behavioral\ reactions$$

e.g.,   happy   birthday   laughing
        sad   pet's funeral   crying
        angry   quarrel   yelling

One's own emotion is identified by noting either the situation or one's reactions.

Another's emotion is identified by noting his or her reactions; correct identification is seen as restricted only by the location of the observer and his or her attentiveness to those reactions.

Control over emotion is accomplished in either of two ways: (1) may pretend by displaying a reaction different from one normally elicited by the situation (e.g., joking after a quarrel); (2) may alter the emotion itself by changing the situation giving rise to the emotion in the first place (e.g., making up after a quarrel).

Effects of emotion. Young children merely note that positive emotions have positive effects and negative emotions have negative effects. There is no attempt to explain them.

Stage II: 11 years and older

$$Emotion = situation + own\ and\ others'\ behavioral\ reactions\\ + inner\ mental\ states$$

One's own emotion is best identified by reference to inner mental states.

Another's emotion is difficult to identify, since visible reactions are seen as an unreliable guide to inner mental states, and an observer may fail to identify another's emotion accurately.

Control over emotion can be exercised in several ways:

1. May pretend by displaying a response different from that normally elicited by the situation. Such a pretense is complicated, however, by the resulting conflict between outer display and inner mental state.
2. Masking of the inner state.
3. Redirecting the inner state.
4. Altering the situation to control the experience of the emotion.

Effects of emotion. Older children provide more mentalistic explanations of the effects of emotion.

We have seen earlier that it is possible that some children with voice disorders may also have problems with interpersonal relationships. Sometimes they may not understand how their own emotional responses are perceived by others or the need to consider the effect of their feelings on their vocal behavior. The information in the preceding section may help the clinician to recognize the child's stage of awareness concerning the feelings he or she and others may be experiencing. It may also help the clinician plan therapy strategies to teach children to identify their feelings and describe them as they relate to vocal expression and productive coping strategies.

Social Development

One of the most important skills young children need to learn is that of gaining entry to a group of peers during play. This is a critical social task for children, and it is probable that vocal behavior significantly affects the process of assimilation into groups. The group entry process has been referred to as "assimilation" (Phillips, Shenker, & Revitz, 1951), "access" (Corsaro, 1981), and "initiations" (Vandell & George, 1981). Whatever the process is called, it is evidently a difficult one to learn. Kindergarteners were studied by Corsaro (1981), who found that young children's initial efforts to enter a peer group were rebuffed by their peers approximately 50% of the time. Studies have also shown that there are developmental changes in the strategies children use to enter groups and that as children grow older the strategies become more sophisticated.

While differences in strategies used by children have been studied in relation to the child's age and stage of development, they have also been studied in other ways. Richard and Dodge (1982) found that popular children generated more strategies, as well as more competent strategies, than did children who were unpopular with their peers. Putallaz and Gottman (1981a, 1981b) studied second-grade children and found that unpopular children were more likely to use "hovering" behavior and self-referent speech than did popular children. Neither of these strategies resulted in acceptance by peers. Coie, Dodge, and Coppotelli (1982) subdivided unpopular children into two groups. They referred to children who were not liked by peers, or were actively disliked, as rejected children. Those who were not liked, but were not disliked either, were called neglected children. Dodge, Coie, and Brakke (1982) found that rejected and neglected children behave differently from popular children, both in the classroom and on the playground.

Studies of children in laboratory situations and naturalistic settings have resulted in some interesting findings about the strategies employed by children categorized as popular, rejected, and neglected. The group entry behavior of rejected and neglected children seems less likely to involve group-oriented statements and more likely to involve self-oriented statements and behaviors. Peers seem to perceive the rejected children as aggressive and disruptive. This appears to be related to the frequency with which rejected children try to enter a group with active or loud behavior that interrupts the group's activity. They also seem more often to respond negatively to statements initiated by peer hosts or established group members. Neglected children, however, engage in fewer entry attempts than other children. Neglected children appear to employ nonassertive approaches, such as waiting and hovering around a peer group. Hovering was the most frequent strategy used by neglected children, even though it is typically ignored by peers. The different entry strategies used by popular, rejected, and neglected children only partially explains the responses of peers. Researchers have also noted that peers may be favorably biased toward popular children because of other factors, such as physical attractiveness.

Although documentation of social competence is incomplete, studies of entry behaviors have yielded some findings that are of interest to the clinician designing voice therapy intervention programs. Undoubtedly, individual children vary in the degree of social awareness and competence they exhibit. Some children who develop vocal problems related to abuse may also exhibit patterns of social behavior similar to those described by children categorized as rejected. Similarly, children who are handicapped because of vocal disorders may at times exhibit nonassertive approaches to group entry and be ignored by their peers, in the way that children described as neglected are ignored. The part played by vocal behavior in the perception of general physical attractiveness is also not completely understood at this time. More research is needed before we can explain the part the voice plays in the process of peer acceptance. Nonetheless, it is certainly useful for us to review the strategies that psychologists have identified as entry behaviors, and consider the way in which voice use may or may not contribute to their success. Then, when we identify children with voice problems who are repeatedly unsuccessful in their attempts to gain access to peer groups, we can teach alternative patterns of vocal use and relate them to meaningful social goals. A coding system explained by Dodge, Schlunt, Delagach, and Schocken (1982) and developed from systems used by others (Dodge, 1981) isolates strategies such as those listed below. Such a list may be used by the voice clinician to observe children's behavior (see Table 2-3). It also provides useful information that can be helpful in enhancing motivation and structuring discussion of reasons for changing behavior during implementation of voice therapy programs.

Group-oriented statements and behaviors (e.g., questions and statements about the group or the activity) are the most effective strategies and are used more by older children and by children perceived as popular. Dodge *et al.* (1982) have suggested that such strategies are related to the Piagetian process of decentration. In order to make a statement that is group-oriented rather than self-oriented, the child must adopt the frame of reference of the group. This involves orientation to the behavior of others over oneself and is not consistent with egocentric thought. Deviant children are more likely to use strategies (such as disruptions and attention getting) that draw attention to themselves. They are less likely to use group-referenced strategies. Researchers have noted that deviant children frequently move from peer goup to peer group, attempting to gain entry but failing to join in. Dodge, Coie, and Brakke (1982) have observed that in the classroom and on the playground deviant children, particularly neglected children, approach each other infrequently. They suggest that the withdrawal of these children may occur as a result of a series of failures to establish positive peer relationships. Such children may not, therefore, respond to encouragement to join in. They may need to be specifically taught alternative strategies for initiating peer contacts.

A low-risk strategy, one in which the probability of a decisive outcome (either positive or negative) is small in comparison to the probability of a neutral outcome, is usually tried first, especially by children who are not acquainted. The best example of a low-risk strategy is hovering around a peer group and waiting to be invited to play. The

Table 2-3 **Strategies Used by Children Approaching Peers**

Strategy	Identifying Behaviors
Wait and hover	approaches a group observes activity for more than three seconds does not speak

Attention getting	verbal or nonverbal attempts
	  (nonaversive)
	tries to attract attention
	tries to interrupt play
	(*example:* bounces a ball on the table
	  where other children are
	  playing
	  clowning, shouting, etc.)

Group-oriented statements	verbalizations refers to the children or the play activity (*example:* "That looks like a fun game you are playing")

Question	child directs a question to the group
	  members
	requires or expects a response
	(*example:* "What are you doing?"
	  "What is your name?")

Self-referent statement	verbal statement referring to self verbal statement describing self (*example:* "I've got lots of cars like that" "I want a turn")
Disruption	verbal or nonverbal aversive behavior interrupts peers' play disrupts peers' play (*example:* grabs toys knocks over building blocks)

Mimicking	imitation of the behavior of the group
	attempts to integrate by engaging in same
	  behavior as group
	(*example:* parallel play with toys
	  playing basketball
	  singing)

Other	any other behavior initiated by entry child

peer-group entry process is one of taking increasing risks as the entry process proceeds. Dodge *et al.* (1981) have proposed that children employ low-risk strategies during initial stages of the entry process and higher-risk strategies during later stages. Some common sequences of children's strategies are:

1. Waiting and hovering ⟶ group-oriented statement
2. Waiting and hovering ⟶ mimicking of peer group
3. Disruption ⟶ disruption
4. Waiting and hovering ⟶ mimicking ⟶ statement regarding peer group (most successful)

Similarly, it seems easier for children to use high-risk strategies with children with whom they are already acquainted. Examples of high-risk strategies include making statements, asking questions, and mimicking the behavior of the group during the approach. Children seem to minimize the risk of rejection by employing such strategies only after they have been successful with lower-risk strategies. It is possible that socially incompetent children have not learned the progression from low-risk to high-risk strategies. They may either remain at the stage of employing low-risk strategies or jump too soon into high-risk strategies. The former pattern may be perceived as shyness and the latter pattern as disruptiveness. McFall and Dodge (1982) have observed that correct employment of such a progression involves the ability to observe accurately the responses of other children.

The successful child is the one who manages to avoid drawing attention to himself or herself during entry and focuses on the group. Putallaz and Gottman (1981a, 1981b) stressed that any strategy that drew attention away from the group was most often met with rejection. Continual group reference may involve such cognitive skills as role taking and empathy, skills frequently associated with social competence (Chandler, 1973; Staub, 1975).

SUMMARY

We have reviewed some of the information drawn from various areas of child development that may have relevance to voice therapy. Some generalizations can be made concerning the way our knowledge of developmental stages can affect the way we approach intervention. It seems, for example, that some interesting changes occur in children's ability to understand certain concepts around the age of 8. Additional research is needed before we can progress to a more complete understanding of the best approaches to remediation with children of different ages. It is probably wise to assume that children younger than age 8 require a more concrete presentation of therapy tasks and may need help with some of the concepts and language used in voice therapy.

Additionally, it is probably important always to assess the child's social and emotional development and how that child's voice use is helping or hindering him or her in dealing with feelings, in interactions with peers, and in attempts to satisfy basic needs for acceptance and attention. Observation of the child's behavior not only in the therapy room but also in the classroom and on the playground may yield important information. This information could be used to enhance motivation for change by ensuring that therapy activities are meaningful and relevant in terms of the child's level of interpersonal skill.

chapter 3
Behaviors Related to Vocal Production

Voice disorders may be categorized in different ways. Pannbacker (1984) provides an excellent review of classification systems. We may decide, for example, to categorize the disorder according to our perception of etiology. Many writers have used the organic–functional dichotomy in order to group disorders this way. Other writers have noted that disorders usually exist on a continuum and that organic difficulties usually include some emotional components and functional problems frequently result in tissue change if faulty habits are perpetuated across time.

Another method of categorizing voice disorders is to group them into perceptual categories according to the problem. Wilson (1972) states that traditionally voice problems have been classified as quality problems, resonance problems, loudness problems, and pitch problems. Deviations in rate may be regarded as a fifth category or classified as a problem of articulation and rhythm. Symptoms may also be described in terms of pattern of muscular activity. Boone (1983) refers to hyperfunctional behavior patterns that occur when there is excessive muscular contraction and force of movement in respiration phonation or resonance. He describes the ways in which hyperfunctional symptoms are exhibited in relation to varied anatomical sites and physiological functions. The opposite set of symptoms, hypofunctional behavior patterns, occurs when there is too little effort or muscle weakness frequently associated with neurological impairment.

Another method of categorizing voice disorders is by referring to sets of voice characteristics subsumed under, or associated with, a primary classification or syndrome. For example, Montague and Hollein (1973) found that Down's syndrome children typically exhibited more breathiness, roughness, and hypernasality than normal children do. Mysak (1971) described the typical voice characteristics of cerebral palsied children as forced or intermittent voicing, phonation on inhalation, difficulty coordinating the initiation of phonation with breath groups, difficulty in shifting from vegetative to phonatory breathing, difficulty with pitch control and stability, breathiness, and spasms of the vocal cords. Hypertension is noted in spastics and hypotension in athetoids. Similarly, children with severe hearing losses are frequently referred to as having "deafy voice," which results from difficulties in monitoring the vocal behavior of self and others. Thus children with hearing losses are often described as having distortions of pitch, loudness, and rate, and cul-de-sac or other inappropriate resonance. Children with "adenoidal" problems are noisy breathers, exhibit hyponasality, and sometimes have laryngeal symptoms related to postnasal drip or dryness of the vocal tract resulting from mouth breathing. Velopharyngeal insufficiency results in a set of voice symptoms that includes hypernasality, reduction in oral breath pressure affecting articulation, and nasal emission.

In medical journals, particularly in articles written by oto-laryngologists, changes in the vocal mechanism that result in changes in vocal behavior usually are categorized according to the type of condition that is manifest. Since these terms may be used frequently in medical reports, it is useful to discuss them here. The first is *congenital*, which refers to any alteration in the structure of the mechanism that was present at birth. Thus, cleft palate, laryngeal web, and laryngomalacia are examples of congenital conditions. The second is *traumatic*, which refers to any condition that results from injury (as in the case of intubation when a child is given oxygen and the folds are damaged) or accident. A larynx may be damaged through trauma in a car accident, or a palate may be injured if a child falls on a sharp stick. The third general category is that of *inflammatory diseases*. Inflammatory and ulcerative changes in the mechanism can be bacterial, viral, or fungal. An example of a fungal disease is histoplasmosis, which is carried by pigeons. *Allergic conditions* affecting the mechanism are considered to be another category, as are *neoplastic* (new growth) conditions. When new tissue is added to the existing mechanism, that tissue may be malignant or benign. Fortunately, malignant tumors are rare in young children. Benign growths, such as nodules, are the additive lesions that occur most frequently in school-age populations. Hemorrhages sometimes occur between the muscle and the squamous lining of the vocal folds. These concentrations of blood in one area, or generalized bruising of an entire fold, may also be described as additive lesions of the folds. An additional category is that of conditions related to the presence of *foreign bodies*. Examples are physical reactions that occur when a child swallows a safety pin or a fish bone or gets a pea lodged in the nasal cavity. The final category used by physicians is *psychosomatic*, and this encompasses any changes in the state or use of the mechanism that are directly related to an individual's reaction to stress or emotional disturbance.

THE RELATIONSHIP BETWEEN CLASSIFICATION OF PROBLEMS AND THEIR TREATMENT

The way we view or describe a set of symptoms sometimes affects our approach to treatment. A comprehensive framework that allows us to look at a child's problem with a wide-angle lens may be the most valuable. As speech–language pathologists, we are frequently called on to coordinate the intervention program, or at least to discuss the total problem with the child, the family, the teachers, and other professionals. Obviously, we need to be sure always that a child receives appropriate medical referrals, since some problems require very specific surgical and medical treatments. (Congenital conditions frequently can be helped by surgical procedures or prosthetic devices. Inflammatory conditions, such as bacterial infections, respond to medication, such as a series of antibiotics prescribed by a physician; in some severe cases, steroids are used to reduce inflammatory reactions. Psychosomatic problems frequently require help from a psychiatrist, psychologist, or social worker.) We also must be alert to our role in explaining to the child why it may be necessary for him or her to see various specialists, in preparing the child for procedures that may be frightening if the child is unaware of what is to be expected, and in providing ongoing support and encouragement. In addition, we need to assume responsibility for evaluating the extent of the behavioral compensations adopted or perpetuated by the child. Inappropriate vocal strategies will be maintained by some children even after they have been treated successfully to remove the root cause of their problem. Elimination of a medical problem does not always mean that a child automatically reverts to a pattern of normal vocal behavior. We always need to remember that, as educators, we are concerned with maximizing the child's abilities and coping skills in all aspects of an intervention program.

Thus it is probably useful for us now to consider the basic areas of behavior that are important in the development and maintenance of appropriate vocal performance. When we evaluate any child with a voice problem, we need to be aware of his or her abilities in the following critical areas: respiration, phonation, resonance, and interpersonal communication. We shall discuss each of these areas in turn. Since speech–language pathologists are familiar with basic anatomy and physiology, however, and since other texts are available for a review of this information (Minifee, Hixon, & Williams, 1973; Wilson, 1972; Boone, 1983; Bless & Abbs, 1983), we shall not focus on the normal anatomical and physiological processes of respiration, phonation, and resonance. Rather, we shall highlight some of the important abilities in these areas that affect the way an individual's voice is used and perceived. We shall note the contributions of each area, the way behaviors are coordinated and sequenced, and factors that affect or limit the production of appropriate vocal patterns. In addition, we shall focus attention on some of the abilities related to the area of interpersonal communication that can affect vocal expertise. This will provide a backdrop that will be useful later when we discuss specific procedures for diagnosis and management.

AREAS OF BEHAVIOR RELATED TO VOICE PRODUCTION

Respiration

The primary function of the respiratory system is biological. Through ventilation our blood gases are continually adjusted. The other important function of the respiratory system is to provide controlled and regulated airflow for the production of acoustic signals. Breathing at rest is more frequent (more breaths per minute) and also more rhythmic (more even inspiration and expiration phases) than breathing for speech or singing. Since we phonate during exhalation, the inspiration is usually quicker and the expiration is lengthened during speech breathing. If the vocal signal is to be adequate, the air supply must be carefully controlled and regulated. A detailed review of respiratory behavior during voice production can be found in Zemlin (1981), Hixon (1973), and Weismer (1985).

Baken (1979) lists several criteria that must be met if the airflow is to be controlled sufficiently to produce adequate voice during speech. First, the quantity of air impounded during inspiration must be matched to the anticipated utterance. Utterances vary with respect to length and phonemic structure. Most people replenish air supply at phrase boundaries; however, there may be differences between individuals and between performance on reading and conversational speech tasks. Second, the air reservoir must be refilled quickly so that disruptions in the flow are minimized. Third, the pressure of the alveolar gas must be appropriate. During vegetative breathing through a relatively open vocal tract, the pressure demands are not great. When voice is produced, however, air is passed through high impedances, and the amplitude of the sound is related to pressure variations. Thus the fourth criterion is that the pressure not only must be adequate but also must be regulated. Fifth, all these criteria must be met with the least expenditure of energy so that the system operates with maximal efficiency. Finally, all of the above must be accomplished within constraints imposed by the individual's metabolic gas-exchange requirements.

The foregoing discussion reminds us of some of the abilities that children need in the area of respiration for voice. When we observe children's respiratory behavior, we need to consider the movements of the chest wall (rib cage and diaphragm–abdomen) in relation to each other during both inspiratory and expiratory activity. It is also useful to observe how much air a child expires during expiration when we are considering chest-wall movements. If laboratory equipment is not available, an estimate of the child's ability to prolong the expiratory phase can be made by asking the child to prolong phonemes and timing the duration. It is usually useful to compare durations of phonemes where there is both high and low impedance (e.g., voiced versus unvoiced continuants). We also need to observe the child's respiratory behavior during connected speech. As Baken (1979) observed, a speaker must be able to achieve an acceptable interaction of the vocal tract, rib cage, and abdomen to achieve muscle forces that are both effective and efficient with respect to the amount of energy expended. (See also Baken, 1977, 1979(b) & 1981.)

Some children may try to talk on the inspiration of air rather than during the expiration. Others may not have developed respiratory muscle control sufficient to regulate the airstream in response to specific speaking demands. This may be particularly apparent when the child tries to vary the loudness level of utterances or when utterances of varying lengths and phonemic complexity are attempted. Itoh, Horii, Daniloff, and Binnie (1982) found that during trains of repeated syllables hearing-impaired individuals used speech breathing in much the same way normal hearers do, but that they expended more volume per syllable. The results of kinematics analyses reported by Forner and Hixon (1977) suggested that hearing-impaired speakers initiate speech at lower lung volumes than do normal hearers and many utterances are initiated within the tidal volume range.

An important aspect of respiratory behavior to observe is the way in which a child replenishes the air supply during connected speech. As a young child develops language and joins words into sentences, the timing of pauses and the use of those pauses to replenish the supply of available air assumes greater importance. As utterances increase in length, the demands on the respiratory system during speech also increase. If a child inhales before every two or three words, the flow and rhythm of speech are disrupted. If a child inhales at the beginning of an utterance and not again until the tidal and/or reserve volume are depleted, the voice may be affected by the gradual reduction of available air across time. For example, it may fade or become strained or quavery at the ends of sentences. Most children seem to take in their largest amount of air spontaneously during a deep inspiration when they first begin a sentence and then use phrase pauses to take smaller or replenishing breaths as the meaning allows. These replenishing breaths are sometimes called *catch breaths* and ensure that the available air supply is never markedly reduced until the opportunity for the next deep inspiration occurs. However, some children may not acquire this respiratory expertise for sustained connected speech spontaneously. They need to be taught the concept of replenishing breaths if they are to sustain appropriate voicing during continuous speaking or reading.

A useful analogy when explaining replenishing breaths to young children is that of filling a car with gas during a trip. At the beginning of a journey the driver fills the gas tank. As he travels, he stops to "top off his tank" before it is completely empty. The driver uses this strategy to ensure that he will never run out of gas before he has finished his journey.

The analogy of the car engine fueled with gas and the voice motor driven by the airstream is also useful when explaining to children another important aspect of respiratory behavior related to voice—the coordination of the exhaled airstream with the onset of phonation. The larynx acts as a valve in the respiratory tract, and the timing of the onset of the exhalation of the airstream and the smooth initiation of phonation involves exquisite precision.

In some voice-disordered children the smooth, easy initiation of phonation may be inhibited because of the inappropriate coordination of respiration and phonation. Like an inexperienced car driver who steps too abruptly on the accelerator, some speakers set the vocal folds abruptly into motion with excessive force. An opposite, though also inappropriate, problem is that of attempting to phonate before the airstream reaches the larynx. Thus, in addition to the amount of available air, the coordination of the emitted airstream with initiation of phonation is critical.

Clinical evidence suggests that persons with communication disorders vary in terms of the ways they use their respiratory systems for speech production. Some use normal speech breathing, some demonstrate deviations in lung volume range, chest-wall configuration, and/or the coordination of chest-wall parts associated with lung volume displacements. It is certainly safe to say that some children demonstrate disorders of voice that are associated with speech breathing problems. More research is needed, but at this point in time it does not appear as if specific speech breathing abnormalities can be directly tied to specific speech disorders in any consistent way.

Before leaving the topic of respiration, let us consider some other general points that are relevant to our discussion. Many voice-disordered children are noisy inhalers or even mouth breathers because of the frequent congestion they experience in the nasal cavities. Some reasons for noisy or labored inhalation or the complete inability to inhale through the nose are chronic allergic or infectious rhinitis or sinusitis, and enlarged tonsils and adenoids. Labored inhalation, as well as being distracting to the listener, may affect the efficiency of the inhalation phase of speech breathing. Children with chronically enlarged adenoids that obstruct the nasopharynx usually present a number of identifiable symptoms. They may exhibit pinched nostrils, sleepiness in school, pallor, circles under the eyes, and enlargement of the bridge of the nose, snoring during sleep, and habituated mouth breathing at rest. The mucous membranes of the vocal tract may be dry because of the mouth breathing; this dryness, sometimes in association with an irritating postnasal drip, may also result in hoarse voice quality. (Some of these symptoms may also be noted in children with partial blockages of the upper respiratory tract caused by intermittent allergic or infectious conditions causing swollen tissue.)

An extensive study of the habits, behavior, and breathing patterns of children with adenotonsillar hypertrophy was reported by Baranak, Potsic, Miller-Bauer, and Marsh (1983). Parents of patients completed questionnaires before and after adenotonsillectomy. In addition, sleep sonography was performed to determine nocturnal respiratory patterns. Parents' responses to the questionnaires indicated significant post-surgery improvement in breathing and sleep patterns; children snored less, had fewer episodes of obstructed inspiration, moved less in their sleep, and abandoned unusual sleeping postures (head hanging over side of bed, legs raised, etc., in attempts to position the body so that inhalation could occur more easily). The conclusions were supported by the sonographic analyses of respiratory patterns tape-recorded during sleep. About 67% of the sample showed clear improvement (i.e., less inspiratory effort and greater periodocity of respiration, and virtual elimination of episodes of obstructive apnea) after surgical removal of tonsils and adenoids. Another study of 100 children with adenotonsillar hypertrophy, reported by Pasquariello, Potsic, Miller, and Corso (1983), indicated that this population frequently demonstrates significant diet and nutrition problems. When enlargement of the tonsils and adenoids persisted for a long period of time, some children experienced difficulties and discomfort when eating. They were reported to be slow eaters and preferred soft foods. When the children's growth records were reviewed, more than 25% were below the tenth percentile for weight, although heights were generally age appropriate. Increased appetite and weight gain were reported following adenotonsillectomy.

The findings of studies such as those noted above remind us that when we suspect that a child may have enlarged tonsils and adenoids, we should question parents concerning the child's respiratory behavior during sleep. When the child is upright, the airway may be less obstructed than when the child is horizontal. Periods of sleep apnea, difficulty when eating, or low weight for age may be considered as evidence that medical attention should be sought.

Deep, relaxed breathing is considered by some authorities in allied health fields to be important in achieving general relaxation and reduction of physical and mental tension. The ability to relax and breathe deeply and efficiently at rest may need to be taught to some children with hyperfunctional voice problems. It may be a part of teaching general or specific relaxation techniques. In addition to appropriate breathing patterns at rest, some children with voice disorders may need specific help in developing and maintaining appropriate speech breathing abilities. As noted, these include the manner and depth of the inhalation, the control and length of the exhalation, the use of replenishing breaths, and the coordination of the emission of the exhaled air with the onset of phonation.

Phonation

Changes in the subglottal air pressure (affected by actions of the thoracic and abdominal muscles and recoil forces that change the volume of the lungs) also change the sounds produced by the larynx. An increase in the subglottal pressure increases sound intensity (Isshiki, 1964). Also, the myoelastic-aerodynamic theory of phonation (Broad, 1973) associates increases in subglottal air pressure with increases in fundamental frequency. However, Titze (1980), in his review of refinements of theory regarding myoelastic-aerodynamic fundamental frequency control, believes it to be primarily myoelastic, since stiffness and mass are controlled by muscular contractions. The ability to produce normal phonatory patterns is related both to respiratory control and regulation and to healthy vocal-fold structure and function.

Vocal-Fold Pathology   The human vocal fold consists of a muscle (the vocalis) and the mucous membrane that covers the muscle. The mucous membrane, or mucosa, consists of the epithelium and the lamina propria. The lamina propria is divided into three layers: superficial, intermediate, and deep. Hirano (1981) describes these layers in the following way: The superficial layer appears loose and pliant, and it is here that edema often develops. The intermediate layer is made up primarily of elastic fibers. The deep layer is dense with mostly collagenous fibers. The entire structure consisting of the intermediate and deep layers of the lamina propria is known as the *vocal ligament*. The epithelium and the superficial layer of the lamina propria is described as the *cover*.

Histological descriptions such as the one provided by Hirano (1981) help us understand some of the ways in which pathological states affect the laryngeal sound. Most lesions discussed by Hirano (1981) that occur frequently in children seem to invade the cover and affect mass and stiffness. The vocalis muscle does not move as vigorously as the mucosa during vibration of the folds. Thus, alterations in the mucosal cover seem to affect how the voice is perceived. Hirano lists the following aspects of pathological states that may interfere with normal vibratory function: location of the pathology, glottal incompetence, symmetry of the bilateral vocal folds, uniformity within each vocal fold, layer structure, mass and stiffness of each layer, and interference with vibratory movement of the fold on the opposite side. He notes marked interference with vibratory movement of the fold on the opposite side when the following pathologies occur: polyp, polypoid vocal fold, cyst, epithelium hyperplasia, papilloma, and carcinoma. Fortunately, carcinoma is rarely found in children. Histological manifestations of nodules and polyps vary; and intratissue bleeding, hyaline degeneration, edema, fibrosis, and cell infiltration were seen in the adult larynges examined by Hirano. However, nodules and polyps did not invade the vocal ligament. The mass of the superficial layer of the lamina propria increased, and stiffness changes could be observed. For example, when edema predominated, stiffness decreased; whereas fibrosis, intratissue bleeding, hyaline degeneration, and cell infiltration sometimes increased stiffness. Epithelial hyperplasia (any pathology causing hyperplastic thickening of the epithelium as the chief lesion) also increases mass and stiffness of the cover, as does papilloma. Papilloma is a benign neoplasm originating from the squamous cell epithelium and usually entering the superficial layer, and occasionally the intermediate and deep layer, of the lamina propria. Hirano noted that it sometimes may also invade the vocalis muscle itself.

When Hirano studied acoustic measures and tried to relate the findings of laryngeal mirror examinations of 200 patients to patterns of vocal-fold vibration and perceptual impressions, the only direct relationship that emerged was that with fundamental frequency. Increased mass results in a lower fundamental frequency. Hirano (1981) stated his impression that if you can detect a pathology using acoustical analysis, you can also hear the differences in voice and see the pathology with the laryngeal mirror. This statement is reassuring for the speech–language pathologist working in school settings where opportunities for laboratory analysis are limited. A trained ear and awareness of the importance of laryngeal examinations by a physician seem to be of utmost importance for the voice diagnostician.

Changes in the physical dimensions and characteristics of the vocal folds influence the sound produced. The fundamental frequency of the voice is controlled by changes in thickness, mass, tension, and length. We have just seen how some pathological states can change an individual's ability to make laryngeal adjustments. Most of the neoplastic pathologies result in increased stiffness and mass of the folds. Mass and stiffness are also affected by variations in the length of the folds. Longitudinal tension is increased by stretching the vocal folds, and the fundamental frequency of the voice increases as length is increased. Variations in vocal-fold length result from contraction of the cricothyroid muscles (Shipp & McGlone, 1971; Gay, Hirose, Strome, & Sawashima, 1972), but there is also an anteroposterior movement by the arytenoids. The movement of the arytenoids is the result of activity by the interarytenoid and posterior cricoarytenoid muscles, which occurs most frequently during the production of higher frequencies in the modal register (Hollien, 1983).

Broad (1973) summarized some of the ways that changes in vocal-fold dimensions affect the laryngeal sound. He said that the vocal-fold dimensions are determined largely through the motions of the cricoarytenoid and cricothyroid joints. The ability to vary the width of the glottis is determined mostly by the adduction and abduction movements of the arytenoid cartilages. The medial compression of the vocal folds is determined by the adductory squeeze of the arytenoids. Vocal-fold length is determined primarily by the rotation in the cricothyroid joint. Vocal-fold tension and thickness are also determined largely by the relative rotation between the cricoid and thyroid cartilages. Pathologies or neurogenic or psychogenic conditions that influence children's abilities to make these adjustments in vocal-fold dimensions affect the sound of the voice.

Perceptions of Phonatory Behavior   When we listen to a child's voice, we usually make some perceptual judgments about the way the voice sounds. We compare the individual's voice to the voices that we have heard of other children of similar age and sex.

The average perceived pitch, or the acoustic measurement of the fundamental frequency of a person's voice, is affected by anatomical and physiological factors. The length and thickness of the folds is influenced by such factors as the individual's age, sex, and physical size. Thus the most frequently used pitch level, sometimes called the *habitual pitch*, is usually structurally determined. However, other factors, in addition to the basic structural constraints, need to be considered. Imitation, faulty learning, and excessive tension in the larynx may affect the way that the structures are habitually used.

In addition to the pitch level used most frequently by a speaker, we may need to be interested in the entire range of pitches available to that speaker. Again, the limits of the range are structurally determined. We need to remember that there are both physiological and musical limits of the voice. At both ends of the entire pitch range it is possible to emit sounds that are not musical.

The lowest musical sound that can be produced by a speaker is defined as *basal pitch*. At the upper limits of the musical range, postpubertal males can produce falsetto voice and some trained sopranos can produce what is known as a *laryngeal whistle*. Falsetto is produced with a vibratory pattern that differs significantly from the regular vibratory mode. The vocal folds are stiff, narrowed bands, tightly approximated, and the airstream forces them to vibrate rapidly along the extreme edge of the approximating surfaces. Beyond the top of the musical range, it is possible to produce nonmusical sounds, such as those emitted during emotional states involving a high degree of tension. Shrieks and cries fall into this category. Another nonmusical sound that can be produced at the lower end of the pitch range is referred to as *vocal fry*. This sound is difficult to describe and is usually likened to the sound made by a creaky door or by popcorn popping. We can describe vocal fry physiologically as the sound made when the folds are extremely relaxed and loosely approximated. This pattern is different from the vibratory pattern used during regular phonation. It is important to remember that true vocal fry is a completely relaxed sound. Our voices sometimes trail off into vocal fry when we are tired or speaking with minimal effort. It should not be confused with the tense, strained, irregular vibrations produced during hyperfunctional voice use. Children will sometimes use glottal fry when they are playing and making sound effects with their voices. They also, of course, will use strained vocalization patterns that sound somewhat similar when they are imitating engines and trucks. The differentiating feature between true vocal fry and other nonmusical sounds produced is the absence of tension associated with vocal fry.

Many clinicians investigate the extent of the pitch range during voice evaluations. It has been noted that voice-disordered individuals frequently exhibit a restricted pitch range. Conversational pitch range, or the limits of the rise and fall of the voice during conversational speech, is also of interest to the clinician. Some speakers have a restricted conversational range because their entire available range is limited. Other speakers may use a narrow conversational pitch range, or monotone, because of factors unrelated to the availability of other pitches.

Occasionally, pitch breaks will also be observed in children. They are not considered to be a problem if they occur around the time of puberty. Curry (1949) found that they occur when rapid pubertal changes take place. If pitch breaks occur in children who are not approaching puberty, they may reflect the use of an inappropriate pitch level. Clinical experience suggests that when the level is too low, the voice breaks upward, and when the level is too high, it breaks downward; hence the clinical dictum that "the voice breaks in the direction it wants to go."

When we listen to children's voices, we are interested in habitual level, available range, variability, and the way pitch changes reflect meaning and feeling.

The loudness level of a child's voice during conversational speech is also of interest to a clinician. We are interested in the level that the child habitually uses and the ways in which the child can vary his or her loudness in response to situational and contextual demands. It is usually important to consider respiratory behavior, pitch, mouth opening, body position, and the amount of effort that the child appears to expend when making judgments concerning children's abilities with respect to loudness levels habitually used, the range of available loudness, and the use of loudness variations.

In addition to pitch and loudness variations produced by the adjustments of the vocal folds, there is an overall quality of the voice perceived by the listener. This perceived quality, or timbre, of the voice is affected by airflow, the laryngeal structure and function, as well as by the resonance characteristics. The size and mass of the folds, as we know, change across time because of predictable factors related to age and sex. There are also intermittent changes that are less predictable and occur as the result of the way an individual's laryngeal structures react to emotional states, physical conditions, and environmental influences and demands. Thus an individual's voice quality may vary at different times of a day, week, or year.

The way in which the folds approximate, or come together at the midline, is very important in any consideration of quality deviation. Normal healthy vocal folds approximate evenly along the free margins during vocal-fold adduction. We have seen that edema and growths change the margins of the folds and interfere with normal laryngeal adjustments. When the folds approximate to some extent, but vibrate intermittently or irregularly, and the smoothness or evenness of the vibratory pattern is disrupted, we describe the behavior as *dysphonia*. The phonation is present, but it is disturbed. In some cases an individual's vocal behavior may be predominantly dysphonic with periods of complete aphonia occurring intermittently or occasionally. *Aphonia* is the term used to describe the absence of voice during attempted phonation.

We have probably all experienced short periods in our lives when we have tried to talk with an acutely irritated vocal tract and felt that our voices "cut out" during a sentence. When children are aphonic for relatively short periods of time, this distressing loss of voice is usually the result of acute infections or prolonged or intense use of the voice (e.g., cheering at ballgames). If aphonia occurs for longer periods of time, it may be the result of neurological or psychogenic difficulties.

Fairbanks (1960) used three descriptive terms to describe quality deviations. One is *breathiness*. Spectrographic analyses of breathy voice usually show reduced definition of a periodic soundwave. The listener usually hears an audible escape of air, suggesting that the free margins of the folds are not approximating optimally. There are, of course, degrees of perceived breathiness, ranging from what some children describe as "a very airy voice" to an almost imperceptible degree. Boone (1983) writes that we frequently hear breathiness at the beginning of an utterance and that the vocal folds may approximate slowly after the initiation of the outgoing airstream has already begun.

Hoarseness is the term used most frequently to describe laryngeal-quality disorders. Moore (1971) said that hoarseness may be related to mucus, additional mass on the folds, or relative flaccidity of one or both folds. Some writers differentiate between hoarseness and *harshness* by suggesting that more tension is present in harshness. Others, such as Darley (1965), say that a hoarse voice quality combines the acoustic characteristics of harshness and breathiness. Harshness is difficult to describe, but it usually creates an unpleasant reaction on the part of the listener. The speaker seems to be using too much effort to speak, may exhibit observable tension in the neck, and may initiate phonation with hard glottal attacks. In Boone's 1983 description of harshness, he also refers to the frequent presence of "metallic aspects of resonance" that are sometimes observed in a harsh voice.

Spectrographic analysis is useful when describing the characteristics of quality deviations, since the aperiodicity of laryngeal vibration can be seen. The Visipitch is also useful for providing both diagnostic information and feedback to the child during therapy. Changes in periodicity of the signal and differences in types of voice onset can be demonstrated and improvement can be quantified when such instrumentation is available. Quantification is especially important because vocal symptoms frequently occur inconsistently and vary in terms of perceived severity. When instrumentation is not available, the speech–language pathologist will need to define symptoms carefully and help children chart the occurrence of specific symptoms.

Hoarseness is sometimes reduced when the loudness level of the voice increases because the speaker adducts the folds more vigorously. An increased pitch level also can, sometimes, improve the extent of closure, reduce the aperiodicity in the vibratory pattern, and decrease perceived hoarseness.

It is not uncommon for a child who has additive lesions of the vocal folds, such as vocal nodules, to produce a clearer voice quality when talking or singing loudly. The voice also may sound clearer on higher pitches. This is usually most noticeable when the nodules (either unilateral or bilateral) are small or moderately sized. As the nodules increase in size, greater and greater effort is necessary in order for the child to adduct the folds forcefully enough to compensate for the lesions during fold closure. Also, as the size of the nodules increases, their effect on increasing the mass of the vocal folds and consequent lowering of the habitual pitch of the voice may be more obvious.

Thus, when children are dysphonic because of vocal nodules, there is always the danger that they will compensate for their hoarseness by learning to overadduct the folds and talk more and more loudly. In such cases the problem is exacerbated by excessive effort and strain. When such behavior is habituated, the place where the folds first make contact at the point of their maximum excursion (i.e., the junction of the anterior one-third and posterior two-thirds of the folds) is repeatedly irritated. Therefore, although this effortful production may make the voice sound clearer in the short term, the long-term effect will be that the nodules may increase in size, and the vocal quality will deteriorate.

Other compensations that are sometimes adopted by dysphonic children are the frequent use of glottal stops. When a glottal stop is produced, the arytenoid cartilages are completely adducted to close the glottis. The sudden release of the blocked air results in a characteristic burst, which is perceived as a pop or click. This sound may be heard as a substitution for a plosive (as in the word "bo*tt*le"). This sound is similar to the abrupt phonatory onset heard when children initiate stressed vowels at the beginning of words with a hard glottal attack. This abrupt, almost grunting, sound differs significantly from a normal easy onset of phonation. It also differs from a breathy attack, which occurs when the airstream begins to pass through the laryngeal valve before the folds approximate. Since the breathy attack is diametrically opposed to the hard glottal attack, it is usually taught as a substitute technique during the beginning stages of therapy to eliminate hard attacks. Both kinds of voice onset, however, may be decribed as the result of deviations in the exact timing and coordination of the airstream with the beginning of the vibratory cycle.

Phonation breaks are sometimes noted in association with quality deviations. This term is used to describe short periods of aphonia that occur on syllables, words, or phrases. It is usually associated with hyperfunction and may appear most frequently on unstressed syllables when the speaker reduces his or her effort level. It may also be related to difficulty maintaining appropriate air pressure (e.g., on the final syllable of a breath group). Sometimes it signals vocal fatigue if the speaker has been attempting to increase effort (e.g., by raising the pitch, trying harder to talk) during a prolonged period of talking. Sometimes the speaker will try throat clearing, coughing, or swallowing to remedy the problem.

Throughout our discussion of phonation we have referred to the effect of size, mass, and tension changes in the folds and the extent of vocal-fold closure on perceptions of pitch, loudness, and quality.

It has been noted that the laryngeal structures react to environmental and physical changes. The laryngeal surfaces are composed of mucous membrane and are frequently subject to irritation by airborne substances and viral and bacterial infections. Reactions of the laryngeal structures can range from extreme dryness of the membranes to excessive secretion. Both dryness and wetness can lead to irritation of the structures, inflammation, and swelling. When such conditions are present, an individual is particularly at risk if abusive vocal behaviors occur repeatedly. It is important to remember that abusive vocal behaviors include the use of excessive amounts of effortful talking or singing, hard glottal attacks, inappropriate use of loudness or pitch levels, and excessive throat clearing and coughing. Compensatory behaviors adopted by an individual trying to talk with an irritated or altered laryngeal mechanism sometimes lead to habituated hyper-functional vocal behavior that exacerbates the original problem. Children's abilities in the area of phonation should always be considered in relation to available medical information concerning conditions (e.g., allergies and infections) that may increase their susceptibility to adopt abusive compensatory practices. While the majority of voice problems in children seem to be related to vocal abuse, it should be emphasized that children will also present with organic problems unrelated to abuse. Other structural deviations, such as papilloma, laryngeal webs, and paralyzed vocal folds, may be seen. In these cases, as in other less frequently seen organic pathologies, the medical report will be the critical factor in evaluating and treating the problem. In some cases, also, emotional problems and faulty learning will result in abnormal use of the vocal mechanism. Whatever the etiology of a disorder involving abnormal use of the laryngeal structures, however, the vocal symptoms themselves need to be described specifically. This includes a description of the onset, the extent of vocal-fold adduction, and the smoothness and evenness of the perceived vibratory pattern.

Resonance

The complex laryngeal tone is modified still further by the supralaryngeal structures. The voice is affected by the size, configuration, and coupling of the supraglottal cavities. Adjustments of the shape and acoustical properties of the vocal tract are known as *articulation*. The vibrating airstream may be changed by variations in tension size and shape of vocal tract structures. Direct emission may be through the nose or the mouth, depending on the position of the velopharyngeal closure mechanism, and the vibrating column of air may be converted to a series of speech sounds. As we know, when the lips, tongue, or palate block the airstream, plosive sounds are generated; when the airstream is constricted and turbulence occurs, fricative sounds are produced.

Since many of the same structures influence both articulaton of speech sounds and resonance, it is sometimes difficult to discuss resonance independently. This is why many writers say that resonance problems are actually articulation problems. One distinction that can be made is that between speech intelligibility and vocal acceptability. These two aspects are obviously related, and yet there are some advantages in considering them separately. Intelligibility of speech sounds is a function of the distribution of energy within the speech sounds. This is accomplished by precise predictable movements of vocal tract structures (such as the lips, tongŭe, and palate) that are capable of generating recognizable phonemes. The distinctive features of speech sounds are well known and are similar for all speakers of a language. Problems with speech intelligibility can result from inadequate velopharyngeal closure during the production of oral sounds. In such instances, vowels may be produced nasally, and consonants requiring oral breath pressure are frequently distorted. The acceptability of the voice quality is also affected and perceived as hypernasal. When voice is perceived as hyponasal, substitutions such as b–m, d–ŋ, and g–n are frequently noted and attributed to obstruction of the nasal cavities. Thus, when speech intelligibility is affected, the misarticulations are generally also accompanied by a perceived change in the acceptability of the voice quality. An acceptable voice during speech involves an appropriate balance of both oral and nasal resonance. As well as specific articulatory adjustments necessary for intelligibile production of speech sounds, however, there are changes in the gross configuration of the vocal tract itself that contribute to the production of acceptable voice.

Let us consider the way that resonance characteristics are altered during voice production. The musculo-membranous tube above the larynx is made up of the laryngopharynx, the oropharynx, and the nasopharynx. This pharyngeal cavity is lined throughout with mucous membrane and communicates with the tympanic, oral, laryngeal, and nasal cavities, as well as with the esophagus. Because of the softness of the tissues lining the pharynx, reinforcement of overtones is not a major contribution of this cavity during voice production. Because of the presence of the pharyngeal constrictor muscles, however, this cavity can be differentially tensed or relaxed. There are individual structural differences in the length, size, and shape of the pharynx, and individual differences in the muscular tension of the walls of the pharynx during voice production. The fauces, the oral cavity itself, and the buccal cavity are also lined with mucous membrane and are highly variable in shape and dimensions. Individual differences occur with respect to basic structure of these cavities and range of variability during voice production.

It is obvious that the mouth is certainly the most movable and adjustable of the cavities of the vocal tract. The degree of mouth opening and movement during communication significantly affects oral resonance, affects facial expression, and provides important visual cues that supplement vocal communication. The mouth's most important biological function is, of course, to provide a port between the external world and the respiratory and digestive tracts. It initiates the digestive process through the production of saliva. On occasion we encounter a child in voice therapy who has problems with excess saliva production or inappropirate swallowing of saliva. Excessive moisture in the corners of the mouth or obvious drooling may be observed. When such symptoms are noted, it may be necessary to observe such relevant behaviors as head position (since gravity may be a factor), mouth closure at rest, and frequency of swallowing (children should swallow at least once every 40 seconds). At the Hospital for Sick Children in Toronto, Canada, important work has been done on the treatment of drooling problems in children, and this work reminds us of the importance of considering the biological as well as nonbiolgocial functions of the oral cavity.

The nasal cavities are paired and separated by the nasal septum. They communicate with the exterior by way of the nares, with the nasopharynx through the velopharyngeal port, and with the paranasal sinuses. The surface of the nasal cavities filters, moistens, and warms the air as it is inhaled. Nasal passages may become dried out, irritated, or both under certain conditions, or they may produce excess secretions that diminish or block nasal resonance.

Descriptions of Perceptual Characteristics   During normal voice production there is a shifting balance of oral resonance and direct and indirect nasal resonance. Let us consider some of the terms used to describe resonance patterns.

Vowel sounds and all consonants in English with the exception of /m/ /n/ and /ŋ/ are produced with a preponderance of oral resonance—in other words, the direct emission of the vibrating air column through the mouth. Since the velopharyngeal port is closed during the production of oral sounds, there is minimal direct air emission through the nasal cavities. So we can say there is no direct nasal resonance. Nevertheless, some indirect nasal resonance may occur during the production of oral sounds. Vibrations may sometimes be felt on the bones of the face and nasal cavities during projected speaking or singing of oral sounds. These vibrations reverberate through the craniofacial bone structures and add richness and color to the tone. In order to maximize indirect nasal resonance, some teachers and singing coaches use images such as "place the sound in the mask" or "use forward projection of the voice" or "think that the sound is vibrating the bones of the head." It is usually suggested that "forward tone focus" or concentrating the resonating energy in the front of the face helps a student to maximize both oral resonance and indirect nasal resonance.

During the production of /m/ /n/ and /ŋ/ when the velopharyngeal port is open and the vibrating column of air is emitted directly through the nose, there is a preponderance of direct nasal resonance in the voice. If the nasal cavities are obstructed because of structural constraints (e.g., enlarged adenoidal tissue) or the presence of foreign bodies or excess secretions, the voice is described as denasal, hyponasal, or "blocked." This is the sound we hear when someone sounds as if they have "a cold in the nose" (Greene, 1972; Boone, 1977).

In a recent study by Rastatter and Hyman (1984) perceptual judgments of denasality were found to be dependent on speaking task. The results suggest that the listeners were able to categorize nasal resonance problems accurately when they were caused by rhinologic disorders such as edemic adenoids and allergic rhinitis. Both VCV syllable using the nasals /m/ /n/ and /ŋ/ and sentences proved the best tasks for listeners to detect hyponasality, since when denasal children prolonged isolated vowels, the listeners judged them to be exhibiting nasal resonance characteristics close to normal. Another interesting finding was reported by Rastatter and Hyman (1984) on six children ranging in age from 8 to 14 years who each had an anteriorly deviated septum of traumatic origin. Listeners judged these children as having essentially normal resonance. The researchers point out that these results should not be overgeneralized, since deviated septums vary with respect to severity and origin and may accompany other pathological nasal conditions (Ryan, 1968).

Hyponasality is the opposite of hypernasality. Whereas hyponasality describes too little direct nasal resonance on /m/, /n/, /ŋ/, hypernasality refers to an excessive amount of direct nasal resonance on sounds other than /m/, /n/, and /ŋ/. Hypernasality is always the result of inefficient valving of the velophyaryngeal sphincter mechanism. This may be the result of structural or neurological deficits or may be functional in origin. The degree of the velopharyngeal insufficiency and the nature of the compensations adopted will influence whether speech-sound generation is also impaired.

It is also important to mention *assimilated nasality*. Assimilated nasality is the term used to describe a resonance pattern that results from imprecise timing of the movements of the velopharyngeal valving system during running speech. Assimilated nasality is usually a behavior learned through imitation (as in the case of speakers representing certain regional speech patterns) and is usually not considered to be a resonance disorder unless a speaker aspires toward a career in professional voice use. It is sometimes also observed in speakers who have mild velopharyngeal inadequacy or faulty learning where speech-sound intelligibility is not impaired but resonance characteristics are. Essentially, assimilated nasality results from the influence nasal consonants exert on adjacent or neighboring oral sounds. For example, if a vowel is preceded or followed by a nasal sound and the velopharyngeal port is not opened or closed quickly or precisely enough, some hypernasality may occur during production of the vowel itself. Similarly, if an oral consonant is embedded in a cluster of nasal consonants, such as in the word "ven*t*nor," nasal emission or plosion may occur on the /t/.

The perception of appropriate oral–nasal resonance balance in speech depends on the interplay of a number of related factors. Rapid connected speech involves a series of precise articulatory and resonatory adjustments. When we observe a child's behavior in the area of resonance, we consider his or her ability to generate both oral and nasal phonemes appropriately and to adjust the size, shape, tension, and configuration of the oral and nasal cavities. It is important to remember that only excessive nasal (hypernasality) or oral (hyponasality) reso- nance is of clinical concern.

The most important prerequisite for appropriate resonance is an intact and operational velopharyngeal closure mechanism. If any doubt exists concerning the efficiency of this mechanism, velopharyngeal assessment should be obtained (e.g., X-ray study, cinefleurography, nasopharyngoscopy).

INTERPERSONAL COMMUNICATION

Communication takes place when a message is transmitted by a speaker to a listener. This interaction between speaker and listener is basic in the true communication of information and feelings. When communication attempts involve little regard for the listener, the act may provide satisfactory self-expression or even catharsis for the speaker, but satisfying communication rarely occurs. A self-absorbed speaker does not capitalize on the responses of the listeners, and the communicative interaction is therefore inhibited.

Vocal communication involves the transmission of meaning on a number of levels. The sounds and words produced carry semantic content, and their arrangement in phrases and sentences, or the syntactic pattern, adds further information. In addition to the phonological, semantic, and syntactic factors, however, · information is provided by the paralinguistic aspects of the utterance. Such features as rate, timing stress, and prosodic patterns add immeasurably to the transmission of meaning and feeling. It is interesting to note that the larynx is exquisitely sensitive to the emotional state of the speaker. We all know from experience that the intensity and degree of feeling affect our ability to control the sound of our voice voluntarily. When we are just a little anxious or nervous, for example, we can usually manage to prevent our anxiety from affecting our vocal communication. If, on the other hand, we are absolutely terrified, our control diminishes. At such times it is unlikely that we even think about how our voice sounds to a listener, and if we do attempt to conceal our emotional state voluntarily, our attempts do not succeed.

Speaker Characteristics

Researchers such as Fonagy (1981) and Davitz (1964) have summarized some of the predictable phonatory patterns associated with intense emotional states. Studies have focused on the acoustic analysis of intensely emotional speech patterns in real-life situations, as well as in lines spoken by actors and actresses. Many different languages have also been studied, and the generalizations reported here are consistent across languages. Some writers have suggested that the biological function of the larynx, described by Darwin (1872) in his discussion of the "flight or fight" phenomenon, may account for the consistent laryngeal patterns observed. Fonagy stresses the dynamic nature of distinctive features occurring during emotive speech and says that if the symptoms of emotive behavior are vestiges of a once purposive activity, vocal and prosodic features may be interpreted in terms of symbolic bodily movements.

We shall summarize some of the behaviors that Fonagy (1981) associated with specific emotional states beginning with his description of anger. Forceful expirations and very intense activity of the expiratory muscles are observed. There is imperfect phonation, such as breathy voice. The speaking rate is faster than normal. Fonagy also noted that the vocal strategy is entirely different for aggressive versus tender emotive speech. Tender voice is characterized by a complete but smooth contact of the vocal folds, and the false folds and laryngeal ventricles are widely separated. In contrast, in hatred the laryngeal ventricles are compressed, probably because of the spasmodic contraction of the adductor muscles. Thus, in anger it is likely that the false folds are approximated and may disturb the vibrations of the true folds. Because of the extent of the muscle contractions, and in spite of the high subglottal pressure caused by the effort of the expiratory muscles, the intensity of the sound produced may be less than a sound produced with much less effort during tender speech. Slower rate and slower gradual pitch changes are observed in affectionate tender speaking. During a prolonged state of fear or anguish, the use of an extremely narrow pitch range is observed consistently.

Fonagy's research findings support some of the vocal stereotypes commonly held in our society. There is no doubt that certain stereotypes of sets of vocal characteristics associated with certain personality types exist. These are learned as part of the acculturation process, and there are some similarities and differences between cultures. For example, many American female speakers are perceived as speaking too loudly by members of Oriental cultures. Within the American culture, particular vocal patterns have become associated with certain personality stereotypes. These have not been exposed to extensive empirical scrutiny but seem to have achieved some measure of general acceptance. For example, the effeminate male voice is generally characterized by high pitch level, exaggerated pitch inflections, prolongation of vowels, and light vocal timbre. The *macho* male voice is described as having a low pitch level, less vocal variety, shorter and less elaborate sentence structures, and a larger proportion of falling inflections (denoting decisiveness) at the ends of sentences. The sensuous female voice is characterized by a breathy quality, higher pitch level, reduced loudness, slower rate, and increased frequency of pauses. Aggressiveness in females is characterized by greater loudness, lower pitch level, fewer questioning or tentative inflectional patterns, faster rate, and precise articulation. In general, slow rate, increased frequency of pauses, and restricted variability of both pitch and loudness tend to suggest lower cognitive function in speakers of both sexes.

The importance of the media in establishing and reinforcing vocal stereotypes cannot be estimated precisely, but it is undoubtedly significant. Anyone who has listened to the Saturday morning cartoons on television can identify the "good guy" and the "bad guy" voices, even when not watching the picture on the screen. Children are undoubtedly influenced by all the voice models they are exposed to and probably internalize them and identify with certain vocal patterns. Thus, as we consider a child's vocal behavior, we need to be aware of the influences that contribute to his or her cultural conditioning. We also need to be aware of the close relationship that exists between children's emotional state and level of general physical tension and its relationship to voicing patterns. While it is expected that vocal behavior will fluctuate across time in response to varying feeling states, the presence of consistently excessive emotional and physical tension reflected in vocal behavior may be diagnostically significant.

Listening Responses

As mentioned, true communication involves an interaction between a speaker and a listener. In other words, a message has to be received and processed as well as transmitted. A good communicator, therefore, is an effective listener as well as an effective speaker. An effective listener is usually an active listener; that is, messages are received, processed, and acknowledged. Clinical experience suggest that listening responses, those verbal and nonverbal responses that indicate a message has been processed, may be developed late in the sequence of language acquisition. Very young children seem to demonstrate few listening responses that are not purely egocentric. If you observe preschool children, and even children in the early elementary school grades, you may notice that they rarely verbally acknowledge that they have processed what has been said to them. Older children and adults usually provide evidence of active listening by facial expressions, gestures, interjections, questions, and confirmations such as "I see." This may be because as one's communicative competence grows, one's awareness of the need to provide more explicit feedback to the listener develops. For example, an adult who is working on a project in the back yard will usually respond when someone calls from the house to say lunch is ready. The need to assure the speaker that the message has been received is acknowledged, either by a wave or other nonverbal signal or by a sentence such as "I'll be there in a minute." A young child playing in the back yard when called for lunch may give no indication that the message has been received. This may be why a parent sometimes feels compelled to call, "Did you hear me?" or "Are you deaf or something?"

This example provides a vivid reminder to many of us of the frustration we feel when someone we are speaking to is unaware of the need to provide us with feedback through listening responses. One could speculate that listening responses are the highest and, therefore, last aspect of communicative behavior to be mastered. Some individuals may never fully master this communicative skill, even as adults. Lecturers are often grateful for members of an audience who demonstrate a high frequency of nonverbal listening responses. Those are the audience members who nod, smile, laugh, and otherwise indicate active processing of the information they are receiving. Because such active listening is reinforcing and reassuring to a speaker, a lecturer may tend to look at, or focus attention on, listeners who actively respond. If we think about people we enjoy talking to in one-to-one or small-group conversational settings, we also realize that the reassurance that our thoughts and feelings are being received and processed is always important. We gain most satisfaction from talking when we feel we have the active attention of our listeners. We know listeners are attending to us

Eye contact is probably the most critical listener response.

when they acknowledge us, and our messages, through their listening responses. Eye contact is probably the most critical listener response. In our culture, we expect the listener to look at us when we are talking and to demonstrate continued interest by maintaining eye contact. We react to a listener's wandering gaze by thinking that they are losing interest. If a listener's eyes wander, and there are other signs (such as rising from a chair, shifting the feet, or moving away from the speaker), we usually assume that the conversation is being terminated. Naturally, depending on the level of awareness of the speaker, these signs may be interpreted and acted on or not. Some speakers will immediately interpret such nonverbal signals as meaning that the conversation is terminated. Others may try to compensate for the wandering attention of the listener by talking more quickly, more loudly, or more dramatically. Some speakers, and we have all encountered them, seem completely unaware of the reactions of the listener and continue talking *ad infinitum*, choosing to ignore all but the most blatant verbal evidence of communication breakdown.

When children talk incessantly and ignore listening responses, it is important to consider the reasons that might be causing such behavior. If they are very young, it is possible that they may not yet have developed expertise in attending to and interpreting nonverbal signals. Children 8 years old and younger may not yet have learned either to transmit or to interpret a variety of explicit listening responses. Children who are older than 8 may also at times demonstrate a lack of awareness and skill in this area of communicative competence. In such cases, the behaviors may need to be taught to them by explicit demonstration, analysis, and discussion.

There may be some elementary school children who seem to have developed the communicative competence to encode and decode listening responses, and who understand both the semantic meaning and the emotional tone of messages, and yet they frequently ignore listening responses. All children, of course, do this occasionally when they are extremely uptight or upset. The emotionality of the moment may obscure everything else. An example of this occurs when a child bursts into a classroom and interrupts a teacher who obviously does not want to be interrupted. If the child is extremely excited or anxious, the need to tell the teacher what has just occurred on the playground is so intense that the teacher's initial negative reaction is disregarded completely. When this behavior occurs frequently, however, it may be assumed that a particular child's anxiety level, or need for attention, is unusually strong. Frequent interruptions, incessant bids to seek and hold attention, very loud talking, very fast talking, and repeated disregard of listener responses may indicate not only immature communicative skills but also could indicate unresolved emotional conflicts or inadequate satisfaction of basic human needs.

The most satisfying communicators vary their listening responses according to the needs of the speaker. They observe and respond appropriately to the verbal, nonverbal, and paralinguistic features of a speaker's messages. For example, when a speaker is very upset or agitated, a sensitive listener is aware of that speaker's need to express his or her feelings or tell his or her story in an uninterrupted manner. Thus, such a listener, sensing that the goal of the interaction is primarily catharsis, provides understanding by murmuring supportive responses and sympathetic interjections that reflect acceptance of the speaker's feelings. A less sensitive or less skillful listener, in a similar situation, by attempting to interrogate or give advice might antagonize a speaker who has a primary need to ventilate his or her feelings and to be understood. Thus, listening responses are usually geared to the interaction that is occurring: At times they are reflections of understanding a speaker's situation; at other times they may be more direct attempts to clarify or analyze or debate issues.

It is important for clinicians to consider the range of communicative behaviors used by the children they teach. Some voice-disordered children may not demonstrate a well-developed range of listening responses. Such children may be so intensely involved with their own anxieties or needs that they are unable to focus on the demands of varied communication settings or on the needs of others. For example, the frequent use of talking primarily for self-expression may sometimes be seen in children referred to the clinician because of vocal abuse. Incessantly loud talking or other abusive vocal behaviors may sometimes be related to immature listening skills or may be a symptom of unsatisifed personal needs. Such one-sided attempts at communication rarely result in satisfying interpersonal interactions.

Question-Asking Skills

As we have seen, many questions are primarily listening responses. However, there are many types of questioning behaviors, and these need to be considered. The informational question appears very early during language development, and the *Why?* question is frequently heard in young children's speech patterns. We know from our study of language acquisition that tag questions ("That's mine, isn't it?") appear earlier than interrogative reversals ("Isn't it mine?"). Children ask questions to find out information, to gain attention, to seek comfort and reassurance, to elicit repetitions of pleasing verbal patterns and make verbal connections with others. Questioning is a strategy for coding personal experience. We check our own perceptions and understanding of feelings and events in this way. Bloom's 1956 taxonomy provides us with a model of the different levels of questioning that teachers may use. Questions can be designed to elicit information ("What is today's date?") or can involve interpretation ("What is important about today?"). Questions can also elicit analysis and synthesis of information. For example, a skillful analytical question can encourage the listener to break down information in different ways, and synthesis questions can encourage reorganization of ideas in a variety of formats. An example of an analytical question is, "What times during the day do you talk a lot?" An example of a synthesis question is, "If you talk most during recess, how much recess talking-time do you have each week?" Evaluation questions that involve some judgment are the most complex question forms to answer. In order to evaluate and form opinions, children must first organize their thoughts and consider pertinent information. Therefore, a question such as, "Why are some people better listeners than others?" might prompt a child who has been discussing specific listener behaviors to form opinions about specific behaviors that seem especially important. The child might respond, "Some people are better at showing you they are listening to you. They look at you, nod when they agree, and ask questions about what you are saying."

The Amount of Talking

The amount of time that a child spends talking each day varies according to situations and opportunity. The classroom organization and the amount of discussion and oral activity encouraged by the teacher are, of course, significant factors during school hours. The peer group and play activities engaged in during free time also exert an influence, as does the kind of family interaction. In addition, each child has a unique personality, and some children are naturally more verbal than others. The amount of self-generated talking varies from individual to individual. We can break down the amount of self-initiated talking further by considering the purposes of the talking. Some children will spend the greater percentage of their talking time in self-expression. Others will spend less time telling about themselves, and their talking may involve fewer purely egocentric statements and a greater number of oral attempts to manipulate the listener. The range of purposes exhibited, and the variety of topics covered, allows us to gain further insight about the child's needs and his or her strategies for need satisfaction through vocal behavior.

We can, therefore, describe the child's vocal behavior by considering how much he or she talks and how often he or she initiates conversation. We can further analyze it by observing how much of the talking is self-expression, how many questions are asked, the type and purpose of the declarative and interrogative forms used, and the type and frequency of what seem to be satisfying communicative exchanges.

Sex Differences

We do not have research data concerning the differences in communication strategies used by girls and boys. Some information pertinent to our discussion of interpersonal communication can be gleaned from studies of adult speakers. Informal behavioral rules often seem to dictate different behaviors for men and women in the same situations. In our culture it seems that men "hold the floor" more and interrupt women more than women interrupt men. Strodtbeck and Mann (1956) found that because men tend to talk more by giving more opinions than women, they appear more competent to discuss the issues. Piliavin and Martin (1978) demonstrated that authority figures who tend to reinforce males cause females to contribute less in terms of task participation.

Frances (1979) confirmed that men talk more, take longer turns in conversations, and thus hold the floor longer. They also engage in a greater variety of body postures during conversations. Interactions between 88 students conversing with a stranger of the same sex and one with a stranger of a different sex were videotaped. The time spent talking, number of turns taken, and number of interruptions were counted. Analysis demonstrated that men talked more and took longer turns; women did more smiling and laughing, as prescribed by the script for feminine role expectations.

Geis, Carter, and Butler (1982) say that interruptions by men often go unnoticed; if a woman interrupts, however, she is violating the dominance–deference script and appears aggressive. Langer, Blank, and Chanowitz (1978) conducted three field studies showing that scripted routines are followed automatically regardless of content or importance. In most interactions women may be expected to be accommodating and thus may be viewed as uncooperative if they do not comply. Geis, Carter, and Butler (1982) suggest that this "accommodation script" sometimes means that women's behavior is evaluated negatively when they fail to act in an accommodating way.

Rosen and Jerdee (1974) found that whatever reasons a woman gives, her demands or decisions appear less credible and justified than the same reasons given by a man. As a result, a woman would have to be more assertive to get her way than would a man; hence, she would be seen as "uncooperative," "arrogant," and "inflexible," as well as presumptuous. Thus the same reward costs a woman more than it does a man. The stereotype that women should be accommodating can lead to unintentional exploitation if they conform to expectations and penalty if they refuse to conform.

The possible influence of sex-coded scripts in daily interactions, and the probability that "rules" for men and women differ somewhat in our culture, are important considerations for the speech–language pathologist. We always need to be careful that we do not unwittingly reinforce girls for stereotypical "feminine" behavior in communication interactions. We need to teach the sharing of talking time and focus on equal participation of all children in the open debate of issues and in the sharing of ideas and feelings.

Racial and Social Differences

Efforts have been made in recent years to study differences in speech and language development related to race and social status. More research is needed in order to understand these differences completely and to ensure that therapy programs are designed to meet the needs of children representing diverse backgrounds. Writers such as Pletcher *et al.* (1978), Adler (1979), Evard and Sabers (1979), and Wiener *et al.* (1983) have stressed the need to improve the validity of speech and language evaluations of children whose primary linguistic background is not standard American English. In addition to understanding the articulation and language differences associated with ethnic, cultural, and socioeconomic background, we also need to understand more about nonverbal communicative differences, that is, vocal cues such as pitch, loudness, rate intonation, and rhythm. Nonverbal behavior is a critical component of communication, and the interaction of the verbal and vocal dimensions during speech and language acquisition is not well documented. While writers such as Egolf and Chester (1973) and Courtright and Courtright (1983) have studied nonverbal communication skills in relation to disordered communication, little attention has been given to differences in nonverbal patterns exhibited by children representing various minority groups within the United States.

Although we have little research evidence concerning the developmental progression of specific vocal behaviors and how these may or may not be affected by factors such as race and status, we can gain some insights by considering some related research. Clinicians' expectations of appropriate vocal behavior are naturally shaped by such factors as knowledge of predictable differences between subgroups within a culture, amount of exposure to representatives of subgroups, and unconscious attitudes and biases. Since the evaluation of appropriate vocal behavior relies heavily on perceptual judgments, it is important that we examine the possible effects of unconscious bias. No matter how well intentioned we are, we may perpetuate subtle forms of bias in our expectations concerning children's performance. This is significant; Rosenthal (1974) found that one person's expectations about another, however unfounded, can influence the other's actual behavior. Because our expectations are the product of our own past experience, factors such as our own racial or social identity may cause us to misperceive children who represent alternative racial and social characteristics.

Snyder, Berscheid, and Tanke (1977) had men and women strangers get acquainted by phone, and they made audiotapes of each partner's conversation. Before the conversation, each man was shown a photo and told that it was a picture of his conversational partner. Half the men were shown a picture of a beautiful woman, and the other half were shown a picture of an unattractive woman. Results showed that the voices of the women believed to be beautiful were evaluated as more warm, open, and responsive than the voices of the women whose partners had seen an unattractive picture.

Word, Zanna, and Cooper (1974) had subjects interview other subjects for a highly desirable summer job. Half the subjects interviewed were black, and half were white. Videotapes were made, and a sample of evaluators later judged the black interviewees as less qualified than the whites. A new sample of interviewees, this time all whites, was then "interviewed" using the videotapes of the original interviewers. Those whose interviewer tapes had been made while interviewing a black applicant were judged less qualified than those whose interviewer tapes had been made with a white. Subsequent analysis of the interviewer tapes revealed subtle differences in vocal intonation and inflection and in body posture. Interviewers' unconscious expectations about the competence of their interviewee created subtle cues that then elicited confirming responses from the interviewee.

Studies such as the ones cited above indicate that our expectations concerning vocal characteristics may at times be affected by attitudes that are unconscious. Factors such as physical attractiveness and racial identity may influence our perceptions of others and our reactions to others. Discrimination that is invisible is especially detrimental because it has the potential to become a self-fulfilling prophecy. Low expectations can therefore seem to confirm negative stereotypical attitudes. High expectations often result in support, affirmation, and encouragement that enhance children's opportunities for success. As Allport (1954), Campbell (1967), and others have noted, disadvantaged groups do in fact share a number of behavioral traits. However, what they have in common may in fact be inferior social status. Sherif *et al.* (1961) demonstrated how estimates of performance are related to social status in a group. Adolescent boys at a summer camp pitched baseballs at a bullseye target wired to record the point of impact but covered with an unmarked canvas face. Onlookers recorded their estimates of each boy's score. The perception-based evaluations bore no relationship to the objectively recorded scores but closely matched the thrower's relative social status in the group.

A heightened awareness of the way in which factors such as perceived status, racial and social identity, and physical attractiveness can influence our perception of children's vocal behavior is an important prerequisite for eliminating bias in clinical interactions. Discrimination is less likely to occur in clear-cut situations. It is more likely in more ambiguous situations that require interpretation. Since it is frequently unconscious and unintentional, it is invisible to the perceiver. It is hoped that the more alert we are to the possibility of inadvertent discrimination, the more sensitive we can be to the subtle differences in children's vocal patterns that reflect experiential diversity.

SPECIFIC COMPONENTS OF THE FOUR GENERAL AREAS

Vocal Production

We have already discussed the four general areas of behavior that provide the support framework for vocal communication. For vocal production to occur optimally, all parts of the mechanism must be structurally intact and exhibit a maturity and level of function commensurate with the chronological age of the child. The importance of the anatomical and physiological state of the mechanism is especially important in the areas of respiration, phonation, and resonance. Although we have discussed these three systems separately, it is obvious that during voice production the child must be able to coordinate the contributions from each area of behavior. Implicit in the notion of adequate function is the ability to sequence a series of behaviors efficiently, smoothly, and with appropriate timing. The mechanics of optimal voice production depend on the presence of intact functional structures capable of supporting coordinated sequences of respiratory phonatory and resonatory activity. This aspect of production, the generation of signals or messages, is referred to in communication theory as *encoding*. Some of the components that contribute to optimal vocal encoding are listed below.

A. *Respiration*
 1. Intact respiratory structures.
 2. Adequate breathing patterns for speech.
  a. Depth of inhalation.
  b. Type of inhalation.
  c. Length of exhalation.
  d. Control of airflow (stopping–starting/decreasing–increasing).
 3. Appropriate timing.
B. *Phonation*
 1. Intact laryngeal mechanism.
 2. Ability to make precise adjustments.
  a. Vocal-fold excursion/closure.
  b. Vocal-fold mass/stiffness.
  c. Vibratory onset/termination.
  d. Smooth continuity of vibratory pattern.
 3. Appropriate timing—durational aspects.
 4. Adequate sensory feedback.
 5. Coordination of respiration and phonation.
  a. Adjustment of airflow.
   i. loudness
   ii. pitch
   iii. duration
  b. Appropriate pausing for air intake.
   i. deep inhalations
   ii. replenishing breaths
  c. Synchronized muscle activity.
C. *Resonance*
 1. Intact supraglottal tract structures.
 2. Adequate coupling of oral and nasal cavities.

3. Precise adjustments of velopharyngeal sphincter during oral-nasal, nasal-oral transitions.
4. Adequate oral breath pressure for production of speech sounds.
5. Adequate sensory feedback.

We have listed some of the optimal components subsumed under the respiratory, phonatory, and resonatory systems. These three systems could be described as providing the technology of voice production. To produce an appropriate voice the "machinery" must be structurally and functionally viable. In addition to possessing the appropriate technological potential for encoding and monitoring voice signals, however, an individual must operate in a psychological domain. It is this psychological domain that we discuss next. Technicians can build machines, such as voice synthesizers, to generate a variety of voice signals, but dynamic vocal behavior seen in its interpersonal context is uniquely human.

Vocal Competence

The fourth area of behavior, that of interpersonal factors affecting voice, relates to the decoding aspects of vocal behavior. Vocal performance, or the encoding of signals, does not occur in a vacuum. There is always an effect on self, on others, or on both. Depending on the level of competence we have achieved, we are able to monitor, understand, modify, and evaluate our vocal products and respond appropriately to the feedback provided by others. Our competence or our knowledge of the rules of vocal and nonvocal behavior is developed by observing others, from explicit instruction, and by trial and error. A child's level of competence will be affected by such factors as age and cognitive and affective development. Some examples of rules concerning vocal behavior that are internalized as competence develops are (1) when to talk and when not to; (2) how loudly to talk in a given situation or context; (3) the ways in which emotion is expressed in voice; and (4) the rules for expressing emotions appropriately. Vocal competence, as an aspect of total communicative competence, is reflected in the way the child adapts vocal behavior in response to personal needs, the reactions of others, and the constraints of his or her world.

Some important interpersonal factors that contribute to the development of effective vocal behavior are listed below. The list is certainly not exhaustive.

Interpersonal Factors

1. Appropriate emotional adjustment/self-esteem.
2. Awareness of feedback from others.
   a. Listens to others' words, meanings.

   b. Observation of nonverbal aspects.

   eye contact   loudness
   facial expression   pitch
   gestures, postures   intonation
   use of space   silence, pauses

3. Providing feedback to others.
4. Seeking feedback from others.
   a. Asks questions.
   b. Checks to see if meaning is understood.
   c. Pauses to allow others to respond.
   d. Talks slowly enough so that others can process information.
5. Shares talking time.
   a. Takes turns.
   b. Does not interrupt.
6. Awareness of differences between people.
   a. Adapts to status of listener.
   b. Adapts to needs of listener.
   c. Adjusts production if listener does not understand–respond.
7. Awareness of differences in situations.
   a. Adapts to physical constraints.
   b. Adapts to formal–informal aspects.
   c. Shares–controls feelings appropriately.
8. Awareness of needs and interests of others.
   a. Shows interest in what others are doing–feeling.
   b. Respects others' property, ideas, feelings.
   c. Allows others to finish what they are saying.
   d. Does not talk only about self.
9. Understanding of the relationship between vocal output and own feelings and needs.
10. Understanding of the relationship between vocal output and effect on others.

SUMMARY

We have described the four general areas of behavior that are important for appropriate vocal production. We have emphasized certain abilities that contribute to efficient function in each area. The checklists that follow (see Tables 3-1 through 3-4) are useful guides when observing children's skills in the four areas just discussed.

   Chapter 4 provides a more detailed format for analysis of children's behavior, and Chapter 5 describes in-depth diagnostic evaluation techniques.

Table 3-1 **Observation Checklist: Respiration**

(Circle One)	Specific Behavior	Description of Inappropriate Characteristics	STIMULABLE? YES (How Achieved— State Cues)	NO
adequate/ inadequate	1. Type of inhalation			
adequate/ inadequate	2. Depth of inhalation			
adequate/ inadequate	3. Length of exhalation: _____ number of seconds			

adequate/ inadequate	4. Control of airflow
	  a. Number of /p/ and /b/ sounds in 20 seconds
	  /p/ _____ /b/ _____			

adequate/ inadequate	b. Produces discernible crescendo on one prolonged exhalation: _____ number of seconds			
adequate/ inadequate	5. Timing of air intake (coordinated with meaningful pauses during reading)			

Table 3-2 **Observation Checklist: Phonation**

(Circle One)	Specific Behavior	Description of Inappropriate Characteristics	STIMULABLE? YES (How Achieved— State Cues)	NO
adequate/ inadequate	1. *a.* Vocal-fold excursion. Prolongs /s/ for ____ seconds			
adequate/ inadequate	*b.* Vocal-fold closure. Prolongs /z/ for ____ seconds			
adequate/ inadequate	2. Vocal-fold mass/tension adjustments *a.* Imitates series of different pitches while phonating /u/: ____ number of different pitches produced			
adequate/ inadequate	*b.* Produces pitch variability when singing "Happy Birthday"			

adequate/
inadequate

3. Onset of phonation
   (words beginning with
   vowels):
   _____ number of trials

adequate/
inadequate

4. Prolongs vowel smoothly
   for _____ seconds

Table 3-3 **Observation Checklist: Resonance**

(Circle One)	Specific Behavior	Description of Inappropriate Characteristics	STIMULABLE? YES (How Achieved— State Cues)	NO
adequate/ inadequate	1. Prolongs vowel sounds with appropriate oral resonance: ___ number of seconds ___ (note vowels produced)			
adequate/ inadequate	2. Prolongs nasal consonants with appropriate nasal resonance: /m/ ___ number of seconds /n/ ___ number of seconds			
adequate/ inadequate	3. Produces a— ŋ m— a appropriately: ___ number of trials			

adequate/
inadequate

4. Produces plosives and
   fricatives with appropriate
   oral breath pressure:
   ____ (note consonants
   produced)

adequate/
inadequate

5. Reads "oral" sentences with
   appropriate resonance

adequate/
inadequate

6. Reads sentences loaded with
   nasals with appropriate
   resonance

adequate/
inadequate

7. Reads passage with
   appropriate balance of
   resonance

Table 3-4 **Observation Checklist: Awareness of Interpersonal Factors**

(Circle One)	Specific Behavior	Child's Responses	WITH PROMPT	
			YES (How Achieved— State Cues)	NO
adequate/ inadequate	1. Interprets nonvocal behavior of others: ___ eye contact ___ posture ___ facial expression ___ gesture ___ use of space	(Check One) ___ unaware ___ notices presence/ absence ___ describes ___ characteristics		
adequate/ inadequate	2. Interprets vocal behavior of others: ___ loudness levels ___ pitch changes ___ duration changes ___ silence, pauses			

3. Interprets vocal behavior of others in relation to

_____ situation _____ purpose
_____ formality _____ emotions
_____ differences between people
_____ needs and interests

adequate/inadequate

4. Provides feedback to others (vocal and nonvocal)

adequate/inadequate

5. Understands relationship of own behavior to others' responses

adequate/inadequate

6. Adapts own behavior according to others' responses

adequate/inadequate

7. Shares talking time

adequate/inadequate

8. Describes how feelings and purposes affect own vocal behavior

adequate/inadequate

chapter 4
Theoretical Bases for Decision-Making

When we start out on a car journey, we usually have some idea of our final destination and a map to guide us in finding our way. If we have been there before, we may have a cognitive map rather than one drawn on paper. Similarly, as we consider the assessment of children it is helpful to have some kind of map or framework to guide us. Basically, assessment is a data-gathering process, and we gather two general kinds of data: We observe behavior and we consider relevant information. We can observe the child's behavior either in naturalistic settings (e.g., playground, lunchroom, classroom) or in a structured way in the therapy room as we elicit samples, ask questions, and present specific tasks. As a result of what we see and hear, we first identify certain symptoms or signs. Symptoms or atypical signs are like red flags that alert us. We then begin to look at the supporting behaviors that may be generating or perpetuating these symptoms. We develop hypotheses concerning the way the mechanism is being used, the appropriateness of individual pieces of behavior, and the sequencing of the behaviors during voice production. We look at the coordination of various areas of activity and make inferences about the ways one part of the mechanism may be compensating for another. We consider the effectiveness of the general communication strategies used and how these strategies are helping or hindering the satisfaction of personal needs. The medical report and case history provide important information and help us interpret the behavior we observe.

Therefore, the first step in the decision-making process is direct observation. As clinicians, we are trained to focus on the observable aspects of children's behavior. We watch and listen and make an initial judgment concerning the appropriateness or inappropriateness of what we see and hear. If we decide that there is something inappropriate about the child's voice, we move to the next stage of the process of assessment, that is, to make inferences concerning the underlying behaviors that may be generating or maintaining the observable symptoms. Our inferences are educated guesses or hypotheses that we develop concerning the possible reasons for the symptoms we observe. Inferences usually arise from our direct observations of behavior and then are checked against additional information we glean from such sources as case histories and reports from other professionals. As we sift through the salient clues obtained from direct observation of the child and the pertinent background information, we are looking for patterns. Our past experience and training help us to do this. Our knowledge of anatomy and physiology and the four areas of behavior important in voice

Figure 4-1   Stages in the assessment process.

A. The child's behavior

Observable symptoms	clinician's observations of
audible	what is seen and heard.
visible	

Observable symptoms
  audible
  visible
— clinician's observations of what is seen and heard.

Negative aspects of critical behaviors
  respiration
  phonation
  resonance
— clinician's inferences concerning maladaptive uses of the mechanism.

Patterns of behavior
  sequencing
  coordination
  compensations
— clinician's inferences concerning the interrelationship between behaviors.

Communicative effect
  personal adjustment
  interpersonal factors
— clinician's inferences concerning relationship between vocal behavior and satisfaction of needs.

clinician's decisions re
  1. Referrals
  2. Consultations
  3. Programming

B. Information about the child from pertinent medical and case history information

Case history information
  family models
  family history of voice problems
  environmental factors
  educational factors
  psychosocial factors
— clinician's generalizations concerning the nature and severity of the participitating and maintaining factors.

Medical information
  anatomical constraints
  medical conditions
  medication

production help us to zero in on any negative aspects of critical behaviors that may be demonstrated. We then look at the interrelationships between critical behaviors and speculate about the possibility that some negative aspects may be compensatory devices. We also consider the way behaviors are sequenced and coordinated. Finally, we develop some additional inferences concerning the relationship between the child's vocal production and his or her overall communicative effectiveness.

When we have developed a set of inferences based on direct observation and checked those inferences against relevant background information, we arrive at the next stage of the decision-making process, the formulation of our clinical impressions concerning the nature and scope of the problem. Clinical impressions are generalizations that can be supported by our available data. We formulate our generalizations against a backdrop of our previous direct experience and our knowledge of the literature. It is important that our generalizations be supported by evidence. In our assessment reports we always need to summarize the data we have collected to substantiate the generalizations we make. This organization of the data also helps us to think about each individual child's pattern in relation to the overall available body of knowledge concerning children with voice disorders. For example, what does this pattern suggest in relation to etiology? What referrals should be considered? What approaches to remediation have been described in the literature as especially helpful for patterns of this type? Our data-referenced generalizations help shape our approach to management. Some children's patterns will not resemble any others that we have seen or read about. These cases are the ones that prompt us to search for additional information, new sources, and second opinions. A schematic representation of the assessment process can be seen in Figure 4-1.

GENERALIZATIONS CONCERNING THE VOICE MECHANISM

It is important to look for patterns in children's behavior during the assessment process. Some symptoms cluster together, and we can sometimes identify commonalities in behavioral patterns.

Although each child is unique and each voice is different, it is convenient to group negative aspects of behavior frequently observed in children with voice disorders. This is useful for review purposes because it focuses attention on some predictable patterns and accommodations. An example of symptoms that typically occur in combination is the hypernasality of voice quality and the distortion of consonants requiring oral breath pressure that occur in the presence of velopharyngeal inadequacy. Similarly, certain predictable compensations or accommodations correlate with some specific deficits. To compensate for velopharyngeal inadequacy, many children attempt to valve the airstream by using laryngeal movement (i.e., glottal stops), pharyngeal movement (i.e., pharyngeal fricatives), and alae constriction (i.e., nasal grimaces).

Earlier we discussed the four general areas of behavior that are important to voice. We also listed some optimal behaviors under each of the four areas. We noted that while it is not always necessary for each child to exhibit all of the optimal behaviors in order to have an adequate voice, a knowledge of some of the optimal behaviors is useful for the clinician in planning remediation programs. Similarly, it is useful to know some frequently occurring patterns involving negative aspects of behavior that are observed under the four general areas. This enables us to be alert for them when we are assessing an individual child's pattern.

Patterns of Muscular Activity

One way to characterize behaviors is to describe the level of muscular activity inherent in the mechanism during vocal production. There is an optimal state of muscle tension and amount of effort used during appropriate voice production. It is also possible to demonstrate an inappropriate degree of tension and effort. Boone (1983) has referred to hyperfunctional voice problems as those characterized by too much force and contraction of muscles concerned with respiration, phonation, and resonance. A child who is using too much effort may be working very hard at the task of producing voice and yet failing to produce a result that is pleasing. The harsh sound that is heard (symptom) results from an excessive level of muscular activity in the mechanism that may be localized in one site or may be pervasive. If a *hyper*functional pattern of behavior is habituated, the muscle state will "feel" normal to the child. The opposite state is that of *hypo*function where the degree of tension during muscle contraction and/or effort is insufficient to produce appropriate voice. This state occurs less frequently and is usually associated with neurological or emotional disturbance. We shall summarize some important considerations to bear in mind in relation to both hyperfunctional and hypofunctional patterns of behavior.

Hyperfunctional Patterns   Listed below are some generalizations that can be made concerning hyperfunctional patterns of behavior.

1. May be desirable or undesirable accommodations to structural deviations (e.g., malformation, laryngeal web, papilloma, paralysis, tracheostomy, velopharyngeal inadequacy).

2. May be temporary or habituated responses to acute or chronic medical conditions of the upper respiratory tract (e.g., allergies, infections, effects of medications).
3. May or may not result in tissue change (e.g., swelling, hemorrhage, hyperkeratosis, polyps, nodules).
4. May involve use of false (ventricular) folds.
5. May be related to deviant sensory system (e.g., hearing loss, neurological impairment).
6. May be related to social or emotional adjustment (e.g., aggression, anxiety, inappropriate self-concept, faulty learning).
7. May be related to cognitive function (e.g., mental retardation).
8. May be a component of cerebral dysfunction (e.g., spasticity in children with cerebral palsy).

The following negative behaviors may occur in association with hyperfunctional patterns:

A. *Respiration*
   1. Quick, shallow inhalation.
   2. Inspiratory voicing.
   3. Inefficient control of exhalation.
      a. Talks on residual air.
      b. Does not take replenishing breaths.
      c. Runs out of air at ends of sentences.
      d. Air escapes in a rush at beginning of utterances.
B. *Phonation*
   1. Abrupt initiation of phonation (hard glottal attacks).
   2. Folds approximated too tightly; voice sounds strained or tight.
   3. Adduction of false folds.
   4. Limited use of rate and pause variation.
   5. Observable tension in neck muscles.
   6. Loudness level inappropriate for situation.
   7. Loudness variation limited to increases.
   8. Pitch level inappropriate.
   9. Phonation breaks.
   10. Pitch variation limited to getting higher.
   11. Uses laryngeal valve (not respiratory muscles) to control exhaled air.
   12. Sounds hoarse, harsh, diplophonic, ventricular.
C. *Resonance*
   1. Tension in supraglottal resonators.
   2. Sounds strident, muffled.
   3. Lack of reverberation of sound on bones of face.
   4. Minimal mouth opening—tight jaw.
   5. Insufficient balance of oral–nasal resonance.

    6. Tense or posterior carriage of tongue, or both.

D. *Interpersonal communication*
    1. Talks too much; does not take turns.
    2. Tries to get and hold attention by talking loudly.
    3. Limited awareness of effect of own tense behavior on others.
    4. Does not ask questions or asks them constantly.
    5. Few "other"-referenced statements.
    6. Does not adjust vocal behavior to feedback.

It is important to remember that any one child with a hyperfunctional pattern will not exhibit all the negative behaviors listed and that there will, of course, be differences in the severity. In some cases excessive tension can be observed in only one area. In other cases more than one area may be involved, but a pattern of generalized tension can be observed in only one area. In still other cases more than one area may be involved, and a pattern of generalized tension can be seen across areas.

Hypofunctional Patterns   Listed below are some generalizations that can be made concerning hypofunctional patterns of behavior.

1. May be secondary to structural deviation or damage (e.g., bowing of folds, neurological impairment, atrophy of folds, postintubation changes, surgeries).
2. May be related to accommodations to acute or chronic upper respiratory tract conditions (e.g., soreness).
3. May be indicative of social or emotional adjustment (e.g., reticence, hysteria).
4. If severe, may necessitate use of substitute communication system (e.g., ventricular phonation, artificial larynx, sign language).
5. May occur in combination with altered sensory feedback (e.g., dysarthria, dyspraxia, impaired hearing).
6. May be a component of cerebral dysfunction (e.g., weakness or flaccidity in children with cerebral palsy).
7. May occur subsequent to prolonged hyperfunctional use.

Wilson (1979) describes hypofunction as resulting from overly lax muscular tonus. This may be specific to one area or generalize across areas. For example, children who are severely hypotonic may have difficulty maintaining an erect head, neck, and thorax, as is sometimes observed in children with cerebral palsy. The following negative aspects of behaviors can sometimes occur in association with hypofunctional patterns:

A. *Respiration*
    1. Inhalation insufficient in depth and timing.
    2. Exhalation weak.

   3. Exhalation of short duration.

   4. Inadequate control of exhaled air.

   5. Weak muscle tone and movement.

   6. Inadequate use of replenishing breaths.

B. *Phonation*

   1. Breathy initiation of phonation.

   2. Inadequate laryngeal valving.

   3. Excessive air escape during phonation.

   4. Voice sounds breathy, aphonic.

   5. Weak laryngeal tone.

   6. Low pitch levels.

   7. Minimal vocal variety.

   8. Low vocal intensity.

   9. Voice fades at ends of phrases.

C. *Resonance*

   1. Inadequate amount of oral resonance.

   2. Inadequate amount of nasal resonance.

   3. Minimal movement of lips and tongue to shape oral cavity.

   4. Vibrating column of air not projected forward.

   5. Voice sounds thin, weak.

   6. Lack of resonance may affect intelligibility of speech sounds.

   7. Inadequate movement of velopharyngeal sphincter mechanism.

D. *Interpersonal communication*

   1. Initiates spontaneous speech infrequently.

   2. Minimal facial movement or expression.

   3. Does not adjust loudness level to situation or listeners' needs.

   4. Withdrawn, reticent.

   5. Responds minimally to questions.

   6. Does not volunteer for participatory activity.

   7. Does not share feelings.

Factors Related to Daily Use

A number of factors can be identified that, individually or in combination, may negatively affect the state of the vocal mechanism. Appropriate vocal hygiene involves avoidance of excessive demands on the mechanism, particularly at times when it is especially vulnerable. The mechanism seems to be especially at risk when there are changes in the mucosa—redness, swelling, dryness, or the presence of excessive mucus—as a result of physical, emotional, environmental, and chemical factors. If a child engages in demanding or prolonged vocal activity during times when an atypical condition already exists in the larynx or upper respiratory tract, or in both the effect of the vocal activity will be more pronounced than when the tissues are healthy. Thus the condition of the mechanism during the time that it is in use influences the possible effect of that use. Punt (1967) discussed the importance of adequate lubrication of the vocal tract. Too much mucus may lead to frequent coughing and throat clearing; too little may cause dryness and heighten susceptibility for irritation of vocal structures if folds are adducted vigorously or with excessive tension. Persistent mouth breathing (e.g., when a child is congested or has enlarged adenoids), medication (such as antihistamine and decongestant), a dusty dry environment, or restricted fluid intake may all contribute to dryness of the vocal tract. The effect of vocal abuses can be magnified if structures are already dry or irritated.

Characteristic patterns of vocal abuse in relation to the demands made on the mechanism have been noted by clinical writers. Wilson (1979) distinguishes between vocal abuse (sudden straining of the voice or continuous use of harmful practices) and vocal misuse, which involves incorrect pitch and loudness. Use may be influenced by a child's interests and life-style (e.g., athletic activities, choir, drama group, cheerleading), permanent or temporary alterations in the mechanism (e.g., compensations), medical conditions (e.g., infections), emotional and social adjustments (e.g., vocalization style and frequency of vocalization), and vocal models (e.g., learned behaviors).

With respect to assessment of factors influencing susceptibility, the clinician should be alert for any indications of temporary or permanent conditions affecting the vocal mechanism and try to discover if there is a repetitive pattern in the child's amount or kind of voice use. The identification of situations and interactions with the potential for negative vocal practices should be attempted during interviews with parents and teachers. Open-ended questions that elicit descriptions of children's preference for, and participation in, various activities seem to yield the most useful information.

The lists below show negative behaviors that can be ascertained from informants and observed by clinicians.

A. Negative behaviors to be ascertained from informants
   1. Protracted talking above noise.
      a. In cars with windows open.
      b. Over TV or stereo.
      c. Competing for attention in groups.
   2. Excessive talking and singing.
      a. Amount of talking time.
      b. Activities involving vocalization.
      c. Time spent in quiet activities.
   3. Habituated responses.
      a. Repeated vomiting (e.g., bulimia).
      b. Sound effects and imitations.
      c. Scaring others (shrieks and screams).

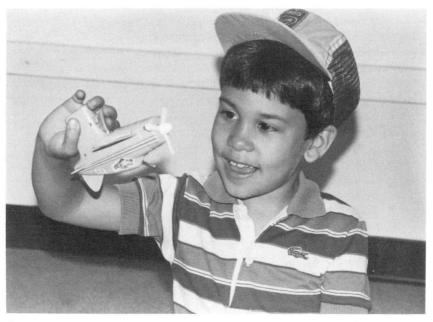

Some sound imitations can be produced without abuse to the vocal mechanism.

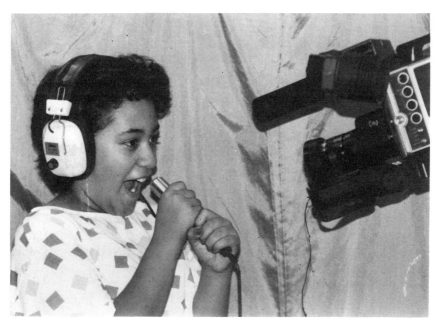

Prolonged or strained loud singing accompanying records or cassettes is a frequent form of vocal abuse.

      d. Emotional outbursts (tantrums, prolonged crying).

      e. Expressions of anger, excitement, etc.

      f. Coughing, throat clearing, wheezing.

      g. Yodeling.

      h. Smoking.

B. Negative behaviors to be observed by clinician

    1. Excessive amount of talking.

    2. Very loud talking.

    3. Hard glottal attacks.

    4. Fillers (ah's, um's produced with strain).

    5. Strained vocalizations.

    6. Sudden shrieks.

    7. Forced laughter, overloud laughter.

    8. Shouting, screaming, cheering.

    9. "Funny" voices used to get attention.

   10. Throat clearing, coughing, wheezing.

   11. Imitation of nonspeech sounds.

   12. Strained singing–very loud singing.

Atypical Sound Production (a substitute sound source—dysphonia plicae ventricularis)

A maladaptive behavior sometimes observed is the effortful compensatory strategy of phonating with the false vocal cords. This compensation is seen in children who do not have true vocal folds or who have congenital malformations of the folds. Brodnitz (1971) said it may be adopted also by children who have had surgery to remove benign tumors of the true folds or children who have suffered from laryngitis. Parisier and Henneford (1969) reported that dysphonia plicae ventricularis occurred in a patient who had surgery for removal of juvenile laryngeal papillomas. These wartlike growths on the laryngeal structures are thought to be caused by a virus and may be potentially life threatening if they impede the airway. Papillomas are not related to vocal abuse or misuse, although hoarseness may be a symptom of their presence. Parisier and Henneford's 1969 patient with papillomas subsequently had surgery also to remove a laryngeal web. Later a laryngologist observed his use of the false folds for phonation. Children sometimes use the false folds for phonation to draw attention to themselves or because of other psychogenic problems. Sometimes phonation of both the true and the false folds occurs simultaneously, and the listener perceives a "double voice." The predominant characteristics of ventricular phonation are extreme tension, hoarseness and aperiodicity, and restricted pitch range. When the child is seen under laryngoscopy, the false folds approximate during phonatory activity but do not approximate during quiet breathing or vegetative activity such as throat clearing, coughing, laughing, or crying. Ventricular phonation may be viewed as an extreme phonatory compensation, often associated with a general pattern of hyperfunctional activity. Tension in the shoulders, neck, and jaw may be observed, and the respiratory pattern sometimes is found to be shallow, tense and inefficient.

Consistency of Symptoms

Another characteristic of patterns of behavior that is diagnostically significant is the consistency. When a child exhibits the symptom of hoarseness, for example, we are interested in the frequency of occurrence and the situations in which it occurs. Intermittent hoarseness may be the result of accumulation of secretions on the folds if it occurs in an allergic child at certain times or seasons of the year. If the voice is hoarse only in the morning and clears as the day wears on, drainage from the nasal cavities may occur during sleep. If the voice is clear in the morning and becomes hoarse at the end of the school day or after participation in or attendance at athletic activities, the symptom may be related to abusive or excessive voice use. If the onset of symptoms occurs in close association with a psychologically traumatizing event in the child's life or is observed only when a child is in a particular context or speaking to particular listeners, emotional factors may be diagnostically significant. Intermittent symptoms also may suggest that permanent tissue changes have not occurred.

Intermittent symptoms that occur in association with fatigue may suggest that there is a neurological component to the problem (e.g., a child who begins to read a passage quite clearly but who becomes increasingly hypernasal as the reading progresses and the control lessens). A marked increase in certain symptoms only at the ends of sentences may suggest that the child's respiratory support is inefficient.

CHANGES IN THE MECHANISM RELATED TO ABUSE

Organic changes that can be linked to effortful vocal practices include thickening of the folds, vocal nodules, polyps, and hyperkeratosis. Wilson (1979) discussed these pathologies in detail and noted that vocal nodules are the most frequently observed pathology in children. A child's susceptibility for developing additive lesions of the folds may be affected by constitutional factors (Arnold, 1963; Kelly & Craik, 1952; Luchsinger, 1965). There seems to be evidence that additive lesions occur more frequently in some families than in others. However, it is unclear whether this is because of a constitutional predisposition or a

Table 4-1 Incidence of Vocal-Fold Pathology

Type	Boys	Girls	Total
Nodules	126	36	162
Thickening	122	26	148
Polyps	15	6	21
Other	15	7	22
	278	75	353

Source: Reported by Robert A. Baynes, "Voice Therapy with Children—a Global Approach" (paper presented at the American Speech and Hearing Association convention, 1967).

pattern of learned behavior. Table 4-1 illustrates the incidence of vocal-fold pathology by type and sex. The total number of children examined was 612.

It can be seen from the Baynes's data that structural changes in the mechanism occur with a higher frequency in males than in females. Senturia and Wilson (1968) reported that voice deviations occur twice as often in males as in females and that laryngeal nodules and localized hyperplasia are the most common benign lesions in children. The lesions occur bilaterally more often than unilaterally. The same researchers also noted that secretion is present in the nasal fossae and the arytenoids are reddened, edematous, or both in a high percentage of voice-deviant children. It is unclear why some children seem to be particularly at risk, while other children who engage in frequent strenuous vocal activity remain unaffected (Anderson & Newby, 1973). Wilson (1979) concluded that nodules are probably the result of a combination of factors. It may be that a number (or certainly more than one) of the high-risk factors noted below may contribute to a pattern of heightened susceptibility for the development of these additive lesions of the folds.

High-Risk Factors Relating to the Development of Vocal Nodules

Clinical writers have noted that some of the following factors may predispose an individual to develop vocal nodules:

1. Constitutional tendency (Arnold, 1963; Kelly & Craik, 1952)
2. Chronic upper respiratory problems (Withers, 1961)
3. Psychological living environment, e.g., size of family (Wilson, 1979)

4. Physical living environment, e.g., air pollution (Wilson, 1979)
5. Personality and adjustment (Arnold, 1963)
6. Endocrine imbalance, especially thyroid (Withers, 1961)
7. Vocal abuse: sudden straining of the voice (Wilson, 1979); continuous use of abusive practices
8. Vocal misuse: incorrect pitch and loudness (Wilson, 1979)[1]

Nodules appear on the edge of the free margin of the fold at the junction of the anterior and middle thirds. There is a progression of development from a slight swelling and reddening in the initial stages, then gradual thickening, and finally fully developed growths consisting of fibrotic tissue (DeWeese & Saunders, 1973). Grey (1973) and Withers (1961) have provided additional information about the maturation sequence of nodules. Although nodules are never painful, they result in size–mass changes that affect evenness of adduction and the vibratory pattern of the folds. As the nodules increase in size, vocal symptoms such as hoarseness become more apparent. Moore (1971) noted the relationship between the size of the mass and the amount of air leakage, or breathiness, but said that the hardness of the nodule is also a factor. A noncompressible nodule may result in audible symptoms even if it is quite small in size. In order to compensate for the nodules, children often use more effort in adduction, thus pressing the folds more tightly together to minimize the irregularity in the margin of the folds. By talking more loudly or at a higher pitch level some children compensate for the alteration in size and mass. These strategies, however, tend to exacerbate the condition of the mechanism. Eventually, if the nodules become larger, the child may exhibit periods of aphonia.

Negative Behaviors Associated with Vocal Nodules

1. *Phonation*
    a. Hoarse or breathy phonation, or both.
    b. Pitch level may appear low for age and sex (increased mass).
    c. Aphonia on unstressed syllables.
    d. Hard glottal attacks on words beginning with vowels.
    e. Voice clearest when phonating loudly; poorest when phonating softly.
    f. Voice clears somewhat in upper part of pitch range.
    g. Reduced phonation time on prolonged /a/.
    h. Difference in duration time of unvoiced versus voiced continuants.
    i. Restricted pitch range.
    j. Hyperextension of head and neck.

[1] Adapted from D. Kenneth Wilson (1979).

    k. Repeated nonproductive throat clearing.
    l. Vocal variety limited to increases in loudness.
    m. Intermittent diplophonia (two-toned sound caused by uneven distribution of weight on folds).
2. *Respiration*
    a. Shallow inhalation.
    b. Inefficient use of exhalation.
3. *Interpersonal*
    a. Aggressive style of vocal interaction.
    b. Incessant talking.

Since vocal nodules are the most frequently occurring vocal pathology in school-age children (Baynes, 1967; Senturia & Wilson, 1968; Wilson, 1971; Wilson, 1979), it is useful to discuss some of the behaviors such children frequently exhibit. Figure 4-2 summarizes assessment information obtained following an evaluation of an 8-year-old boy who was referred by his classroom teacher.

Figure 4-2   A profile of Brett—age 8 years.

A. *Behavior*
   1. Audible and visible symptoms
      i. Hoarseness (lessens as loudness increases).
      ii. Hard glottal attacks.
      iii. Excessive loudness level during conversation.
      iv. Observable tension in neck and jaw.
      v. Observable tension in shoulders.

Pattern = hyperfunctional

   2. Negative behaviors
    a. Respiration

Excessive effort and muscular tension observed in all three areas

      i. Clavicular inhalation.
      ii. Short exhalation phase.
      iii. Inefficient control of exhaled airstream.
    b. Phonation
      i. Leakage of air during phonation.
      ii. Aperiodic vibratory pattern.
      iii. Inappropriate initiation of phonation.
      iv. Variety limited to getting louder.
    c. Resonance
      i. Reduced oral resonance on sustained continuants (z, ʒ, ð).
      ii. Reduced nasal resonance on sustained continuants (m, n, ŋ).
      iii. Reduced mouth opening.
      iv. Inappropriate tone focus.
      v. Tension of supraglottal structures.

Brett was a typical vocal abuser who personified many of the characteristics noted in the literature. His demands on his vocal mechanism were excessive, and he exhibited few of the optimal behaviors necessary to support loud vocalization combined with strenuous activity. An allergic condition increased his susceptibility for irritation of the mechanism. He compensated for his poor respiratory support for sustained speaking by increasing the effort he was using in the laryngeal area. Supraglottal resonance was not well developed, and lip and tongue movement was minimal. His attempts to improve intelligibility were limited to using more laryngeal effort and increasing the tension in his whole body. Brett needed to learn to use more productive vocal strategies, since the compensatory behaviors he was using were not effective. Telling Brett he should never talk loudly was not a feasible solution, given his life-style.

---

3. Compensations
   i. Uses laryngeal valving to compensate for lack of respiratory muscle control exhalation.
   ii. Uses excessive laryngeal effort to compensate for reduced resonance and articulatory precision.

Hearing sensitivity within normal limits bilaterally

   iii. Uses increased loudness as only means of "clearing" tone and varying voice.
4. Interpersonal Behaviors
   i. Does not listen well.
   ii. Uses few "other-referenced" statements.
   iii. Uses many "self-referenced" statements.
   iv. Does not adapt to feedback or situational constraints.
   v. Does not share talking time.
   vi. Uses loud talking to get and hold attention.

B. *Information*
1. Medical report
   i. Mature bilateral nodules.
   ii. Allergic to mold; cat and dog dander.
2. Family history
   i. Youngest of five children.
   ii. One older sister (a cheerleader) had vocal problems.
3. Environmental
   i. Has a dog that sleeps in his room.
4. Vocal demands
   i. Active in neighborhood peer group; sporting activities; church choir.
5. Other
   i. Teacher reports that he is a very active, noisy child in class.

Brett's profile is a typical one, frequently seen in active, talkative boys of his age. We have noted some negative behaviors under the "interpersonal" category of Brett's profile. We do not mean to imply that there is a causative relationship between these behaviors and the development of vocal nodules. There is no research in this area to suggest such a connection. However, clinical experience suggests that some children with vocal nodules need to develop improved interpersonal skills in order to facilitate vocal improvement. It is also possible that a child such as Brett may need even better interpersonal skills than other children in order to protect and improve his voice.

CONSTRAINTS THAT REDUCE VOLITIONAL CONTROL

Affective Constraints

Since the voice is a bridge between an individual and his or her world, disturbances in voice and the withholding of voice have been noted in the literature as symptoms of affective disorders. Voice reflects emotional states and reactions to life stress. Goldfarb (1961) studied child schizophrenics and described a variety of vocal characteristics. In a later study (Goldfarb *et al.*, 1976), also with schizophrenics, no specific set of symptoms was observed but there was a basic loss of control and regulation of speech.

The terms *elective* and *selective mutism* have been used in the psychological literature (Kolvin & Fundudis, 1981) to describe the withholding of voice and speech by young children. Psychiatrists suggest that such children have severe psychological disturbances, frequently come from conflicted families, and may use withdrawal behaviors to manipulate their environment. In most instances of mutism of this type, the children have previously developed speech and language and may continue to use voice in certain situations or with certain people but withhold oral communication consistently for long periods of time.

This lack of voice or disordered voicing may be viewed as a manifestation of psychological disequilibrium. Extreme anxiety, depression, conversion reaction, or personality disorder can interfere with normal volitional control over phonation (Aronson, 1980). Wilson (1979) says that hysterical aphonia is not common in children, though dysphonia is relatively common. In some children a normal voice returns quickly, whereas other children require help from a clinical psychologist or counselor. Wilson (1979) also noted that some children may have bowed vocal folds as a result of a hysterical condition. In older children mutational falsetto is thought to be related to a conflicted response to sexual maturity (Van Riper, 1972) or problems in a relationship with the parent of the same sex. For example, a postpubertal male may maintain a high-pitched voice because of a reluctance to identify with his father.

In very young children, when voice use is withheld completely or restricted because of psychological factors, the problem may at first seem to be merely shyness. An example of this kind of problem can be seen in the following case history:

Rosie, a 5-year-old kindergartener, was referred to the speech-language pathologist by her classroom teacher because she did not talk at all during the school day. She smiled when people spoke to her, hung her head, or used gestures. Great effort was expended by school personnel to coax Rosie to talk. She was given extra privileges and treats and special attention, which she seemed to enjoy, but she could never be encouraged to vocalize. She was neat and careful in her written tasks and assignments and seemed extremely cooperative and well behaved. The speech-language pathologist interviewed the parents and described to them some of the problems that Rosie's "excessive shyness" was causing her. The parents' response was surprising. They smiled and said, "So she's making fools out of you all at school here. We don't have any problem at all at home. She talks to us all of the time. It's just at school and on the bus that she won't do it. You're the experts, and it's your problem obviously." The parents' reaction indicated that a psychological consultation was needed, and the family was eventually persuaded to seek family therapy. The psychiatric report to the speech-language clinician indicated that it seemed likely that the parents were hostile to authority figures and were subtly encouraging Rosie's responses. It was recommended that school personnel (including the bus driver, lunchroom supervisor, etc.) refrain from becoming caught up in the "game" of coaxing Rosie to talk, as such attempts were seen as rewarding to her and were in fact reinforcing the undesirable behavior. Instead, it was suggested that Rosie be rewarded for any nonverbal attempts to relate positively to others and that significant adults at school should try to establish warm, accepting relationships with her. It was two years before Rosie used appropriate vocal behavior in the school environment.

In Rosie's case, the child's withholding of vocal behavior was related to a severe psychological disturbance that involved a conflicted pattern of family interaction. The example emphasizes the need for team assessment of such problems and the fact that the reactions of all school personnel are important in determining the way the symptoms are maintained. Rosie's "aphonia" was a response to entering a different (i.e., school) environment. In other cases, the appearance of such behavior can occur suddenly after many years of vocalizing appro-

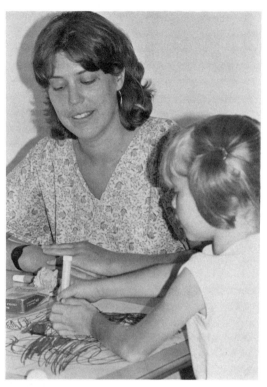

Children who withhold vocal communication may be encouraged to express their feelings through nonverbal tasks. A warm, trusting relationship with the clinician can then develop gradually.

priately in a particular environment. Such was the case of Misty, who exhibited a sudden onset in response to traumatizing occurrences in her home life.

Misty, age 11 years, was in a special education classroom for mildly mentally handicapped children. She had been enrolled in language therapy for some years and exhibited normal patterns of phonatory behavior and articulation, but depressed receptive and expressive language skills. She had been seen by the speech-language pathologist for her regular session on a Friday and participated normally in the session. When Misty came to school on Monday, she seemed withdrawn, offered no voluntary communication, and responded in a whisper when she was asked questions by her teacher. When Misty's occasional whispering continued to be her only attempt at communication, a case conference was scheduled. The mother reported that Misty could not be encouraged to vocalize at all at home. She attributed Misty's withdrawal to the father's sudden departure from the family. Psychiatric counseling further revealed that Misty had recently begun to menstruate and had been frightened and apprehensive. Her depressed language skills made it more difficult for her to understand and cope with the physical and emotional changes that occurred. After six months of counseling in combination with speech-language therapy, Misty's appropriate vocal behavior was reestablished.

As can be seen in the preceding examples, the way a voice is not used, or withheld, can be indicative of an individual's psychological adjustment. It seems to be important to consider the child's relationships with significant adults in the home and school environment, since such relationships are critical in helping a child cope with adjustments to painful events and situations.

Neurological Constraints

The volitional control of voice may be diminished by impaired neurological functioning resulting from disease or congenital problems. Occasionally, young children will be seen with myasthenia gravis (Wilson, 1979). Poor control of the musculature results in hypernasality, dysphonia, and reduction of loudness levels. Symptoms increase as the system fatigues. More commonly, the effect of impaired neurological function is seen in children with cerebral palsy. Mysak (1980) has described the variety of voice problems occurring in this population. The symptoms depend on the type and severity of the condition. Westlake and Rutherford (1961) provide some helpful guidelines for assessing the voluntary control necessary for sustained voicing. Table 4-2 is adapted from their ideas.

Table 4-2 **Respiration**

Prerequisite Behaviors	Inadequate Behaviors
1. Voluntary control of inhalation	Panting: fewer than 3 quick breaths in 5 seconds. Reverse breathing (upper chest depressed during inhalation).
2. Voluntary control of exhalation	Involuntary movements during exhalation.
3. Sufficient air to sustain phonation	Fewer than 4–5 seconds exhalation.
4. Breathing rate that allows for continuous phonation	A rate of 30 breaths per minute or higher in children over 2 years.

Table 4-3 **Phonation**

Prerequisite Behaviors	Inadequate Behaviors
1. Ability to initiate phonation rapidly	Less than once per second (repeated /ha/).
2. Sustain phonation for phrases of more than 2 or 3 words	Fewer than 5 seconds. Normal children can sustain for 10 seconds or longer.
3. Voluntary control of laryngeal movements	Erratic involuntary spasms and movements of laryngeal muscles (heard in fluctuations and breaks in sound).
4. Appropriate muscle tonus in head, neck, torso	Unable to lift head easily when shoulders are held down (weak neck flexors). Hyper- or hypotonicity of musculature. Inappropriate posture.
5. Differentiation of muscle activity	Vocal-fold adduction associated with extensor patterns (e.g., hypotonic child may extend trunk and neck to assist adduction; hypertonic child may hyperextend jaw).

Phonation may be observed during periods of involuntary activity (such as laughing, crying, sighing, coughing) and in voluntary tasks. See Table 4-3.

Cognitive Constraints

The incidence of voice problems in retarded children is higher than in the normal population. Voice symptoms associated with Down's syndrome have been studied by Montague and Hollein (1973), Novak (1972), and Weinberg and Zlatin (1970). While mental retardation is not the primary cause of voice disorders in children with Down's syndrome (Novak, 1972), some evidence suggests that modal frequency levels may deviate from normal levels; hearing loss occurs with greater frequency; and breathiness, roughness, and hypernasality are often observed. In Novak's 1972 study, laryngeal examination found only slight thickness of the vocal-fold mucosa but signs of atrophy and dryness in the pharyngeal mucosa.

Metabolic disorders are sometimes seen in connection with mental retardation. The thyroid, an endocrine gland, produces thyroxin, which regulates the body's metabolic rate. Individuals who suffer from hypothyroidism have a lowered metabolic rate. Their voices may be excessively low in pitch because of edema of the folds (Aronson, 1980). Brodnitz (1971) stated that some vocal symptoms of extreme thyroid deficiency are roughness and hoarseness. Cognitive deficits also may affect children's ability to understand the language used during assessment and therapy and to process feedback and adjust behavior.

Sensory Constraints

Voice problems frequently result from difficulties in monitoring one's own voice and the voices of others. Auditory, visual, and kinesthetic awareness can be disturbed in a variety of ways. Some disturbances are transitory; others are permanent. Children with structural abnormalities of the vocal mechanism, supraglottal tract, or both receive distorted sensory feedback during the speech learning period. An example of this is the child with a cleft palate. Tactile, kinesthetic, and auditory feedback is affected even during prespeech vocalization. In most instances, specialists try to alleviate this by the early fitting of speech appliances and early initiation of surgical procedures. Since multiple procedures are frequently needed, these children are constantly adapting to changes in the structures and consequent changes in feedback over a period of years. Another example is that of a child with enlarged tonsils and adenoids who undergoes a tonsillectomy and adenoidectomy. It is commonly believed that some children with a normal velopharyngeal mechanism can take up to six weeks to adjust their behavior and exhibit normal resonance following surgery. Before surgery, they may have made closure against the enlarged adenoidal pad. After surgery, they sound hypernasal until they adopt more vigorous velopharyngeal movement. During the adjustment period, they are adapting to altered auditory and proprioceptive feedback. Children who have laryngeal surgery also need time to make adjustments in their motor behavior as they learn to adapt to new sensory information. This is why we need to be alert, for example, to possible problems in children who have multiple surgeries to remove papilloma.

The most dramatic examples of voice deviations resulting from altered feedback are seen in children with hearing loss. Fuller (1970) noted that voice quality is disturbed when children have flat audiograms with threshold levels greater than 50 dB. It is also disturbed if losses are 40 dB or greater in the low frequencies accompanied by a greater loss in the high frequencies. Some factors that affect the extent of the voice problem include the severity and type of loss, the use of amplification, the training received in use of residual hearing (Calvert & Silverman, 1975) and the emphasis given to voice in speech–language therapy. Ling (1975) states that it is important to focus on the control of breathing and vocalization early in the remediation program. Frequently, if too much emphasis is put on language stimulation and articulation skill, and respiration, phonation, and resonance patterns are ignored, inappropriate voicing patterns become habituated. Audiologists frequently consider inappropriate loudness levels to be clues that are of interest diagnostically. A child with a conductive loss may speak too softly, since he or she is able to monitor through bone conduction, and a child with a sensorineural loss may need to speak very loudly, even in quiet environments, in order to monitor the voice auditorally.

Vocal Symptoms Associated with Hearing Loss Some vocal symptoms identified as occurring in persons who have impaired hearing are listed below. The degree of loss affects type and severity of symptoms.

A. Faulty resonance
   1. Hypernasality.
   2. Hyponasality.
   3. Cul-de-sac resonance.
   4. Posterior tongue carriage.
   5. Insufficient velopharyngeal closure.
   6. Oral–nasal imbalance.
   7. Difficulty habituating appropriate patterns.
B. Inappropriate loudness
   1. Level.
   2. Variation.
C. Inappropriate pitch
   1. Modal pitch.
   2. Variation.
D. Inappropriate rate
   1. Breath groups.
   2. Prolonged duration and diphthongizations.
E. Inappropriate initiation of phonation
   1. Not matched with expiratory cycle.
   2. Hard attack.
F. Tendency to develop nodules
G. Inappropriate prosodic patterns

CONSTRAINTS RESULTING FROM SPECIFIC STRUCTURAL DEVIATIONS

Velopharyngeal Inadequacy

Since the velopharyngeal closure mechanism is responsible for separating the oral and nasal cavities, an inadequate mechanism results in hypernasality of vowels and nonnasal consonants, and distortion of consonants. Consonants that require intraoral breath pressure are particularly affected. When the velopharyngeal mechanism is structurally intact but functionally impaired, as in the case of paralysis, the problem is usually referred to as *velopharyngeal incompetence.* When the term *velopharyngeal insufficiency* is used, it suggests structural deficiency. Structural defects include unrepaired clefts of the palate (overt, submucous, or occult), short palates (congenitally short or the result of surgical repair of a cleft), lesions due to trauma, abnormally large or inactive pharynges, and inappropriate relationships between structures (sometimes seen in craniofacial anomalies associated with a variety of genetic syndromes).

A team approach to assessment is usually the procedure of choice. Velopharyngeal adequacy is best evaluated in a medical center where information from videofluoroscopic, endoscopic, or radiographic analyses is available. There are also a number of noninvasive instruments, such as accelometric devices, that can provide information concerning the adequacy of velopharyngeal closure. These instruments are sometimes available in speech science laboratories in universities and medical centers. The plastic surgeon, orthodontist, and prosothodontist play important roles in the assessment and habilitation process. Surgical procedures and the various kinds of speech appliances and obturators have been described in the cleft-palate literature. A secondary surgical procedure that is sometimes used with good results is the construction of a pharyngeal flap. In this procedure a piece of mucosal tissue from the pharynx is permanently attached to the velum to form a bridge. When air is emitted through the nose (as in breathing or the emission of nasal consonants), it passes on either side of the flap. To accomplish closure of the port, pharyngeal wall activity is necessary so that the sides of the pharynx close around the bridge of tissue. Bzoch (1972) reported that hypernasality and problems with nasal emission were reduced in patients who had undergone this surgery. We mention this secondary procedure not because it is necessarily the method of choice for all patients but because it is a fairly common example of a permanent alteration in structures that requires accommodation and relearning.

Negative Behaviors Associated with the Velopharyngeal Inadequacy Negative behaviors frequently associated with velopharyngeal inadequacy and problems that cause difficulty for children who have undergone procedures to improve insufficiency are listed below. In some cases symptoms persist even after structural adequacy is achieved. In other cases procedures do not always produce the desired result. We must emphasize that while certain behaviors occur frequently in such a population, each child must be evaluated carefully and individually. Following surgical or prosthetic intervention, periodic reevaluation is encouraged. In some instances revisions may be necessary.

A. *Phonation and resonance*
   1. Breathiness.
   2. Hoarseness.
   3. Hyperfunctional use of phonatory mechanism.
   4. Laryngeal attempts to compensate for inadequate velopharyngeal valving (e.g., glottal stops).
   5. Nodules.
   6. Hypernasality of vowels (especially apparent on high vowels /i/ and /u/).
   7. Hypernasality of oral consonants.
   8. Hyponasality of nasal consonants (sometimes apparent subsequent to pharyngeal flap surgery). If accommodation does not occur as a result of therapy, revision may be necessary.
   9. Nasal emission of airstream.
B. *Articulation*
   1. Distortions of consonants dependent on intraoral breath pressure, particularly fricatives and affricatives.
   2. Substitutions most frequent on plosives (e.g., glottal or pharyngeal stop).
   3. Voiceless consonants more difficult than voiced.
   4. Consonantal blends misarticulated frequently.
   5. Nasal snort–posterior nasal fricative.
   6. Nasal grimace–constriction of nares; /s/ may be lateralized, palatalized or produced with pharyngeal friction.
   7. Omissions of pressure consonants.
   8. Substitution of nasals for pressure consonants.
   9. Connected speech may be unintelligible.

Vocal-Fold Paralysis

Paralysis of the vocal folds is relatively common in children (Holinger & Brown, 1967) and may be congenital or acquired. It represents about 10% of all congenital anomalies of the larynx and may be bilateral or unilateral. Laupus and Pastore (1967) note that the abductor muscles are most usually affected. If one or both folds are fixed in an abducted position, breathing is not restricted, but voice use may be impaired. Symptoms will depend on the degree of involvement and the compensations that are possible with respect to closure. For example, if only one fold is affected and the other is able to approximate it, the leakage of air during phonation will be minimized. Some degree of breathiness will be present if one or both folds are fixed in the paramedian position. If one fold is fixed at the midline, voicing will not be impaired since the other fold will move to the midline appropriately during phonation. Some difficulty in breathing, especially during physical activity, will be noted, however, since the airway is reduced. If both folds are fixed at the midline, and the airway is blocked, the child will need to breathe through a tracheostomy tube. Such a child may need help in dealing with the disturbance in respiratory and phonatory activity and in personal and interpersonal adjustment. Paralysis of the left vocal fold is frequently more serious than that of the right, and more difficult to ameliorate, since it is often associated with anomalies of the heart and blood vessels (Holinger & Brown, 1967).

Symptoms Associated with Vocal-Fold Paralysis

Respiratory difficulties
Breathiness; hoarseness
Reduced loudness levels
Reduced vocal variety
Hyperfunctional compensations
Personal adjustment difficulties
Impaired interpersonal skills
Ventricular phonation
Stridor
Stoma noise (if tracheostomy necessary)

Laryngeal Trauma

It is difficult to generalize about the patterns of symptoms displayed by children who have undergone traumatic experiences affecting the larynx, since the insults vary considerably with respect to the type of damage. Prolonged intubation is a common cause of trauma in children. Clinicians should be alert to the need to question parents concerning episodes of respiratory distress in a child's medical history or operations that may have involved intubation. Endotracheal tubes and nasotracheal tubes can result in temporary or permanent damage, as can aspiration of foreign objects, direct trauma to the neck, or inhaling toxic substances.

Problems Resulting from Trauma

Hoarseness
Breathiness
Dysphonia
Aphonia
Damage to joints or musculature
   of larynx (Arnold, 1966)
Fractures of cartilages
   (Hilinger *et al.*, 1952)
Inflammation of folds
Edema of folds
Pain on swallowing
Asymmetry of fold approximation

(Bowman, Shanks, & Manion,
   1972)
Dyspnea
Social and emotional reactions
Habituated compensatory
   behaviors (e.g., talking too
   softly and carefully even after
   healing)
Ulceration of folds
Glottal web—high-pitched voice
   (Arnold, 1966)

SUMMARY

We have discussed some typical symptom patterns that are sometimes seen in association with specific etiologies. We have also listed a wide range of symptoms that can occur in conjunction with some of the most common problems. We emphasized the importance of always considering each child as a unique individual. It is certainly unwise to assume that one can ever be sure that a child with a specific problem will automatically exhibit a predictable set of symptoms. Nevertheless, it sometimes helps us organize our thoughts and our planning strategies if we are cognizant of the way some symptoms cluster together. In Chapter 5 we describe specific assessment strategies.

chapter 5
Techniques for Evaluating Vocal Behavior

The first step in the evaluation process is usually screening. In many school districts, screening of all children is conducted by the speech–language pathologist at regular intervals. At such times, the voice screening is a part of a process that also involves hearing, articulation, and language. The clinician, for example, listens to the child's voice during brief conversation, reading, or both, or asks the child to count. Many screening forms have been developed by clinicians as aids to sharpening their focus on specific aspects of behavior. Most forms include the opportunity to note any deviations in pitch, loudness, quality, and resonance. Many clinicians include prolongation of vowels in the screening in order to check duration time and any deviations such as breaks in the continuity of voicing. The s-z ratio (Eckel and Boone [1981]), is also becoming more popular as a screening technique used if quality deviations are suspected. If, during the screening, the clinician is unsure that a problem is permanent or transitory (as in the case of a child with an upper respiratory tract infection), then a follow-up screening is usually scheduled.

In school districts where periodic screening of all children is not standard procedure, the speech–language pathologist must rely on referrals. These referrals are made primarily by teachers; but sometimes parents, school nurses, and physicians ask that a child be seen for voice evaluation. When clinicians depend on referrals alone, they need to ensure that information concerning voice disorders is disseminated. Regular in-service programs for teachers and other school personnel need to be organized so that symptoms of vocal disorders can be identified. Programs on voice hygiene for music teachers, physical education teachers, nurses, bus drivers, lunchroom supervisors, parents, and others can be provided. Posters and notices can be used effectively to raise awareness. For example, one innovative clinician placed small colorful signs on each table in the teachers' lounges in one school district. On each stand-up sign was written: *If any children you know have voices that sound unusual (e.g., hoarse, raspy, nasal), please send them to the speech teacher to be checked.* Informal discussions with individual teachers can also stimulate interest and help focus attention on vocal behavior.

It is usually helpful to initiate and maintain cordial professional relationships with otolaryngologists in the community. When new physicians move into the clinician's district, a friendly call or letter describing the services available for children with voice problems may be mutually advantageous. Some established physicians who rarely refer for voice therapy may nevertheless respond positively to invitations to lecture to speech–language pathologists. Question–answer periods following such lectures can help generate interest in improving communication between physicians and teachers. Clinicians may find it rewarding to ask physicians to participate in team presentations with speech–language pathologists on such subjects as Ear, Nose, and Throat Problems for PTO or PTA groups. Improved communication between physicians and speech–language pathologists usually heightens the physicians' awareness of the speech–language pathologists' areas of expertise and consequently may increase the number of children referred for voice therapy. When physicians do make referrals for voice therapy, they usually respond favorably to short follow-up reports. Some clinicians routinely write to thank physicians for referrals. They use the opportunity to note that they enjoy working with children with voice problems and would appreciate future referrals.

Most clinicians want to be sure that they have obtained adequate

Figure 5-1   Physician's Evaluation Report. (Voice)

Child _____ Age _____

School _____ Grade_____

This child has been evaluated by the speech pathologist. Because of voice symptoms that could be related to psysiological or neurological conditions affecting communication, a physician's statement concerning pertinent medical information is requested.

Speech–Language Pathologist's Findings:_____

_____

_____

Date of Evaluation:_____

Description of Voice:_____

I. Physical conditions that may be pertinent (circled)

allergies   frequent upper   craniofacial

surgeries   respiratory infections   anomalies

medications   excessive mucus   broken nose

deviated septum   thyroid condition   hearing loss

previous intubation   enlarged tonsils   dryness of tract

mouth breathing   and adenoids

other:_____

II. Abusive practices (circled)

throat clearing   crying–screaming   excessive talking   loud talking

sound imitations   impersonations   coughing   smoking   yodeling

other:_____

III. Demands inherent in life-style-environment (circled):

voice models   noisy environment   cheerleading   sporting activities

choir   solo singing   dramatics   stress   other:_____

Please complete the following information and return the entire form as soon as possible. Thank you.

_____

Speech–Language Pathologist

Results of physician's evaluation (e.g., condition of larynx, tonsils, adenoids):

_____

_____

Does the child need medical care related to the communication disorder (e.g., surgery, prosthesis, medication)?   Yes_____   No_____   If yes, please explain:

_____

_____

Please describe any health or medical problems that would affect the communication training: _____

_____

Comments: _____

_____

_____

Date:_____   Signature of Physician: _____

Please return to: Stamped Name:

(Clinician's
name and address)

information on the child's abilities before they make a medical referral. This enables them to send a description of their findings with the child when he or she visits the otolaryngologist. A referral form such as the one suggested by Boone (1983) is helpful, since a form that asks the physician to provide specific written feedback to the clinician concerning his or her findings streamlines the communication between professionals. Most school districts have their own medical referral forms, and frequently the best forms are short and simple so that a busy physician can complete them in a few seconds. It is also important, however, to try to provide as much information as possible concerning the speech–language pathologist's findings. This can help focus the physician's attention on pertinent information that the clinician thinks may be relevant to the medical diagnosis. The Physician's Evaluation Report shown in the next section (see Figure 5-1) allows information of this type to be transmitted to the physician.

EVALUATION PROCEDURES

Unfortunately, no standardized tests are available for clinicians to use during voice diagnosis. Much work remains to be done in this important area of evaluation. However, there are excellent descriptions of methods of assessment to be found in texts such as Wilson (1979), Boone (1983), and Aronson (1980). We shall not attempt to review all the information contained in these texts, but shall note some of the relevant behaviors subsumed under our four general areas and explain some ways in which these may be elicited. Remember as you read the suggestions that the tasks provided are designed to help the clinician formulate subjective impressions about children's behavior. In the absence of normative data, we have no objective method of comparing an individual's responses with other children of similar age, sex, or socioeconomic level. Similarly, our impression of a child's poor performance on any one task is not in itself evidence that a pathology exists. Patterns of difficulty on a number of tasks, however, may help us to formulate hypotheses concerning the nature of the problem and the possible etiology. These hypotheses help us to decide (1) whether the child has a problem that warrants intervention; (2) whether additional information–help is needed, and, if so, what referrals should be made; and (3) which specific behaviors should be translated into possible goals for therapy.

We find it convenient to use the form shown in Figure 5-2 to record the results of our evaluation. This form is divided into sections pertaining to respiration, phonation, resonance, and high-risk factors. At the beginning of each section of the recording sheet the clinician decides whether or not detailed information needs to be recorded before proceeding to

Figure 5-2   Andrews Voice Evaluation Form.

Child's name _____   Date(s) examined: _____

Birthdate: _____ Age: _____   Time of day: _____

School: _____Grade: ____   Examiner: _____

Siblings' names and ages: _____   Room/teacher: _____

_____   Hearing testing results: _____

Cold or allergic reaction at time of testing? Yes _____ No _____

Synopsis of Diagnostic Results
(check areas of concern)

Respiration
Type and depth of inhalation _____
Length of exhalation _____
Control of airflow _____
Use of replenishing breaths _____

Phonation
Vocal-fold abduction–adduction _____
Vocal-fold mass/tension adjustments _____
          pitch _____
          loudness _____
Onset of phonation _____
Evenness of vibratory pattern (quality) _____

Resonance
Oral resonance _____
Nasal resonance _____ Transitions between orality and nasality _____
Tone focus _____
          mouth opening _____
          tongue movement _____
          lip movement _____

Interpersonal Factors
Motivation _____
Environmental factors _____
Social–emotional factors _____

Rate
Phrasing _____
Length of pauses _____
Too rapid _____
Too slow _____

High-risk Factors
Relevant _____
Irrelevant _____

Referral needed: Medical _____ Psychological _____
Enroll in therapy? _____ Yes _____ No

RESPIRATION
     Respiration for speech appears:
     appropriate _____   inappropriate _____ (if inappropriate, complete section
     that follows)

Figure 5.2 (continued)

Characteristics of Breathing Patterns:

1. Coordination of inhalation and exhalation in spontaneous speech:
   rhythmical _____   jerky _____   noisy _____   other _____

2. Chest wall movements: appropriate _____   inappropriate _____

3. Tension sites: none _____   chest _____   neck _____

4. Length of exhalation (average of 3 trials)
   a. Can count on one breath to _____
   b. Sustains s-s-s _____ sec.
   c. Sustains z-z-z _____ sec.
   d. Sustains /a/ _____ sec.
   e. Sustains /i/ _____ sec.

5. Control of exhalation (stopping and starting airflow per breath)
   a. Number of /p/ productions per exhalation _____
   b. Number of /t/ productions per exhalation _____
   c. Number of /g/ productions per exhalation _____
   d. Number of /t∫/ productions per exhalation _____
   e. Number of /h/ productions per exhalation _____

6. Use of replenishing breaths
   a. Number of breaths taken while counting to 50 _____
   b. Number of breaths taken while reading (50 words at
      child's reading level) _____
      (Child's reading rate appears: appropriate _____ fast _____ slow _____)

PHONATION
Phonatory behavior for speech in the following areas appears:

	quality	onset	loudness	pitch	rate
Appropriate	_____	_____	_____	_____	_____
Inappropriate	_____	_____	_____	_____	_____

(if inappropriate, complete section below)

1. Quality in spontaneous speech sample
   a. Normal _____
   b. Breathy_____   Mild _____   Moderate _____   Severe _____
   c. Harsh _____   _____   _____   _____
   d. Hoarse _____   _____   _____   _____
   e. Related observations: pitch breaks _____ phonation breaks _____
      aphonia _____ glottal fry _____ diplophonia _____ tremor _____
      other: _____
   f. Hard attacks noted in spontaneous speech: _____ yes _____ no

2. Onset of phonation

Single Words	Appropriate	Breathy	Hard Attack
a. arm /a/	_____	_____	_____
b. eggs /e/	_____	_____	_____
c. umpire /ʌ/	_____	_____	_____
d. out /au/	_____	_____	_____
e. ooze /u/	_____	_____	_____
f. eight /eɪ/	_____	_____	_____
g. apple /æ/	_____	_____	_____

Figure 5.2 (continued)

Sentences	Appropriate	Breathy	Hard Attack
a. Uncle Eddy eats eggs.	_____	_____	_____
b. Is everyone angry?	_____	_____	_____
c. Amy Anderson always understands.	_____	_____	_____
d. Aunt Ellie ate out.	_____	_____	_____

3. Loudness
   a. Prolonged vowel /a/ loudly: _____ seconds
   b. Prolonged vowel /a/ softly: _____ seconds
   c. Can say the days of the week softly: yes _____ no _____
      Can say the days of the week loudly: yes _____ no _____
   d. Sustained vowels gradually increasing and decreasing loudness (e.g., police car siren coming closer and fading)
      Ability to control loudness: yes _____ no _____
      Limited loudness range: yes _____ no _____
      Tension present: yes _____ no _____
   e. Counting from soft to loud; loud to soft
      Ability to control phonation: yes _____ no _____
      Limited range: yes _____ no _____
      Tension present: yes _____ no _____
   f. Sustained level during reading passage:
      overstrong _____   weak _____
      fading _____   lacking in variety _____
      inappropriate to meaning _____   appropriate _____
   g. General conversational level: appropriate _____ inappropriate _____
      Describe if inappropriate:
      Comments:

4. Pitch
   a. Reading and conversation: habitual level:
      Appropriate to age and sex _____ too low _____ too high _____
      Voice breaks to higher pitch _____
      Voice breaks to lower pitch _____
      Variability: appropriate _____ limited _____ monotone _____
   b. Ability to imitate extremes of pitch range (isolated vowels):
      good _____ fair _____ poor _____
   c. Ability to discriminate pitch differences (pitch pipe; noise makers):
      good _____ fair _____ poor _____
   d. Ability to imitate a given pitch (isolated vowels):
      good _____ fair _____ poor _____
   e. Ability to imitate a sequential pitch pattern (isolated vowels: e.g., low/high/low): good _____ fair _____ poor _____
   f. Ability to imitate pitch inflections (phrases):
      e.g.,   It's mine?   It is?   She's eaten it?
               It's mine!   It is!   She's eaten it!
      good _____ fair _____ poor _____
   g. Consistency of appropriate pitch level, range and variability in conversational speech:
      always _____ sometimes _____ never _____
   h. Does the child's age and physical development indicate the possibility of pubertal voice changes?
      Yes _____ No _____

Figure 5.2 (continued)

RESONANCE

Overall resonance in reading and conversation appears:
appropriate _____ inappropriate _____ (if inappropriate, complete section below)

1. Ability to sustain a hum: nasal resonance present _____ weak _____ absent _____

2. Word pairs (vowels in nonnasal vs. nasal contexts)

	appropriate	hypernasal	hyponasal	assimilated nasality on vowels only
hat/ham	_____	_____	_____	_____
pat/mat	_____	_____	_____	_____
bat/man	_____	_____	_____	_____
towel/town	_____	_____	_____	_____
cow/now	_____	_____	_____	_____
pout/noun	_____	_____	_____	_____

3. Oral sentences (to check for hypernasality)

   She eats cheese chips.   (nares open)   same ____ different ____
     "   "   "   "   (nares occluded)

   Charley has a fat cat.   (nares open)   same ____ different ____
     "   " " " "   (nares occluded)

4. Nasal sentences (to check for hyponasality)

   My mommy makes me mad.   (nares open)   same ____ different ____
     "   "   "   " "   (nares occluded)

   Ned knows Nancy's not nice.   (nares open)   same ____ different ____
    "   "   "   " "   (nares occluded)

5. Circle observed characteristics of possible velopharyngeal inadequacy:
   snorts/grimaces   nares constriction   nasal emission
   bifed uvula   palatal deviations   distortion of pressure consonants
   Comments:

6. Circle observed characteristics of possible nasal obstruction:
   dark circles under eyes   noisy breathing   mouth breathing
   blocked nostril   swelling of nasal bridge   discharge   congestion
   enlarged tonsils   slow eater
   Comments:

7. Oral-nasal balance:
   appropriate _____ hypernasal _____ hyponasal _____ mixed _____

8. Circle observed characteristics of neurological dysfunction:
   absent gag   weak cough   asymmetrical palatal movement
   Comments:

9. Tone focus (when counting)

	seated near clinician		projecting voice across room	
	adequate	inadequate	adequate	inadequate
mouth opening	_____	_____	_____	_____

Figure 5.2 (continued)

lip movement   _____   _____   _____   _____
tongue movement
   (retracted?)   _____   _____   _____   _____
supraglottal tension   _____   _____   _____   _____

HIGH-RISK FACTORS

High-risk factors appear:
present _____ absent _____ (if present, complete section below)

1. Physical conditions that may be pertinent (circle):

   allergies   frequent upper   postnasal drip   paralysis–paresis
                   respiratory infections

   surgeries   dryness of tract   spasms–tremors

   medications   excessive mucus   hearing loss   deviated septum

   bifed uvula   thyroid condition   mouth breathing   broken nose

   cleft palate   craniofacial anomalies   enlarged tonsils and adenoids

   incoordination of muscles   other:_____
       of face or mouth

   Comments:

2. Abusive practices (circle):

   throat clearing   crying–screaming   excessive talking
   loud talking   sound imitations   impersonations
   coughing   smoking   yodeling
   other:_____
   Comments:

3. Demands inherent in life-style–environment (circle):

   voice models   noisy environment   cheerleading   sporting activities
   choir   solo singing   dramatics   stress
   other:_____
   Comments:

4. Interpersonal behaviors (circle):

   talking too much   ignoring feedback   not seeking feedback
   ignoring differences between people   ignoring differences in situations
   ignoring needs and interests of others   poor self-esteem
   aggressive behavior   reticence   family problems
   other:_____ _____
   Comments:

the next section. The cover sheet of the form is completed last. The check marks on this page indicate areas of concern and help us focus on information that is important to us when we formulate our treatment plan. Following the Andrews Voice Evaluation Form are examples of methods that we have found useful for eliciting samples of relevant behaviors.

Suggestions for Eliciting Samples of Respiratory Behavior

1. Length of inhalation may be assessed by having a child inhale through a straw while keeping a piece of tissue attached to the end of the straw.

2. When checking a child's depth of inhalation, provide a model and cues. For example, for young children a picture of a birthday cake with candles is a helpful visual aid. They can then be asked to take a deep breath so that they can blow out all the candles.

3. Depth of inhalation, as well as length of exhalation, can be observed by using the activity of blowing through a straw into a glass of water. The clinician should model an exhalation of at least 10 seconds, stressing the relationship between depth of air intake and length of time the bubbles can be blown in the water.

4. When the clinician is observing the length of a child's exhalation, it is important that the child understands the concept of continuity. Give instructions such as "Keep going as long as you can" or "Keep making the sound until my finger reaches the end of the table." For young children, it is helpful to use an object moving toward a destination in order to elicit the prolongation (e.g., "Say the /s/ until the snake gets to his cave" or "Say the /z/ until the bee gets to the hive"). Silly Putty can also be stretched to suggest prolongation.

5. When the clinician presents tasks involving control or segmentation of exhaled airflow, a model and clear explanations of the purpose of the activity are necessary for all children. For younger children, a picture of a little pig huffing and puffing a house down (e.g., "He takes in a lot of air—then he lets out one huff like this /huh/ and stops—then lets out some more") or similar visual aids are helpful.

6. When the clinician wants to see the number of syllables, words, or numbers emitted in one exhalation, ask children to count or say the alphabet as far as they can in one breath. For younger children, ask them to name colors of beads threaded on a string. See if they can manage to name more beads (as clinician moves them) in successive trials.

7. In order to help older children understand the concept of replenishing breaths, the clinician may need to use a reading passage and mark pauses in different places to illustrate how the meaning is enhanced or changed depending on where we pause to breathe.

   The use of visual aids (e.g., cars stopping at gas stations, trains stopping at stations, elevators stopping at various floors to let more people in) can help younger children understand the concept of periodically refilling or refueling the air supply.

8. In order to see whether children are stimulable and can produce changes in their behavior when they have an understanding of the

concept of replenishing breaths, try the following: Ask older children to read a passage and note their use of replenishing breaths. Then ask them to mark places in the passage where it makes sense to pause and take in air. After they have marked the pauses, ask them to reread the passage and note if their behavior has changed since the first reading (count pauses for breaths in each instance; also note appropriateness of pauses in terms of meaning of passage). For younger children who cannot read well, use objects or colored blocks or beads arranged in a continuous array. When they "read" them (e.g., "a red bead, a blue bead, a yellow bead"), demonstrate how they can be arranged in groups so that there is time to stop and breathe. See if they can arrange them in manageable breath groups. Then ask them to say them again.

9. In children exhibiting disturbed respiratory patterns (e.g., neurological impairment) it may be valuable to assess the child's vegetative breathing pattern. This can be accomplished by making the following observations:

   a. Number of breaths per minute at rest—bpm's
      (count number during 20 seconds and multiply by 3)

   b. Rhythmic deep breathing (with cues)
      slows rate to _____ bpm's
      appropriate movement of chest wall _____ yes _____ no
      extends exhalation phase during rhythmic breathing when cued _____ yes _____ no

   c. Physical observations
      posture _____ appropriate _____ inappropriate
      hyperextension of neck _____ yes _____ no
      concave chest _____ yes _____ no
      extraneous movements _____ yes _____ no
      other_____

   d. Ability to understand
      concepts _____ yes _____ no
      instructions _____ yes _____ no

Suggestions for Eliciting Samples of Phonatory Behavior

If a structural anomaly is present or if tissue change has occurred as a result of irritation, abusive habits, or both (i.e., nodules, polyps, thickening of the folds), the child may have difficulty approximating the folds evenly. He or she may therefore be unable to produce a clear tone unless using considerable effort. If so, the voice will sound *best* when loud and poorest when soft. In such cases, aphonia on unstressed syllables may occur during soft talking.

1. Ask the child to count from 1 to 40. Ask him or her to do it softly, then loudly. (If the tone is clearest when the child counts loudly, it is possible that there is some pathology present.)

2. Ask the child to sustain the vowel /a/ for as long as he or she can. (Most young children can do this for 10 seconds. If the child lasts less than 7 seconds on repeated trials, sounds clear *only* when loud, has voice breaks or diplophonia, it may be a sign of pathology.) Younger children will need help to ensure that they understand the concept of prolongation. The clinician may say, "Keep going until my pencil stops moving across the paper," etc. Another technique would be to use visual aids and say, "Here is the big brown bear." (Present bear.) "He says /a/ for as long as he can. You be the big brown bear and say /a/ for as long as you can. Like this. . . ." (Examiner models 10-second production of /a/.)

3. Ask the child to produce the /s/ sound for *as long as he or she can*. Then ask the child to produce the /z/ sound continuously. If, on repeated trials, the child always sustains the unvoiced /s/ for *longer* than the voiced /z/, it may be a sign of pathology (Eckel & Boone, 1981). Since the child has the same amount of available air for both phonemes, it is significant if the phoneme /z/, requiring approximation of the folds, is the more difficult.

   Examples of techniques that may be useful for young children include:

   a. "Sammy Snake goes /s/." (Present snake and place house 3 feet from snake.) "Keep going until Sammy Snake gets into his house." (Examiner models 10-second production of /s/ while moving snake into house.)

   b. "The motorcycle goes /z/." (Present car and place garage 3 feet from car.) "Keep going until it gets to the garage." (Examiner models 10-second production of /z/ while moving car into garage.)

4. Onset of phonation may be affected by the loudness level that the child is using. Therefore, in addition to asking a child to produce individual words, it is helpful to ask the child to say the sentence "Uncle Eddie eats eggs" softly and then loudly. Listen to see if he or she begins each word with a hard glottal attack.

5. If a child appears to be using excessive effort during phonation, note any observable signs of tension in the jaw, neck muscles, etc. Then, place your fingers under the child's chin above the larynx. Ask the child to swallow. Then ask him or her to sustain a vowel. If you feel the same muscles being used in phonation as are used in swallowing, it may indicate that the child is using excessive muscular effort.

6. A child who is using excessive effort when phonating because of edema or additive lesions that make adduction difficult may phonate

best when talking loudly or producing the stressed syllables in a word. To check for this, ask the child to repeat multisyllabic words (e.g., Mississippi, Alabama, Mrs. MacIntyre, Mr. Johnson). Note if the child is aphonic on the unstressed syllables.

7. To determine the effect of a more relaxed production on the quality of the sound, ask the child to yawn while producing a vowel sound. For a young child, the following technique may help the child understand the concept: "Look at Baby." (Present baby doll.) "She is yawning. She is tired. Let's pretend you are tired. Take a big breath. Yawn and say /a/." (Examiner models behavior.)

8. Children who are intermittently aphonic may have difficulty with adduction or simply may be running out of air. More air is lost during soft phonation than during loud phonation when the folds are closed for a longer portion of the vibratory cycle. To check to see if there is a pattern in the aphonic production, ask the child to read a passage or tell you about a picture. If, during connected speech, the vocal quality is poorest at the ends of sentences, it may indicate that the child needs help in improving breath support. Make sure you get samples of both soft and loud speech.

9. If aphonia or hoarseness is related to vocal abuse, the folds may be more swollen after prolonged use. On one occasion, test the child late in the day to assess the effects of use and fatigue on the voice.

10. Ask the child to vary loudness, for example, starting loudly and becoming softer (diminuendo) or starting softly and becoming louder (crescendo). Younger children may need the analogy of a siren coming closer or getting fainter as it moves away (e.g., a police car goes "Whoo ..."). For younger children, the following technique may be used to assess loudness variations: "Look, the garage is on fire!" (Present garage.) "Here is a fire engine." (Present fire engine.) "It goes 'Whoo.' It is coming. It is getting louder. The fire engine is going home. It is getting softer." (Examiner models production of "Whoo" at a soft intensity level, followed by an increase in loudness and then decrease. Phonation is accompanied by corresponding movement of the fire engine.) "You pretend you're the fire engine. Start at home, put the fire out and go back home. Remember, it goes 'Whoo.'"

11. To determine if a child understands the concepts of loud and soft, it is sometimes useful to pair a loud sound with a large puppet and a soft sound with a small one. (Present large Mr. Bert puppet. Play the following prerecorded language master card.) "His voice sounds loud: /u/." (Present small Mr. Bert puppet. Play the following prerecorded language master card.) "His voice sounds soft: /u/. Show me who said this." (Examiner plays prerecorded card of production of loud /u/. Repeat for soft /u/. Randomize trials.)

12. Ask the child to hum on a variety of different pitches after being given a model. If the higher-pitched hums are clearer, it may mean that the child can approximate the folds best when there is greater stiffness. This may indicate some tissue change affecting the adjustments of the folds.
13. Ask the child to sing a simple song (e.g., "Happy Birthday"). Note whether the child can vary the pitch of his or her voice appropriately. Restricted pitch variability is sometimes a sign of vocal pathology. Be cautious—this child may just have a "tin ear"!
14. If a child is young or seems to have difficulty with the concepts of high and low pitch levels, it may be advantageous to use visual aids and techniques similar to the ones below:
    a. (Place Mrs. Chicken on top of steps. Play following prerecorded language master card.) "This Mrs. Chicken talks in a high voice /i/." (Place Mr. Bert on bottom of steps. Play the following prerecorded language master card.) "This Mr. Bert talks in a low voice /i/. Show me who said this." (Examiner plays prerecorded card of production of high /i/. Repeat for low /i/. Randomize trials.)
    b. (Present sheep and steps.) "Mr. Sheep says /a/. He goes up the steps." (Examiner moves sheep up steps, producing /a/ one tone higher on each step.) "Make Mr. Sheep go up the steps. Mr. Sheep says /a/. He goes down the steps." (Examiner moves sheep down steps, producing /a/ one tone lower on each step.) "Make Mr. Sheep go down the steps."

Suggestions for Eliciting Samples of Resonance Behavior

1. When the clinician is testing for the presence of hypernasality, the following techniques may prove useful:

    a. Ask the child to say [aŋ] vigorously. Does the velum move up for [a] and down for [ŋ]? Does the velum move symmetrically?
    b. Ask the child to sustain nonnasal sounds (e.g., vowels and fricatives). Listen to see if there is any difference when nostrils are occluded and unoccluded. (Place thumb under child's nostril to occlude.) There should be no perceived difference on nonnasal sounds if there is adequate velopharyngeal closure.
    c. Ask the child to say sentences with no nasal sound, for example:
        "She keeps cheese chips."
        "Charley has a fat cat."
        "Lisa teases Chris."
    Does the resonance sound appropriate? Is there any difference when the nostrils are occluded and unoccluded? (If a child is hypernasal, there will be a difference in the sound when the

nostrils are occluded. If a difference is heard, it is an indication of velopharyngeal incompetence during connected speech.)

   d. Do an articulation analysis of the sounds requiring oral breath pressure (e.g., plosives, fricatives, and affricatives). Children with velopharyngeal problems often have the most trouble with these sounds. (The Iowa Pressure Test is useful.) Additional sentences with pressure sounds and including high vowels are these:

"Chip bits of ice."	"Louise has skis."
"Kitty has fleas."	"Fix the scissors."
"She eats three cookies."	"Squeeze the chopsticks."
"Freeze the peas."	"See Chris kiss."
"Cross the t's."	"She sells six geese."

2. When the clinician is testing for the presence of hyponasality, the following techniques may prove useful:

   a. Observe whether the child is a mouth breather. This may indicate nasal obstruction. Are there signs of tonsilar or adenoidal enlargement? (Does the child snore loudly at night? have circles under eyes? have pinched nostrils? have enlarged bridge of nose? appear listless? have frequent upper respiratory tract infections?) Does the child have allergies that cause nasal congestion? Can air be emitted through both nostrils, one nostril only, or not at all?

   b. Can the child produce nasals (e.g., /m/ and /n/) with appropriate nasal resonance and vibration in nasal area? (Place hands on nasal area to feel vibrations.)

   c. Ask the child to say a sentence loaded with nasals (e.g., "My mommy makes me mad"). Does the resonance sound appropriate? Is it the same whether or not nostrils are occluded? If it sounds the same, the child must not be emitting the nasal sounds through the nose. Additional sentences are these:

"Mr. Norris never knew."	"Coming home is fun."
"My neighbors moved."	"Ring in the new year."
"Don't knock Juan's knees."	"My nose never runs."
"Sing and hum in tune."	"Notice Kevin's nostrils."
"Time my running."	"Hammer nine nails."

   d. Ask the child to prolong a humming sound. (For young children, move a toy car toward a garage.) Inability to hum may indicate nasal obstruction.

3. When the clinician is testing for the presence of assimilated nasality, it is important to listen to the production of vowel sounds adjacent to nasal consonants and those adjacent to oral consonants. Observe how the nasal consonants influence the production of the oral sounds. The following suggestions may be helpful:

   a. Does the resonance sound appropriate when the child says a sentence (e.g., "Charley has a black hat") in which there are no nasals present? Children with assimilated nasality will do this appropriately.

b. Ask the child to say word pairs and observe the quality of the vowel sounds when they are adjacent to nasals. Compare the production of the same vowels in oral contexts. For example:

at	am	dough	know
cat	mat	pat	pam
rig	ring	see	knee
bake	make	beat	meat

c. In order to observe the child's production at the single word level without a model, have the child supply the missing word. For example:

Mother is a woman, Daddy is a _____.
I hit the baseball with a _____.
It doesn't belong to you, it belongs to _____.
With my ears I hear, with my eyes I _____.

d. Ask the child to say sentences such as "Go downtown now, Mrs. Brown." Observe whether the perception of the oral–nasal balance changes during connected speech.

Eliciting Samples of Interpersonal Behavior

1. Engage the child in conversation with one or more other children in the speech room. Try to introduce topics in which the child will become emotionally involved, for example, "Some people think school should continue all summer." "Should the whole class miss recess when one or two children misbehave? Why not?" (Observe amount of talking, turn taking, interruptions, etc.)
2. Notice feedback. Ask children to tell the true meaning of sentences spoken different ways. (Observe their ability to respond to cues.)
   a. I like school.
      (frown; flat intonation)
      (puzzled look; questioning inflection)
   b. He's a good person.
      (negative facial expression; hesitant rate)
      ("He's" prolonged; questioning intonation)
   c. Girls giggle a lot.
      (tight mouth; duration of "girls" prolonged)
      (happy face; questioning inflection)
3. Ask questions. Ask children individually to ask you any five questions that they would like you to answer (or use this technique with a small group of children questioning each other). (Observe the child's ability to formulate questions.)

4. Adapt to different situations. Show the child pictures of different situations, for example, a library (looking at book); a movie theater; a playground (fight); an art gallery. Ask the child to use the same words but say them in a manner that would be right for the different places; for example, "I'm going to tell my mother all about this." (Observe the appropriateness of the child's response.)

5. Show the child pictures of different people and ask him or her to choose the person the clinician is talking to when saying, "I need to talk to you" (e.g., point to the picture; older children may be asked to say why they chose a specific picture)—for example, elderly person, young child, doctor or nurse, police officer, school principal, bus driver, mother. (Observe the child's ability to interpret the vocal behavior used by the clinician. The clinician may be also question the child about why certain choices were made.)

6. Tell the child a sample story and ask him or her to tell you why things worked out the way they did. Ask the child to retell the story with a different ending. (Observe the child's analysis of the needs and interests of others.)

   a. Jim was playing with his train set. His young brother Billy kept asking him if he could play, too. Jim ignored him. Finally, Billy grabbed the caboose and threw it on the floor. Jim yelled at him, "You dummy—you've broken my caboose—I'll get you for that."

   b. Greg and Tom were playing ball. Greg hit the ball over the fence into a neighbor's yard. The neighbor was annoyed because the ball broke a tomato plant in his garden. When he looked over the fence, Greg yelled, "It's not my fault—it's Tom's ball."

   c. Juanita and Maria were giggling on the subway and forgot to get off at their stop. When they were late getting home their mother was angry. They were scared, so told her their teacher kept them, and they missed the train home. Their mother said she would go to the school and complain to the principal the next day. Maria yelled at her mother, "The principal will just think you're crazy!"

Additional Suggestions for Eliciting Samples of Voice during Conversational Speech

1. Describe your best friend.
2. Tell me four things you did in school today.
3. Describe the plan of your house. Start at the front door.
4. How will it be different when you are in Grade _____?
5. What will it be like to be a teenager?
6. Who are the important people in your life? Tell me about them.
7. How would I recognize your family if I met them on the street?

8. Tell me about a movie you saw recently.
9. What would you like to do on your birthday?
10. What are the best and the worst things about this school?

Additional Topics to Elicit Discussion of the Child's Feelings

1. What do people misunderstand about you most?
2. What is something that really bugs you?
3. What do you think about when you can't fall asleep?
4. Say something you like about yourself.
5. What feelings do you have the most trouble sharing?
6. What is something someone did for you today that you especially liked?
7. Who are the people you most like to talk to? What is it about them that is special?
8. What have you done recently that you are proud of?
9. What are you looking forward to this week?
10. What would you most like to change about yourself? your family? your friends? your teacher?

SUMMARY

Naturally, the information we obtain in the voice diagnostic evaluation is considered together with the results of the oral peripheral examination, the hearing testing, the medical report, and the case history. As we put all the pieces together we obtain a picture or a Gestalt of the child's abilities, current level of functioning, the context in which he or she is operating, and the most pressing needs and priorities for the remediation program.

chapter 6
Program Planning and Design Strategies

We looked at some of the components of the four general areas of behavior relating to voice. We constructed checklists of some aspects of vocal production and vocal competence that contribute to optimal patterns of vocal behavior. The checklists are helpful for noting the presence or absence of components when we observe children's behavior. They can also be used to record descriptions of inappropriate or atypical characteristics and to note if an absent, immature, or distorted behavior could be elicited in its appropriate form. In Chapter 5 we discussed in-depth assessment procedures. At this point, however, we need only concern ourselves with a possible repertoire of behaviors that may or may not be observed. The reason we want to call attention to these behaviors is that as prized components of vocal behavior, they may, on occasion, be behaviors that handicapped children need to acquire. An inventory of various components of each of the general areas related to voice is helpful as we consider objectives for therapy. In voice therapy our aim may be to teach behaviors that are absent, substitute appropriate behaviors for inappropriate ones, strengthen behaviors that are weak or inconsistent, and shape and refine behaviors until prized characteristics are habituated. If, as a result of a sequence of treatment (usually referred to as a *program*), we believe a child could acquire particular behaviors, we may state those desired terminal behaviors as our *program objectives*. When we select our objectives, we need to be cognizant of (1) the constraints imposed by any structural or medical conditions; (2) limiting factors such as development stage, ability, motivation, parental support, available time; (3) the repertoire of optimal behaviors from which to choose; and (4) the developmental progression of normal acquisition.

One more point should be made before we turn to the specifics of program planning, and that is the importance of always considering the vocal demands inherent in the child's life-style. We shall illustrate this by some examples. Consider the need for optimal performance in the area of respiratory control. Many children will not need to demonstrate optimal respiratory support in order to produce adequate voice production. If a 7-year-old girl uses her voice mainly in conversational situations and has few demands for projected sustained speaking, it may not be necessary to select objectives from among the optimal behaviors in the area of respiration. Minimal skill may suffice. On the other hand, should a child be active in strenuous athletic pursuits and frequently engage in loud sustained talking in conjunction with physical activity, the demands on the respiratory system may be such that optimal support may indeed be required. Similarly, the child who is the star in the school operetta and makes great demands on the vocal mechanism during singing and speaking may need to develop optimal respiratory behavior in order to avoid the deleterious effects of strenuous unsupported laryngeal activity. Optimal levels of function may indeed be realistic targets for such a child, since interests and needs may enhance motivation for improvement.

Because we have included a listing of optimal behaviors, we do not want to imply that every child we teach must, should, or can achieve all of them. Expectations for each child are always tempered by what is realistic and sensible for the individual. Program objectives must always be individualized. Optimal target behaviors should not be considered as a set of behaviors that all children must acquire. They could be considered as landmarks that define potentials for growth and change.

PROGRAM OBJECTIVES

Depending on the nature of a child's problem, objectives are usually drawn from one or more areas. If the child exhibits deficits in all areas, the decision to work on objectives from each area simultaneously or sequentially will be made based on the child's level of functioning and the priorities established by the clinician. Some children can handle work on all areas at once and benefit from an approach that emphasizes interrelationships; others may be confused by such an approach. The selection of the objectives is based on what seems to be realistic for a child to achieve in a given period of time. The objectives are the long-term goals, or the behaviors the child will have achieved by the end of a therapy program. They are always stated in terms of the child's behavior, and action verbs are used because the behaviors must be specific and observable. Standards and criterion levels are also needed. It is usual and helpful to develop a task that can be used as a pretest and a posttest for each objective. This test then enables the clinician to measure the progress made as a result of the therapy program.

Once the terminal objective has been stated and the pre- or posttest has been specified, a behavioral hierarchy is established. We look at the overall behavior that we hope the child will finally learn and break it up into an orderly sequence of smaller pieces of behavior. These pieces of behavior are arranged in a sequence proceeding from the simplest or easiest to learn to the hardest or most complex. Our knowledge of the normal acquisition of the behaviors helps us develop this sequence. We know, for example, that children use vegetative breathing before they develop speech breathing; we also know that vocalizing isolated vowel sounds is easier than vocalizing words, phrases, or sentences. Each individual behavior that we select and arrange in a cumulative series of difficulty becomes a short-term or intermediate goal. These short-term goals are the building blocks of the program plan. They specify the prerequisite behaviors, or the foundation, necessary to achieve the objectives of the overall program. The following example illustrates what we do first, that is, specify the overall objective and pretest–posttest:

General Area:　Laryngeal behavior.

Specific Symptom:　Limited vocal variety.

Terminal Objective:　Child will produce "word pictures" on verbs, adjectives, and adverbs with 90% accuracy; one per sentence.

Pretest–Posttest:　Fifteen simple sentences read and tape recorded. Count sentence correct if underlined word is emphasized in any of the following ways (pitch, loudness, or rate changes).

Once the terminal objective is stated, we then state the short-term goals and arrange them in a meaningful sequence.

The following list illustrates a behavioral hierarchy that might constitute short-term goals of the first part of the therapy plan. You will notice that this is an "awareness" not a "production" hierarchy.

1. Identification of "picture words" and "nonpicture" words (verbs, adjectives, adverbs versus articles, prepositions, pronouns).
2. Identification of voice strategies to make picture words (e.g., loudness, pitch, rate changes).
3. Matching picture words with a strategy (e.g., noisy = loud voice; velvety = soft voice; crawled = slow voice; galloped = fast voice; dropping = voice goes down; climbing = voice goes up).
4. Choosing picture words to underline in simple sentences.
5. Describing strategies another person demonstrates.
6. Judging the appropriateness of another person's word pictures.
7. Describing better strategies for another person to use (e.g., "You could make the word longer").

SHORT-TERM GOALS AND EXAMPLES OF STRATEGIES

In addition to stating what behaviors the child will learn and the order in which they will be acquired, we need to plan how the steps will be mastered. Each behavior needs to be taught, and so a teaching strategy must be developed for each goal. A strategy operationalizes a goal. The common strategies we use in voice therapy are the same as those used in other forms of therapy. We explain and describe and model the target behaviors. We also provide stimulation and cues (visual, auditory, tactile, and kinesthetic) to facilitate learning. We always need to know what we are planning to say and do (the stimulus) and what we expect the child to say and do (the response). We need to know in advance whether we will accept an approximation of the target response or whether we expect perfect accuracy. We need to plan the number of trials, the kind of trials, and the method of scoring and evaluation. The strategy we use is really our lesson plan. It is a script we follow as we work with the child. There are many lesson-plan formats, but most of them require that the stimulus and the response, and the criteria, are stated explicitly. The materials we use and the reinforcement provided are also stated on many lesson-plan forms. An example of a short-term goal with a matching strategy is as follows:

Short-term Goal

The child will hum with appropriate tone focus and resonance for 10 seconds, given a model and visual and tactile cues (100% accuracy, five trials)

Strategy

1. The clinician will model the sound while holding the child's hand against the clinician's face and lips. The clinician will explain how her lips "tickle" as the sound vibrates. The clinician will ask the child to produce the sound, pressing the child's lips against the clinician's hand and against her own hand.

2. The child will hum (while the clinician watches the secondhand of the clock) for 10 seconds. The child will press her lips against her own hand to feel the vibrations.

3. The clinician will time five trials. Verbal descriptive statements will be used as reinforcement, for example, "I can feel the tickling on my hand as you hum. I can feel the vibrations on your face. Your humming sounds rich and

full. I can hear how the sound is
tickling your lips."

It will be helpful now to discuss some specific behavioral goals and
describe a variety of strategies that may be used to achieve them. We
shall select goals from only one general area, that of respiration. Our
terminal objective might be for the child to demonstrate appropriate
speech breathing by the end of the therapy program.

Terminal objective: The child will use appropriate breathing
   patterns (100% correct on fifteen trials) when speaking
   spontaneous sentences.
Pretest–Posttest: Fifteen sentences spoken by the child; clinician
   rates (*a*) type of inhalation; (*b*) efficient use of exhalation.
   Sentences elicited by use of 15 picture cards[1] and the instruction "Tell me what is wrong in this picture."

Short-term Goals and Strategies to Achieve Them

1. To increase the depth of the inhalation
2. To increase the length of the exhalation
3. To increase control of the exhaled airstream

Strategies or techniques to achieve these goals can be described
according to their effectiveness in highlighting specific aspects of the
targeted behaviors. For example, techniques that emphasize the sensory
and kinesthetic awareness of the desired behavior usually involve
postural change that facilitates appropriate movement and provides
heightened awareness of a particular part of the body. We shall explain
only a few of the basic strategies used to modify respiratory behavior in
order to develop efficient patterns of speech breathing and will describe
why some techniques are helpful in achieving goals.

Strategies to Achieve Increased Depth of Inhalation (Goal 1) The
most common mistake that children make during deep inhalation is
moving the shoulders and upper chest instead of increasing the depth
and width of the lower chest cavity where the lungs inflate most
efficiently. Therefore, any posture that decreases the likelihood of
movement in the shoulders and upper chest can be used to help achieve
this goal. Exercises that involve postural change to decrease the
likelihood of excessive movement or tension of the shoulders and upper

[1] "What's Wrong Here?" Level 1, Catalogue #85–230 (Hingham, MA: Teaching Resources,
n.d.).

chest frequently position the upper part of the body so that gravity assists. For example, an exercise undertaken by a subject lying flat on the floor facilitates a lowered, relaxed carriage of the shoulders and decreases the likelihood of movement in the upper chest during inhalation. Postural positioning also is used to increase kinesthetic awareness of movements of the abdominal and lower thoracic muscles. Contact of the abdomen and lower chest with hard surfaces, or other body parts, provides a form of biofeedback that helps an individual monitor the presence and extent of required movements. For example, an inhalation achieved as the individual rests the upper part of the body against the thighs ensures that the chest movement is felt on the thighs and upper legs. Such an exercise begins with the candidate seated in a chair. The upper part of the body is then moved forward until the torso rests on the upper legs. Deep inhalation is then repeated so that the movement of the lower chest is felt against the upper legs. Variations of this exercise that use pressure against hard surfaces include sitting the subject in a chair in front of a desk or table so that forward movement of the thoracic wall results in pressure against the table or desk edge. When an individual lies in a prone position on the floor and inhales, the pressure of the movement of the abdominal and thoracic muscles is felt against the floor. This effect can also be achieved to illustrate movement of the back of the chest cavity by having the subject stand against a wall or lie with the back flat on the floor. Movement of the sides of the thoracic cavity can also be monitored by placing the hands on the sides of the lower chest above the waist so that the upward and outward movement of the rib cage is felt. Resistance in the form of a loose elastic band tied around the rib cage so that the elastic stretches during inhalation can also heighten kinesthetic awareness during inhalation. Naturally, it is important that a child engaging in this kind of exercise not wear restrictive or tight clothing. Belts and tight waistbands that cramp the movements can detract from the efficacy of the technique.

Another approach to monitoring the desired movements of the respiratory muscles during deep inhalation is through the placement of an object on the lower chest. If this object moves as the direct result of thoracic expansion, a child can see, as well as feel, the effects of the desired movement patterns. Young children seem to enjoy lying on the floor on their backs and watching an object (e.g., a stuffed animal) moving up and down as they breathe in and out. A book is often used in a similar way with older children.

Some children experience difficulty with deep volitional inhalation. This difficulty sometimes is seen in children who are neurologically impaired or extremely tense. Retarded children also may need more specific cues related to the onset of the inhalation task. We know that forceful explusion of air from the lungs is a means of capitalizing on the internal versus external air pressure differential. We also know that there is elastic recoil of the lungs that encourages air intake subsequent to air expulsion. We use this information when we apply techniques such as pressing down on the lower chest and abdominal cavity just before instructing a child to inhale. Another similar facilitating technique is to ask a child forcefully to "snort out" all the air in his or her lungs before inhalation. "Snorting out air" involves expelling the air through the nose with the mouth closed. The respiratory muscles help force the air out as the chest walls collapse and the abdominal wall moves in. Reverse movements occur as the child inhales and the abdominal wall moves out and the thoracic walls expand. Five or so rapid "snorts" alternated with deep air intakes can be used to demonstrate the contrasting physiological states. Sometimes two or three "snorts out" are suggested prior to deep inhalation in order to create an intense need for a deep inhalation to follow. (Caution needs to be exercised to ensure that children do not hyperventilate.)

Coordination of Inhalation and Exhalation   The tying together of the contrasting patterns of exhalation and inhalation and repeated practice of the rhythms of slow deep breathing is a beneficial transition from goal 1 to goal 2, which is to increase the length of exhalation. In the initial stages of teaching speech breathing, it is usually beneficial to slow down the rate of vegetative breathing (i.e., decrease the number of breaths per minute). As the rate of breathing slows, the depth of breathing increases. With the length of the inhalation equaling the length of the exhalation during slow rhythmic breathing the child can be asked to concentrate on how the body feels. The teacher then verbalizes descriptions of what is happening in the body during the "in" and "out" phase. Repeated quiet descriptions of this kind can help a child understand the concepts and associate each idea with a specific sensory awareness. Such an activity has the added benefit of relaxing the child and developing in the child a feeling of the naturalness and ease of the behavior. A child, who may be predisposed to try too hard "to do the exercises" and become tense as a result, can thus experience the naturalness of act. A teacher can assist in this by quietly repeating such statements as "Your body *knows* how to breathe—relax and feel how easily your muscles move—the muscles help your chest grow big as the lungs fill with air—then gradually the air is going out again—in—out—in—out—one, two, three in—one, two, three out."

Images can also be used for vividness of understanding. For example, "Your lungs are like two balloons slowly growing bigger and bigger. Now they are growing smaller and smaller." Once an awareness of the even rhythm of vegetative, quiet breathing has been learned, the next step in the sequence is to shift gradually from the "equal in–equal

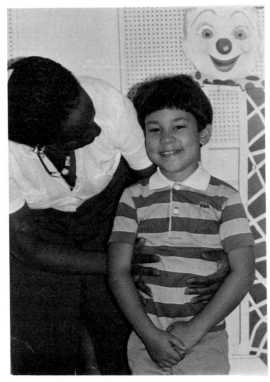

The clinician helps the child develop an awareness of the movement of the lower chest during deep relaxed breathing.

out" phases of nonspeech breathing to the "quick, deep in–long, controlled out" phases of speech breathing. This can be accomplished by changing the counting rhythm. For example, "This time we will take longer to breathe out. Breathe in, one, two, three and out, one, two, three, four, five."

Strategies to Achieve Goals 2 and 3   A common mistake that children make when they do not use the exhaled airstream efficiently for speech is to allow too much air to rush out during the first few words, leaving them with insufficient available air to finish the sentence. Thus, some children need to learn to conserve the air that they have inhaled and to ration it out across an entire utterance. The concept of a steady stream of air exhaled gradually can be learned by practicing exercises that focus on the gradual emission of air for increasing durations of time. Another mistake some children make is to attempt to control the emission of the airstream by blocking the flow with excessive tension in the larynx. When this occurs, the valving action of the larynx is used to compensate for ineffective respiratory muscle action.

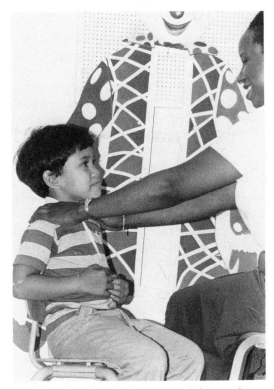

Upward movement of the shoulders is discouraged during deep inhalation.

Exercises to achieve both increase in the length of the exhalation (goal 2) and control of the exhaled airstream (goal 3), therefore, can be described in terms of their helpfulness in avoiding the likelihood of such errors. Any exercise that emphasizes the gradual elongated emission of air and simultaneously prevents the control of the airstream by closure of the vocal folds is optimal. Examples of such exercises are prolongations of unvoiced continuant fricative consonants. Prolongation of /s/ for increasing lengths of time (measured in seconds) is an excellent strategy to use to help achieve goal 2. The advantages of this strategy include the open glottis, since /s/ is unvoiced, the opportunities for monitoring the evenness and continuity of the air emission by tactile (feeling the airstream), visual (watching the effect of the airstream moving a feather, etc.) and auditory feedback. Other consonants that can be used are / θ / and / ∫ /. These breathed continuants, because of their place and manner of articulation, share the advantage of focusing the child's attention on the forward projection of the airstream, which helps to distract attention from the laryngeal area. This side benefit is especially helpful if the child is inclined to use excessive laryngeal tension. The use of such fricative sounds has the added advantage of allowing for a smooth transition to the next goal in the therapy process. After the child has achieved competence in emitting a lengthened controlled flow of air, the addition of voicing is easily achieved by requiring the child to produce the voiced cognates of the unvoiced phonemes. Thus, a child can be instructed to add voice to /s/ and prolong /z/ instead. Similary / θ / can become / ð / and / ʃ / change to / ʒ /. The adding of voicing midway through the emission of the airstream, initially, can be especially helpful in creating the appropriate preparatory set with respect to respiratory control, before the addition of laryngeal activity.

Another set of exercises sometimes used to help achieve goal 3 involves activities related to the segmenting of the exhaled airstream. Skill in "chunking" the airstream is required, since speaking involves a series of modifications of the exhaled airstream. Thus, exercises such as producing as many short /p/ productions as possible during an exhalation phase are useful. Since /p/ is an unvoiced bilabial, its production is helpful in focusing the attention on the lip movement rather than laryngeal valving. Again, the subsequent addition of voicing results in the production of the cognate /b/, and the alternation of /p/ and /b/ allows for practice of seriated unvoiced and voiced productions during a single exhalation. It is possible to count the number of products achieved during one exhalation and thereby to work toward increasing both length and control of the exhalation phase. Other techniques sometimes used to establish improved control of the air available for exhalation include emission of the air in two, three, or four segments. In other words, a child might be instructed to divide his or her available air into equal halves, thirds or quarters. If the child uses an unvoiced phoneme, such as /h/, to emit the "air chunks," he or she is forced to rely on respiratory muscle control alone, since no valving of the airstream occurs at the laryngeal or articulatory levels.

UNIQUE ASPECTS OF VOICE THERAPY PROGRAMMING

We have reviewed some of the basic terms used in programming. Although it is apparent that voice programming is similar to other kinds of programming, some important differences need to be mentioned. In articulation therapy, when a child misarticulates a phoneme, the target phoneme is already known to the clinician. When a child exhibits a voice disorder, the identification of the target vocal behavior is sometimes more complex. The standard used to judge the child's best voice is less clearly defined. Vocal behavior varies depending on age, sex, and anatomical and psychological constraints. Sometimes there are anatomical constraints that are permanent and irreversible. Examples of such constraints are severe structural malformations or neurological impairments. In such instances a child's best voice may never be a perfectly "normal" voice but a voice that is the result of the best possible compensations. The task of eliciting a target voice may frequently involve the manipulation of a number of different behaviors. Thus the clinician and the child together must embark on a trial-and-error search for the most efficient vocal production. Compounding the problem is the fact that the clinician's most easily available model is that of an adult voice. While an adult's production of any specific phoneme is not markedly different from a child's target phoneme, an adult voice is usually different from a child's voice. Thus, at times the use of tape recordings of samples of children's voices may be an important part of a voice therapy strategy.

GENERAL APPROACHES TO DEVELOPING TASK SEQUENCES

There are a number of different approaches to vocal remediation, and one could argue that no single approach is necessarily better than another. Nevertheless, certain approaches will be better suited to some individuals' needs and some patterns of symptoms than others. Much depends on the number of inappropriate symptoms exhibited by the individual child, the severity of the symptoms, and the interrelationship of symptoms. In previous discussions we have focused on the different areas of behavior, on selecting objectives and goals, and on choosing strategies to achieve those goals. We have also mentioned the need for behavioral hierarchies. We now review some different approaches that affect the way we order our therapy tasks.

One approach to planning task sequences in voice therapy probably grew out of traditional voice improvement programs. This is a holistic approach to remediation based on the assumption that if all of the component parts of voice production are overhauled sequentially, the end result will be an appropriate composite voice. Thus, one begins at the beginning of the physiological process (i.e., with respiration) and proceeds in an orderly fashion to link respiration with the onset of phonation, with sustained phonation, then with resonance and articulation. With this approach, the kind of symptoms exhibited by the child does not alter the progression of the tasks. The order is predicated on the sequence of events occurring during normal vocalization. Thus, since respiration always begins the speech act, respiration training is always attacked first. This is so even if it does not appear that the respiratory behavior is explicitly contributing to the vocal symptoms. Implicit in this approach is the assumption that an understanding of the interrelationship of the system; and a strengthening of the control of the behaviors at each level of the entire process, will result in an optimal voice. This approach is obviously more time-consuming than others and requires a high level of sustained motivation on the part of the student. It probably works best with older children, highly motivated children, or children who exhibit severe symptom patterns that involve the entire mechanism (e.g., cerebral palsied children).

In order to illustrate this approach, and the other approaches yet to be discussed in this section, we shall demonstrate how a task sequence might be developed for a child who demonstrates the symptom of hard glottal attacks. We shall proceed through a typical sequence of tasks that might be used to remediate this symptom. Remember that the task sequence is somewhat abbreviated and will not progress through all the steps. We shall not attempt to continue the sequence to the termination of therapy but shall proceed far enough to illustrate the differences between basic approaches. First, let us consider the holistic approach.

Task Sequence I	Child's Behavioral Goals
Respiration	1. I can inhale using appropriate lower chest movement.
Respiration	2. I can exhale evenly on /s/ for approximately 20 seconds (airstream smooth and even; length increases during repeated exhalations).
Coordination of respiration and phonation	3. I can move smoothly and easily from s͟z; h͟m during exhalation phase (no breaks or bumps in the flow).
Phonation	4. I can prolong *h* + vowel (CV's).
	5. I can stop and start *h* + vowel (CV's) (e.g., hey; he; hi; hoe; who)
Resonance	6. I can chant words feeling facial vibrations (e.g., hi/my; he/me; ho/mo; who/moo).
Articulation	7. I can prolong voiced sounds while chanting words (e.g., his͟is; she's͟ill; been͟away; gave͟in; beige͟egg; bill͟Emmy).
	8. I can separate word pairs while remembering to begin vowel sound easily (e.g., his/is; she's/ill; been/away; gave/in/; beige/egg; bill/Emmy). (*Cue:* "Think of the sound on the front of the mouth not in the throat.")
	9. I can say sentences using easy attacks on vowels (e.g., My age is eight; Mom is angry, Amy; May always eats every apple). (*Cue:*

"Feel the vibrations on the lips for the /m/ and keep the feeling of the sound there during the vowels.")

Another approach to remediation is to zero in on the particular symptoms exhibited by the child and isolate the behaviors to be changed. Thus, for example, if hard initiation of phonation is noted, the phonatory system, or the laryngeal mechanism, would be considered as the primary target system. The behavior to be modified is focused on without reference to its relationship to other aspects of the entire process. This highlighting approach usually involves explicit description of the audible or visible characteristics of the undesirable behavior and contrasts them with the characteristics of the desirable behavior that is to be substituted. This approach is more symptom specific than is the previous approach. It tends to emphasize the behaviors by extracting them from their behavioral context. Verbal descriptions of the behaviors are explicit and concrete and frequently modeled by the clinician and repeated by the child. This approach is often used with young children or with children who are working in groups.

Task Sequence II   Child's Behavioral Goals

Phonation
(awareness level)

1. I can tell when the voice starts with a hard sound (isolated vowels).
"I hear a grunt or click."
"The neck is tight."

2. I can tell when the voice starts with an easy sound (isolated vowels).
"I do not hear a grunt or click."
"The neck is relaxed."

3. I can count the hard and easy attacks when other people say words starting with vowels (interpersonal level).
any, every, angel, uncle, eggs, insect

Phonation
(production level)

4. I can feel and describe the difference when I make a hard sound on /a/ and an easy sound on /ha/.

Hard	*Easy*
grunt to start	air comes out first
neck tight	neck not tight
sounds bumpy	sounds smooth

5. I can make an easy start on any vowel when I say /h/ before it.
I/hi; Ed/head; ill/hill

6. I can make an easy start on any vowel when I

think the /h/ sound and then just say the vowel.

(h)ill; (h)is; (h)at

7. I can make an easy start on words in sentences. (*Cues:* Think the /h/ on all of the words. Pause before the vowels.)

"Hi, I'm Amy"; "Who are idiots?"; "Hit it anywhere".

8. I can tell when I've made a hard sound and say it again with an easy sound.

9. I can tell when I am about to make a hard sound because I know the vowels that trick me most. (*Cue:* Mark the hard works before reading the sentence so that you'll be ready for them.)

A third approach that can be employed in voice therapy is that of using specific behaviors from an allied system to cue more appropriate behaviors in another. Thus we synthesize or link up behavioral patterns in order to produce a desired vocal effect. This is essentially another way to describe "stimulability" as it applies to vocal production. We are all familiar with the use of facilitating contexts to elicit target phonemes during articulation therapy. Often in voice therapy we do the same type of thing. We employ associated behaviors, images or contexts to shape the vocal production. If we think about our example of the child with the hard glottal attacks, we can see that her symptom can be remediated by linking the phonatory behavior to resonance and/or articulation. We can emphasize easy onset of voicing by focusing attention on "the front of the face" (facial bones) or on the characterisitics of voiced continuant consonants. By redirecting the child's attention to another part of the speech mechanism, we accrue an additional benefit of distracting attention from the laryngeal mechanism. Since the articulatory system is less likely to be adversely affected by excessive effort than is the laryngeal system, a child who is using too much effort may be helped by such an approach. It should be noted that this is a frequently used approach that works with many different symptoms. Boone (1977, p. 109) lists 24 "facilitating behaviors" that are useful in voice therapy. We shall illustrate the use of facilitating associated behaviors in the following task sequence designed to eliminate hard glottal attacks.

Task Sequence III	Child's Behavioral Goals
Resonance	1. I can prolong a humming sound, feeling the tickling on my lips and the vibrations on my face, /m/.

2. I can describe the difference between feeling the sound on the front of my lips and face versus all the sound in my throat. (*Cue:* hands on face and lips.)

Articulation

3. I can prolong the /z/ sound, feeling the vibrations on my teeth.
4. I can prolong the /ð/ and /v/ sounds, feeling the vibrations on my tongue and lip.
5. I can prolong the voiced continuant consonants + vowels (e.g., za; ði; vo; mu).
6. I can repeat the five CV's (voiced continuant plus vowel), keeping the vibrations on the front of my face.
7. I can contrast the forward versus laryngeal tone focus on alternate CV syllables.
8. I can chant CV + V + V + V, maintaining the forward tone focus even on the vowels that aren't started with the voiced continuant consonant, e.g.,

    ma; a; a; a
    zi; i; i; i.

9. I can chant a sentence, keeping the forward tone focus (e.g., "My mom is making me mad"). (*Cue:* Practice sentence cumulatively, e.g.,

    my _____ _____ _____ _____
    my mom _____ _____ _____ _____
    my mom is _____ _____ _____
    my mom is making _____ _____.)

10. I can say the sentence maintaining forward tone focus. (*Cue:* Hum "m" before beginning.)
11. I can say phrases where the first word ends in voiced continuant consonant. (This helps glide into easy start to word beginning with vowel, e.g., I'm eager; I'm anxious; I'm earnest; is Edgar; is Ellie; is Emma; an orange; an apple; an alligator).
12. I can say phrases pausing before vowel yet maintaining easy, smooth onset. (*Cue:* Think of the vowel sound vibrating in the front of your mouth.)
13. I can say sentences full of words starting with vowel sounds. (*Cue:* Keep the sound at the front of your mouth.)

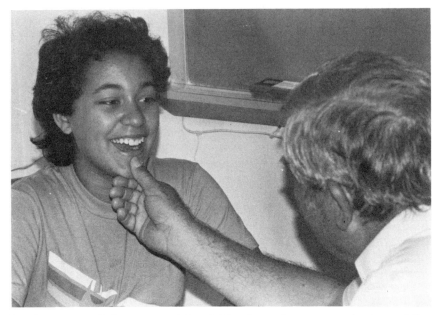

Tactile cues can help to remind the child to keep the voice on the front of the mouth.

14. I can tell when the vowel sounds at the beginning of words are easy and forward versus hard and in the throat.
15. I can predict when I am likely to make the vowel sounds hard and with too much effort in my throat.
16. I can describe what I do to avoid hard attacks on words beginning with vowels (e.g.,
    a. Keep the voice on the front of my mouth
    b. Prolong voiced continuant [sound carrying] consonants
    c. "Think" about linking preceding final consonants to the vowel in the next word
    d. "Hum" in my head to place the sound before saying the vowel).

A fourth approach to therapy needs yet to be considered. This approach differs from the three already discussed in that it does not focus primary attention on the vocal symptoms. The therapy is aimed at the understanding of the interpersonal dynamics precipitating or maintaining the vocal symptoms. Thus, this approach may be used when the clinician feels that the vocal symptoms arise from or reflect problems in personal or interpersonal adjustment. Aronson (1973) has used the term "psychogenic" to refer to voice disorders that result from emotional factors, lack of self-esteem, or disturbed interpersonal relationships. His excellent series of tapes illustrating his approach to diagnosis and intervention with adult patients provides insight into the ways in which maladaptive vocal behavior may stem from psychosocial problems. Obviously, severe problems of this kind are best treated by a team approach. Psychological counseling either alone or coordinated with symptomatic voice therapy is frequently the method of treatment used when a complex or severe problem is identified. Some children, however, who exhibit less severe difficulties, may benefit from a voice therapy approach that emphasizes analysis of the interpersonal factors influencing vocal behavior. Such an approach focuses on awareness of the way our feelings influence our own vocal behavior and the way our behavior is perceived by others. It involves the effects of physiological and emotional states on vocal strategies. To illustrate this general approach we will again consider a task sequence designed for a child exhibiting the vocal symptom of hard glottal attacks. In this instance, however, the approach will not focus so much on the vocal symptom but on understanding the underlying basis of that behavior.

Task Sequence IV	**Child's Behavioral Goals**
Interpersonal level	1. I can listen to tape recordings of voices and describe how I feel as I listen to the individual's voices (e.g., tense/ relaxed/ anxious/annoyed).
	2. I can describe specific feeling states associated with certain vocal characteristics (e.g.,
	angry = loud, tense sound, fast rate
	friendly = pitch variety, relaxed sound, even rate
	scared = soft, quavery sound, pauses, endings fade
	confident = moderate loudness, clear sound, even rate).
	3. I can describe the characteristics of voices and behavior of people I like to talk to (e.g.,
	relaxed body, facial expression and voice
	good eye contact
	don't talk all of the time
	don't butt in when I'm talking
	ask me questions sometimes

seem to really listen to me
voice is easy to listen to
don't talk about themselves all of the time
don't try to be the center of attention always).

Intrapersonal Level

4. I can express different feelings while talking (with facial expression and gesture), e.g.,
    Oh yeah! (angry/happy)
    Answer, anyone! (ordering/coaxing)
    Everyone is out (sneering/questioning)

5. I can explain how it feels and sounds when I talk different ways, e.g.,
    angry "Oh yeah"—neck and jaw tense
    hard attack on "Oh"—voice loud
    and strained

6. I can describe how listeners respond differently to different ways of saying the same words (e.g., they feel irritated, blamed, put down).

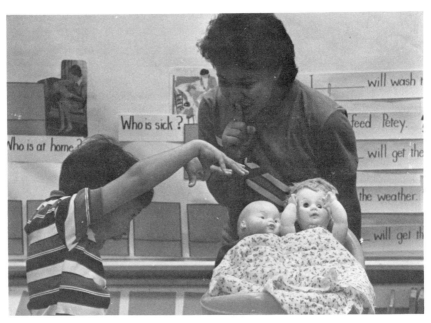

Role-playing allows the child to try out a variety of different vocal behaviors.

7. I can role-play the same dialogue using different feelings in my voice (e.g., friendly/defiant).
   a. I want to talk to you, Al.
   b. Why? What is it all about?
8. I can demonstrate different tricks I can use to make my voice sound: friendly/defiant, relaxed/tense, e.g.,
   relaxed face and body (versus tense)
      easy attacks (versus hard)
      loud (versus moderate)
      fast (versus slow)
      pauses (versus no pauses)
      pitch rises at end (versus pitch falls)
9. I can role-play various situations (switching parts) and analyze the effects I create by using my voice different ways. TAPE RECORD—PLAY BACK—DISCUSS—REDO
10. I can match vocal behaviors with specific situations and expected effects (e.g., situation = talking to the principal).
    How do I want to sound?
    What vocal behaviors will be helpful?
    What vocal behaviors will be harmful?
11. I can analyze situations by using the following questions:
    What do I want to gain?
    What risks are there?
    What vocal behavior should I use?
    How will the listener react?

chapter 7
Phases of Therapy Programs

We have just reviewed some different approaches to organizing individual therapy tasks into meaningful sequences. The approach we adopt influences which short-term goals we select, the priority given to certain goals, and the strategies we design to teach the child to acquire the behaviors stated in the goals. Of course, it takes a large number of short-term goals and task sequences to build an entire therapy program. When we take an overview of a complete, well-organized therapy program designed to achieve long-range terminal objectives, we notice that there is usually a discernible pattern. The program is subdivided into sections made up of similar short-term goals and task sequences. These sections are called *phases*.

The amount of time required to implement an entire voice therapy program will vary depending on a variety of factors. Individual phases of the program will be completed along the way, however, and the success of the entire program will depend to a large extent on how these phases mesh in promoting cumulative learning. In the section that follows we describe and illustrate four distinct phases that are important in voice therapy programming for children. These are (1) general awareness; (2) specific awareness; (3) production; and (4) carryover. Every phase may not always be necessary in every therapy program. Some phases will be more applicable with some children than with others. Nevertheless, it is probably safe to say that there is merit in capitalizing on possibilities inherent in all the phases, not only during the initial stages of program planning but also when problems occur in implementation and program revision seems necessary.

An awareness phase of voice therapy usually involves more complicated planning than does a similar phase in articulation therapy. When a child with an articulation difficulty is taught to focus on distinctive features, the parameters are fairly well defined and are similar for all children. The voice student, however, may present the

Goal 1: Label correctly two contrasted behaviors with 100% accuracy

General Area	Respiratory Behavior	Laryngeal Behavior	Resonance	Interpersonal Skills
(Identification)				
Behavior I	Upper chest breathing	Tense neck	Nose voice [m]	Angry voice
Behavior II	Lower chest breathing	Relaxed neck	Mouth voice [a]	Friendly voice

Goal 2: Describe the visible signs of the two behaviors in others

	Respiratory Behavior	Laryngeal Behavior	Resonance	Interpersonal Skills
(Description)				
Characteristics I	Shoulders raised. Lower chest still.	Neck muscles move. Jaw thrust out.	Mouth closed. Air blows feather near nose.	Face frowns.
Characteristics II	Shoulders down. Lower chest moves.	No movement in neck. Jaw loose.	Mouth open. Air blows feather near mouth.	Face smiles.

Goal 3: Describe to others how to change Behavior I to Behavior II

(Instruction) Verbalizations			
1. Keep shoulders down.	1. Roll head around.	1. Open mouth more.	1. Don't frown.
2. Breathe deeper.	2. Loosen neck.	2. Blow air to move feather.	2. Smile.
3. Put hands on lower chest and push out.	3. Unclench jaw.		3. Loosen face.
4. Move chest walls out at sides.	4. Shrug shoulders.		4. Think friendly thoughts!
	5. Drop jaw down.		

The arrangement of the goals involves a progression from identification to description to instruction.

Strategies that could be used to teach the behaviors stated in the preceding goals might include the following activities:

Goal 1 A. Model plus explanation of behaviors.
           B. Tell me what one I am doing.
           C. You be the teacher and tell me what to do.

Goal 2 A. Tell me how you know which one I am doing.
           B. Put a mark beside the label on the chalkboard and tell me why you chose that one.
           C. Choose the card with the description that matches what I did. Read it to me.

Goal 3 A. Simon says.
           B. Draw a picture of each and explain what you drew and why.
           C. You be the teacher and tell me my mistakes and how to correct them.
           D. Make up some rules and write them on the chalkboard.

clinician with a variety of distorted vocal patterns and some may be rather unusual. In deciding how to describe and define the characteristics of vocal patterns, the clinician is often in uncharted territory. Individual differences in adaptive behavior seem to present more challenges in voice therapy than in articulation therapy. Of primary importance during any awareness phase is the reduction of all behaviors to their simplest form. This enables children to attend to the significant characteristics. Children are taught first to identify characteristics of specific behaviors in others and later to identify what they themselves are doing.

When the clinician first teaches awareness of behaviors produced by others, children are usually better equipped to identify and describe those behaviors in themselves later in the program. An added advantage is the avoidance of feelings of embarrassment and self-consciousness that often result if children are required to focus on their own patterns before they have been trained to observe and describe those behaviors demonstrated by others. One way to approach this kind of observation is to contrast behaviors. When the clinician presents a pairing of basic behaviors, children are given a clear-cut choice, and differences can be made more dramatic. The chart below lists examples of some simple behavioral contrasts subsumed under the four different areas of concern in voice therapy. Simple terms are selected and used to describe what is seen and heard, and practice is given in identifying and describing each aspect of the patterns.

We have just illustrated some simple goals and strategies useful for helping children zero in on significant aspects of contrasting behaviors. By pairing the contrasting behaviors, we tried to emphasize the significant differences in characteristics. This technique is frequently helpful in teaching specific awareness of target behaviors. However, some children may not be motivated or ready to proceed directly into the specific awareness phase of therapy. Sometimes when we begin to work with a child in voice therapy, a more general orientation to the area to be worked on is necessary first. It is unlikely that all children automatically "know" what they are supposed to be thinking about in voice therapy, or why it is important or relevant at all. Until they develop some basic concepts about the area of concern, they may not be equipped to proceed.

GENERAL AWARENESS PHASE

A voice therapy program frequently begins with a *general awareness* phase in which the child is introduced to an area and oriented to significant concepts. If, for example, the area to be considered is respiration, the clinician may begin with a general discussion of breathing: how it is necessary to sustain life, to make sound, and so on. This can by followed by a discussion of how people breathe when they talk or sing; how the amount of air affects the length of the sound; how there are even, smooth sounds or jerky sounds produced when the airstream is emitted in different ways; how air can be taken in and stored by efficient and inefficient methods. If a child is an athlete, the discussion can be linked to the way efficient air use affects athletic performance. If the child plays a musical instrument, the discussion can refer to the relationship between airflow and the musical effect, and so on. What is important is that the child is acquainted with and understands the relevance of the broad area of interest. During the general awareness phase of therapy we teach the background information that the child needs to understand before beginning work on specific symptoms.

Teacher's Goals

1. To orient the child to the area to be addressed in therapy.
2. To develop concepts that are basic to learning in the area.
3. To introduce linguistic terms used to describe characteristics and relationships.

Child's Objectives

1. I can identify the area to be worked on.
2. I can describe why this area is important to all people.
3. I can describe how this area is important to me in my daily life.
4. I can explain the basic concepts relevant to this area.
5. I can define the linguistic terms used in this area.

Steps in the Therapy Sequence

1. I can identify voice as the area to be worked on.
   a. Animals, birds, and people all have unique voices.
2. I can describe why voice is important to people.
   a. we recognize people by their voices
   b. voices tell us important information
      i. age
      ii. sex
      iii. health
      iv. wakefulness/fatigue
      v. emotional state
      vi. intent

     c. people react differently to different voices
        i. familiar/unfamiliar
       ii. pleasant/unpleasant
      iii. natural/artificial
      iv. neutral/emotional

3. I can describe how voice is important to me in my daily life.
     a. it is the "me" others hear
     b. it can help me feel confident/anxious
     c. it can draw others to me/turn others from me
     d. it can help me/hinder me from getting what I want

4. I can explain basic concepts relevant to voice (e.g., parameters of voice).
     a. high/low
     b. loud/soft
     c. tense/relaxed
     d. smooth/rough
     e. even/jerky
     f. easy/squeezed

5. I can define the linguistic terms used in voice (e.g., characteristics of voice behavior).
     a. abrupt/easy onset
     b. slides up/slides down
     c. keeps going/stops
     d. gets softer/louder
     e. too loud/too soft
     f. grunts/clicks/flows/breaks
     g. not enough air/too much air
     h. tight muscles in neck/relaxed neck

SPECIFIC AWARENESS PHASE

Once the child has participated in a discussion of the general area and has acquired some understanding of it and its importance, the work on *specific awareness* of individual behaviors can begin. The symptom pattern dictates the selection of the specific behaviors that the child needs to be able to isolate from the behavioral Gestalt. During this phase the clinician models specific behaviors and uses consistent terms to identify and describe relevant behavioral characteristics. The child then practices using this descriptive language. An example of a therapy sequence for specific awareness that is applicable to any behavior and appropriate for any area of voice therapy follows.

During the specific awareness phase of therapy, we teach the child to focus on the part of behavioral patterns that are most relevant to his or her symptoms.

Teacher's Goals

1. To isolate behaviors relevant to the production phase of therapy.
2. To discriminate between appropriate and inappropriate behaviors.
3. To isolate symptoms to be modified during therapy.
4. To describe the auditory, visual, and kinesthetic characteristics of target symptoms.
5. To provide pertinent information concerning anatomy and physiology (if applicable).
6. To identify reasons for symptoms.
7. To target negative behaviors to avoid or change.
8. To describe alternative strategies.

Child's Objectives

1. The child will identify behaviors exhibited by others (negative and positive).
2. The child will describe the characteristics of those behaviors.
3. The child will discriminate between the appropriate and inappropriate behaviors.
4. The child will suggest ways others can avoid or change inappropriate behaviors.
5. The child will identify own behaviors.
6. The child will explain the characteristics of the behaviors he or she uses now (auditory, visual, kinesthetic characteristics).
7. The child will explain the correct–incorrect physiology associated with the symptoms.
8. The child will identify symptoms and negative behaviors to change.
9. The child will explain how/why/when he or she uses inappropriate behaviors.
10. The child will describe some ways inappropriate behaviors can be avoided or changed.

When the child has been taught to focus on the characteristics of behaviors that need to be modified and understands the perceptual framework and terminology, he or she is in an advantageous position to experience success on production tasks.

PRODUCTION PHASE

During the production phase of therapy we teach the child to produce and monitor target behaviors in a highly structured and controlled situation. Initially, cues and monitoring are provided by the clinician. As the production phase progresses, however, the responsibility for cuing and monitoring is assumed more and more by the client.

Teacher's Goals

1. To elicit the target behaviors
   a. in isolation
   b. in simple linguistic contexts
   c. in complex linguistic contexts
2. To describe the child's responses in terms meaningful to the child
   a. how
   b. why
   c. when
3. To provide techniques to shape consistency and accuracy of responses
   a. imitation
   b. extensive cuing
   c. minimal cuing
4. To encourage child's self-monitoring of responses.
5. To structure increasingly difficult contexts in which the child can practice target behaviors.
6. To reinforce the child's correct responses and/or attempts at extinguishing undesirable behaviors.

Child's Objectives

1. The child will produce a target behavior correctly (in isolation)
   a. with instructions, cues, and model
   b. with instructions and cues
   c. with instructions
   d. spontaneously
2. The child will prolong–repeat the target behavior.
3. The child will stop and start the target behavior at will.
4. The child will demonstrate both the appropriate and inappropriate forms of the behavior (negative practice).
5. The child will produce the target behavior, varying length of utterance
   a. isolated sounds
   b. syllables
   c. words
   d. phrases
   e. sentences
6. The child will produce the target behavior varying complexity of processing
   a. imitation
   b. automatic responses
   c. limited repertoire of responses

d. simple self-generated responses

e. complex self-generated responses

7. The child will produce the target behavior varying the timing of the response

    a. predictable response time

    b. unpredictable response time

8. The child will describe the characteristics of his or her production in terms of

    a. preparatory set

    b. strategies used

    c. reactions of self

    d. reactions of others

9. The child will monitor his or her own production

    a. when cued verbally

    b. when cued nonverbally

    c. after practicing aloud

    d. after thinking about it first

    e. spontaneously

In voice therapy the target is usually less well defined than it is in articulation therapy. Thus the clinician must present opportunities for the child to verbalize descriptions of what he or she is doing to produce the target behavior, and to specify how the behavior sounds, feels, and looks. Monitoring and self-evaluating are achieved most effectively when the processes involved in production are scored and analyzed as well as practiced.

As can be seen in item 4 of the task sequence above, negative practice (Wilson, 1972) may be incorporated into the learning sequence. It is also traditional for the mean length of the response to be gradually increased as a new vocal behavior is learned. During item 5, the traditional progression from isolated sounds (usually vowels or voiced continuants) through gradual combinations of sounds is illustrated. In item 6 we see the graduations that involve cognitive processing. For example, a child who is learning to produce a "new" vocalization pattern usually needs to concentrate full attention initially on the mechanics of production rather than on the ideas expressed. Thus we require minimal cognitive processing initially and gradually increase the complexity of the processing as skill develops.

When a child first learns to produce a new behavior and that behavior is not yet stabilized, it helps if we give him or her plenty of time to produce the target behavior, or a predictable latency between the stimulus (instructions and/or cues) and the expected response. As skill develops, it is advantageous to begin to vary these demands during practice so that the elapsed time between stimulus and response more closely approximates the variability of actual speech interactions. That is why in item 7 of the sample task sequence we include variations in timing. It seems helpful at times to vary timing even when the child is still at the single-sound level. For example, we may wish to employ a strategy such as asking a child to be ready to respond to questions of various lengths with a simple "Oh" or "Ah hah!" Such an activity, while making simple demands in terms of the length of the target utterance, can be useful in terms of requiring the child to be ready to respond whenever the questioner stops talking. An example of such an activity is given below.

1. Area: Laryngeal behavior
2. Goal: Child will produce an easy vocal tone on single vowels in response to oral questions or statements of various lengths (9/10).
3. Strategy:
   a. Clinician tells the child to be ready to produce an easy voice on [ou] and [ʌ] [a] whenever the clinician stops talking (questions or a narrative may be presented)
   b. Child responds immediately when the clinician pauses. The vowel may be varied in terms of pitch inflections to reflect meaning.
   c. Verbal reinforcement is given. Stimulus materials are as follows:
      i. "I like ice cream, but my sister doesn't. Can you believe that?" [ʌ] (with head shake)
      ii. "The news was exciting today. A bank robber dressed in a ski mask held up the downtown bank and escaped with $100,000!!" [ou]
      iii. "No one was hurt!" [a] (with relief)

The preceding example illustrates the interrelationship that may exist between length of utterance, timing of response, and complexity of processing during voice therapy activities. Although in the sample task sequence presented earlier, items 5, 6, and 7 are listed sequentially, the variables of length, timing, and complexity are often difficult to consider in isolation from each other. Since we are always trying to shape behavior so that it will eventually support spontaneous communicative exchange, consideration of conversational timing and interaction between speakers early in the task sequence is often beneficial.

Choosing Materials to Facilitate Responses

We have discussed how we systematically shape the child's responses during the production phase of therapy; however, there is yet another aspect to be considered as we plan therapy during the production phase.

We need to choose practice items geared to facilitate correct responses.

The correct choice of appropriate materials to cue responses and to be spoken during practice sessions is an important part of successful planning. It is self-evident, of course, that the level of all materials used should be appropriate to the child's academic achievement level. The child who cannot read fluently needs materials such as rebus stories (pictures interspersed with printed words in sentences). The child who can read needs sentences and passages commensurate with his or her reading proficiency level. Additionally, the content is chosen so as to correlate with the individual child's interests, ethnic and/or family background, and socioeconomic level. Common sense suggests that the more the child can identify with the characters and the circumstances in stories that he or she is listening to, discussing, or reading, the more involved he or she becomes in the task. Children from single-parent families, for example, may not always feel comfortable reading about or discussing narratives that describe intact family groups. Similarly, children from ghetto areas may not relate well to pictures from glossy magazines depicting luxurious home interiors. While most of us are aware of the pitfalls inherent in the examples just cited, we should also be careful to include in stimulus materials pictures of children who match the ethnic characteristics of the children we are teaching.

Choice of Phonemes Another consideration when we select practice materials is the extent to which the phonemes selected enhance the child's chances of achieving his or her voice production goals. This consideration is a familiar one, since we are aware of the importance of using facilitating phonetic contexts when we work with children during articulation therapy. However, the effect of specific phonemes and phonemic sequences in facilitating vocal production is somewhat more subtle though equally important. Let us consider some examples of phonemes that are helpful in relation to some examples of specific skills worked on under the various areas that are important in voice therapy.

Respiration We have talked about the importance of the exhalation phase of respiration. We know that children must be able to prolong and control the airflow during expiration. When we choose sounds for children to practice to increase the duration of the exhalation phase, we need to remember that voiced continuants will be easiest at first. This is because the vocal folds are closed during voiced sounds, thus restricting to some extent the emission of the airstream. We improve the child's chances of success if we ask him or her to prolong sounds such as /z/ /m/ /v/, since continuant sounds can be prolonged for as long as the air lasts, and the air lasts somewhat longer when the continuant is also voiced.

When success has been achieved in increasing the duration of individual voiced continuants, the next step is to proceed to teach the child to prolong unvoiced continuants. We might begin with /s/ / θ /, for example, since the production of these sounds provides the possibility of capitalizing on a kinesthetic awareness of the air passing through the constriction of articulators in the front of the mouth. During production of these sounds. The evenness of the airflow can also be demonstrated by the use of visible cues, such as the movement of a feather or paper held in front of the mouth. All of the unvoiced fricative continuants will usually be easier than the glottal continuant /h/, in which the airflow is unimpeded at both the laryngeal and oral levels. Thus the production of /h/ may best be reserved to practice until last in such a series.

When children have achieved proficiency in prolonging and controlling the airflow during the production of individual continuant sounds, a clinician may wish to introduce tasks that help develop skill in segmenting the exhalation. Because during running speech the exhalation phase is segmented as voiced and unvoiced sounds are sequenced across time, segmentation (or stopping and starting) exercises are frequently valuable. Examples of these exercises may include stopping and starting the voiced continuants practiced previously, as many times as possible during one exhalation. When this exercise has resulted in improvement in performance, production of a repeated plosive during one exhalation may be attempted. Again, the search for the easiest phonemes to practice first should involve a consideration of the features of voicing, and the place and manner of articulation. Clinical experience suggests that the most difficult task for children who are working on improving the control of the exhalation may be successive repetitions of the voiceless affricative /t ʃ /. Since the oral cavity is relatively open and the vocal folds are apart, the child is required to place more attention on the role of the respiratory muscles. It may frequently be easiest for a child to practice sounds arranged in the following order of difficulty: voiced plosives, voiced affricative, voiceless plosives, and voiceless affricative. Bilabials [p] and [b] that are highly visible provide excellent feedback, since a child can look in the mirror and see how the lips are "helping" the respiratory muscles stop and start the airstream. The phonemes produced with a more open oral cavity (e.g., [t] [d] and [k] and [g] and finally [t ʃ] and [d ʒ]) may therefore not be as easy as the bilabials are for some children. Clinicians may find it useful to experiment in order to see how the features of voicing, and the place and manner of articulation, affect each individual child's performance on tasks involving repetitions of individual phonemes. In this way the most facilitating phonemes can be selected for the initial training of segmentation of exhalation.

Phonation   In the area of phonation, certain behaviors may also be facilitated by the selection of apppropriate vowel and consonant combinations. One behavior focused on frequently in voice therapy is the onset of phonation. If, for example, a clinician is training a child to use a breathy initiation of phonation, the use of voiceless consonants may be extremely helpful in facilitating appropriate responses. We are familiar with the technique of teaching children to practice CV combinations involving [h] + vowel. Another technique (previously noted) involves the child's practice of smooth transitions from unvoiced to voiced continuants during a single exhalation. This allows the child to begin the flow of air during the voiceless phoneme and then to add voicing gradually. We have found the following combinations useful for teaching smooth transitions into voicing:

s   z   (feel the sound on your teeth)
f   v   (feel the sound on your lower lip)
θ   ð   (feel the sound on your tongue)
h   m (feel the sound on both of your lips)

The choice of vowel sounds to be used to practice easy initiation of phonation at the syllable and word levels may also be an important consideration. Clinical experience suggests that the /e/ /i/ /I/ monophthongs (as in "every," "easy" and "ink") seem particularly susceptible to hard attacks when they occur in the initial position of a stressed syllable in words. Because of this, it is often advantageous to begin practicing easy attacks, at the word level, on vowels such as /u/ (as in "ooze"). In general, it may sometimes be observed that the back vowels are more facilitating than the more forward vowels and the lax vowels easier than the tense vowels. With this in mind, the clinician may at times find it helpful to sequence practice materials in an order of difficulty similar to the sequence below:

1. *u* (ooze)
2. þ (Austin)
3. ʒ (Ernest)
4. æ (aspirin)
5. e (any)
6. *i* (eel)
7. ɪ (it)

Sometimes it may be observed that diphthongs are easiest for a child who is practicing easy attacks on vowels, using the technique of "easing into the vowel" and "lingering" on it. At such times, the diphthong [ou] seems more facilitating, for example, than [eɪ]. A facilitating sequence of diphthongs might be similar to that below:

1. oʊ (old)
2. oɪ (oil)
3. aʊ (out)
4. eɪ (ate)

An arrangement of word pairs might then be presented in the following order:

hoe	oh
hoy	oy
how	ow
hay	eh

Selection of vowel sounds that are facilitating is not, of course, a consideration limited only to practice materials associated with the onset of phonation.

When strategies are designed to achieve goals related to quality, pitch, and loudness, the clinician may also need to consider how certain vowel sounds can be helpful in eliciting appropriate target products. For example, the high [i] is frequently used to elicit a high-pitched utterance. In addition to the acoustic characteristics of the vowel itself, words containing [i] vowels frequently evoke helpful associations. Consider words such as "cheep" and "shriek," for example. Similarly, the [ʌ] vowel, as in the word "bump," may facilitate the production of a low pitch. When loudness variations are being taught, a clinician may wish to contrast certain vowel and consonant sequences, such as those in "shush" and "bang," in order to capitalize on the onomatopoeic effect. The voiceless fricatives will be easier for the child to say softly, and the voiced consonants will lend themselves well to louder, more vigorous production.

If the focus of an activity is the smoothness of the vocal quality, practice materials should be chosen so that open relaxed vowels are combined with continuant consonants. The liquid [l] is especially facilitating in this regard, as is the semivowel [w]. On the other hand, unvoiced plosives that require interruption in the continuation of the voicing may need to be avoided during early practice trials. Again, the manner and place of articulation need to be considered. Alveolar consonants (so that the movement of the tongue tip can be the focus of the child's attention) may be especially helpful for a child who is practicing avoidance of excessive laryngeal effort. The following word and sentence lists contain some combinations of sounds that facilitate smooth vocal production.

loom	vein	anvil
ruin	honey	mule
oily	oozing	winning
move	mowing	wailing

1. Lily loves lamb and veal every meal.
2. Oh, no, Julie, the oil is oozing away.
3. Now William loves mowing lawns.
4. Honey is flowing smoothly along.
5. Will Mervyn win more money?
6. Whale oil will ruin Merle's loom.
7. Row, row, smoothly over the wave.
8. Ewes, rams, and silken lambs.
9. Millie and Neville, wave to Mommy.
10. Lovely smooth raven wings.

Resonance   It is traditional in voice therapy to segregate oral and nasal sounds in syllables, words, and sentences used to test and train children to use appropriate resonance patterns. For example, children who are hyponasal will practice materials loaded with nasal sounds.

1. No, no, not now—never!
2. *Never Say Never Again* may be a mystery movie.
3. My mouth moves more than Mary's mouth.
4. Moaning and groaning, mewing and meowing.
5. My mascot is Mickey Mouse.

Children who are hypernasal may need practice materials involving all oral sounds (and particularly vowels *other* than /i/ and /u/ on which nasality is most frequently perceived) in the initial stages of their therapy program.

1. Go, girl go, row, row, row!
2. Kick the ball over the wall.
3. Pick the apple, pick the pear.
4. The ditch is wide, adjust your stride.
5. Twitch, hop, plop, the rabbit has stopped.

The use of stimulus items involving alveolar consonants and forward vowel sounds emphasizes forward movement of the tongue when tongue retraction is a problem. Materials used to correct this problem might include sentences such as the following:

1. Pit-a-pat, what is that?
2. Eight fat cats sat by the rat.
3. "Itty Bitty," he's Bill's kitty.
4. "Tittle tattle," Betty chatters.
5. Therese baked pies with peas.

In cases of cul-de-sac resonance, or inappropriate tone focus, combinations of sounds that facilitate mouth opening and lip movement can be most helpful; for example, open vowels, rounded vowels and bilabial and labiodental consonants.

1. Oh, no, Joe. Don't go below.
2. One blue bottle plopped off the wall.
3. Two for you and two for Stu.
4. Ah, lady, show off the Barbie doll.
5. "Ahoy," shouted the ship's captain.

When resonance is weak, and a voice lacks sufficient richness and carrying power, chanting is frequently effective in creating a kinesthetic and auditory awareness of increased reverberation in the oral and nasal cavities. Chanting involves the prolongation of vowels and voiced continuant consonants. In order to maximize the awareness of the "sound carrying" consonants, and to emphasize mouth opening and lip movement, practice materials should include a high frequency of continuant sounds that facilitate oral movement.

1. Maisie is marrying Vivian Withers:
2. Rosie revs the engine of the Mercedes Benz.
3. Lions lying languidly in the zoo.
4. Come now, one and all, come!
5. "Amen" sing the boys as the organ plays.
6. Eve was living in the Garden of Eden.
7. Beams zoom towards the moon.
8. The treasure is golden coins, rubies, emeralds.
9. Hey Ho, Hey Ho, they all are dwarfs you know.
10. Vandals even live in the Virgin Islands.

In cases when children are mildly hypernasal, and oral resonance needs to be increased to improve the oral–nasal balance, practice materials should highlight open vowels and voiced continuant consonants that facilitate oral movement, but nasal consonants may need to be avoided in early stages of training.

1. Buzz, buzz, buzz goes the busy fly.
2. Tra la, tra la, a gray and white galah (an Australian bird).
3. Zippidy doo dah, zippidy eh.
4. It is, of course, a lovely day.
5. Hey ho, hey ho, it's off to work we go.
6. "Toto, Toto," called Dorothy. "Where are you?"

The examples cited under the area of respiration, phonation, and resonance illustrate only a few of the ways that clinicians can use their knowledge of the articulation of speech sounds in order to enhance children's vocal behavior.

Improvement in vocal behavior usually occurs if the movement of specific articulators aids in (1) an awareness of the interrelationship of behaviors; (2) directing attention away from a part of the mechanism being used incorrectly; (3) opening or shaping the oral cavity; (4) increasing forward tone focus and projection of voice.

Analysis, Self-Monitoring, and Evaluation of Progress

In voice therapy we usually teach a child a perceptual framework and the descriptive language necessary for monitoring and evaluating behavior during the awareness phases of the program. As we enter the production phase, the child is then equipped with the self-regulating speech patterns (Pellegrini, 1982) that are helpful in mediating behavior. Freeman and Garstecki (1973) discussed the importance of children playing an active part in voice therapy. They demonstrated that children can participate successfully in the process of setting their own goals. When specific behaviors are clearly defined and children actively participate in describing the characteristics of behaviors from the outset, evaluation and self-monitoring are integral parts of the therapy throughout the production phase. Children's own descriptions of behaviors can be used to chart the evaluation sequence. As children progress through a series of self-evaluation activities, they can be encouraged to move from retrospective "after the fact" evaluation of their productions to simultaneous evaluation. Finally, they can arrive at an awareness of how the preparatory set for correct and incorrect products can be identified. This process can be helped by visual aids and charts that allow the progress across time to be concretely documented. In this way children can be helped to understand where they are going and the intermediate steps along the way.

An example of how self-monitoring skills can be initiated early in the production phase is the way in which cues are explicitly stated during activities to elicit the target behavior. We know that we can stimulate a child to produce a target voice by evoking images that result in modifications of the vocal tract. We can also use many other cues and techniques as well as facilitating articulatory contexts. Whatever technique is most beneficial in eliciting a required response, the child will be helped if a concrete description of it is provided. This description then becomes part of his/her self-cuing and evaluation during subsequent practice.

1. Getting ready: It helps me if
    a. I take in plenty of air.
    b. I relax my neck and chin.
    c. I don't tense my shoulders.
    d. I open my mouth wide.
    e. I think of how it should sound.
    f. My teacher does it first.
2. Starting: It helps me if
    a. My teacher does it with me.
    b. My throat feels open.
    c. I think of honey flowing.
    d. I use an /h/ as the first sound.
    e. I lengthen the vowel.

In questioning a child concerning the characteristics of a response, it is very important that the child is asked explicit questions. Vague questions such as "How was that?" and "Do you think that was okay?" are not likely to result in specific answers. It is preferable for the clinician to teach the child to evaluate performance in as concrete a way as is possible. Thus the techniques used to cue the behavior can be used as a checklist to evaluate that behavior.

1. *Before* you started were you ready?
    Did you have plenty of air?
    Did you relax your neck and chin?
    Did you drop your shoulders?
    Did you think how you wanted to sound?
2. *When* you started what happened?
    Did you feel your throat open?
    Did you think of honey?
    Did you use an /h/?
    Did you lengthen the vowel?
3. What else could you have done to help?

The previous example illustrates the first step in the evaluation process: the identification and description of relevant aspects affecting production. The presence or absence of facilitating aspects are noted. The next step in the process frequently involves the child in a comparative task such as "Was that one better or worse than the last try? Why?" Repeated trials can also involve an element of evaluation. For example, "This time keep doing it until you are sure it is as good as you can make it." The use of audio- and videotape recordings is especially helpful for post hoc analysis of this kind. If videotape equipment is not available, peers in group therapy or mirrors can be used to provide feedback concerning the visual characteristics of the behaviors. The clinician should try not to be the sole evaluator of the behaviors. Independent written scoring of responses with subsequent comparison of the clinician and students' evaluations is a technique that is especially useful in encouraging children to assume responsibility for judging their own productions. When judgments differ, the tape recordings can be replayed and discussed and reasons for discrepancies identified. Evaluation is an active process, in which the child is a full and responsible participant, throughout the phases of therapy. But it is during the carryover phase of therapy that the effect of an earlier emphasis on analysis and self-evaluation is most striking. Children who are already comfortable and experienced in analyzing and judging their own behavior seem more likely to demonstrate rapid improvement during the carryover phase of therapy.

CARRYOVER PHASE

During the carryover phase we teach the child to habituate the target behaviors for increasing lengths of time in increasingly complex interactions.

Teacher's Goals

1. To design a repertoire of rehearsal and practice activities analogous to those encountered in the child's everyday life (e.g., home, school, recreation).
2. To provide a framework for the child to practice analysis and evaluation of voice use in relation to specific situational and interpersonal demands.
3. To teach the child to accept responsibility for self-monitoring and evaluation.

Carryover activities include examples of situations relevant to the child's own life-style and interests.

4. To develop a hierarchy of practice assignments (to be completed outside of therapy) that is meaningful to the child and allows for documentation of progress.
5. To provide feedback and reinforcement of the child's vocal behaviors and insights.

Child's Objectives

1. I can describe the times in my everyday life when it is hardest/easiest for me to use/maintain my target behaviors:
    a. emotional state
    b. size of group
    c. specific people I know
    d. type of activity
    e. time of day
    f. location of the talking

    g. background noise

    h. physical state

2. I can role-play correct vocal behavior (in the therapy room) simulating situations I identify as difficult:

    a. for short interactions

    b. for longer interactions

    c. with the clinician (one-to-one)

    d. with others present (small group)

3. I can analyze my vocal behavior during role playing:

    a. anticipating problems in advance

    b. evaluating behavior after the event

    c. self-correcting during the role playing

4. I can help design easy practice experiences to be completed outside the therapy room:

    a. short duration (e.g., automatic response, asking directions)

    b. neutral emotional contexts

    c. with strangers

    d. with supportive listeners

5. I can keep data concerning my easy experiences and analyze factors affecting my vocal behavior:

    a. anecdotal records

    b. checklists

    c. logs

    d. charts

6. I can help design difficult practice experiences to be completed outside the therapy room:

    a. longer duration

    b. competing background noise

    c. larger groups

    d. more demanding listeners

    e. more challenging locations

    f. stressful contexts

    g. when I'm not feeling good

7. I can organize and interpret data concerning difficult interactions and analyze factors affecting my vocal behavior:

    a. generalizations drawn from experiences

    b. coping strategies for specific problems and situations

    c. reinforcement for self (strengths and liabilities) (e.g., "Give yourself a pat on the back")

8. I can accept the help of supportive individuals in monitoring my spontaneous vocal behavior:

    a. my classroom teacher

    b. peers

    c. family members

9. I can adjust my own behavior based on the evaluations of supportive listeners.
10. I can monitor and adjust my behavior without external support.

Teaching Self-Reliance

Throughout voice therapy it is important to be specific in noting the characteristics of correct responses when reinforcing the child's efforts. When the clinician follows a good evaluation, with a brief explanation of why the behavior was correct, it helps the child focus on the pertinent aspects. For example, "Good, none of the air came out of your nose that time," or, "That's right, you opened your mouth really wide." Sometimes the clinician will describe his or her reactions to the response. An example of this is, "I really like that easy, smooth voice. I feel calm when you use that voice."

It is important also to note feelings and personality characteristics when evaluating children's work in therapy. When we comment on our own feelings of enjoyment or satisfaction arising from our interaction with the child, we enhance his or her self-esteem; for example, "I always enjoy working with you because you don't let problems get you down," or, "You listen so well to my instructions, no wonder you got all of the sentences correct today," or, "One thing I really admire about you is the way you keep trying no matter how hard the task is." Our expressions of confidence in the child, and in his or her strengths, can help the child internalize positive feelings about his or her part in the therapy process. By our verbal descriptions of the child's predictions, insights, and attitudes, we can help significantly in the development of confidence and reinforce feelings of self-worth.

As we progress through the carryover phase of therapy, it is often helpful to state our expectations, not only in terms of the child's achievement of target behaviors but also in terms of his or her feelings and self-evaluations. Our aim in doing this is to encourage the child to rely less and less on others' evaluations. For example, we might say, "Give yourself a pat on the back because you remembered to use your new voice. Isn't it a good feeling to know you remembered all by yourself?" or, "I'm proud of the way you don't need me to remind you to take replenishing breaths now," or, "Although it's always nice when someone else notices how well you're doing, that's not really the main thing. When you know it's right and feel good about it yourself—that's what really counts, isn't it?"

In setting assignments for children to complete outside the therapy room it is often helpful if we include in our instructions some statement concerning our expectations; for example, "Now you might get discouraged if the first time you try this, it doesn't work out. But knowing you, I bet you'll not let that stop you from trying it again." In addition, a positive attitude on the part of the clinician can help children learn to describe their mistakes and failures as opportunities rather than setbacks. For example, "It's a good thing you tried out your new voice in that situation. Now we know the kinds of situations we need to practice today. You'll be ready for it next time." Although we need to code children's experiences in terms that stress the positive aspects, that is not to say that we should avoid discussing the negative aspects at all. We strive to create a climate in therapy in which children can be open and realistic. We need to accept and not discount their feelings of frustration and anxiety in relation to performance on certain assignments. Telling a child, "Don't worry about it," or, "It doesn't matter," may cause the child to feel "put down." It is usually advisable to acknowledge the feelings first, so that the child feels understood, before rushing in with suggestions or advice. A useful strategy is to ask questions to help the child arrive at solutions that are his or her own. For example, "I can imagine how embarrassing that was when your pitch sounded so high in front of the whole class" (acknowledgment of the feeling). "What do you think you could have done differently?" (question focused on child's ability to solve problems). "Is there any other assignment you'd feel more comfortable trying?" (question focused on child's part in planning).

The carryover phase of therapy presents many opportunities for the clinician to teach children to acknowledge and enjoy the rewards of "being one's own person," learning from mistakes and savoring the satisfaction of knowing they can, by themselves, use their own voice the way they want to.

SUMMARY

We have discussed some general principles underlying the preparation of programs for voice therapy. It can be seen that in many respects, planning a voice therapy program is much like planning any other therapy program (See worksheet, p. 183). There are some important differences, however. One is the need to orient the child to the area to be worked on and to prepare him or her to deal with the prerequisite concepts and terminology needed during the production phase. We have seen how this can be accomplished during the general awareness phase. Another involves the need to specify the relevant behaviors and their characteristics as concretely as possible. We have reviewed some ways in which this can be dealt with during the specific awareness phase.

It may well be that the ultimate success of an entire voice therapy program for a young child depends significantly on the success achieved in the awareness phases. This is because the understanding and motivation developed during the awareness phases can accelerate progress through subsequent phases. In our discussion of the production phase we provided examples to illustrate how facilitating materials can be selected to enhance correct responses. We also noted the integral part played by the child's own analysis, self-monitoring, and evaluation of performance. In our sequence outlining the carryover phase we provided ideas for the gradual removal of external support as the new behaviors are habituated.

WORKSHEET 6-1:
Progress in Self-Evaluation

Child's name _____ School _____

Target behavior _____ Semester and year _____

I am a careful judge   Date

I know when it is right   _____

   —some of the time
   —most of the time
   —all of the time

I am able to explain why it is right   _____

   —some of the time
   —most of the time
   —all of the time

I know what goes wrong   _____

   —when my teacher explains why
   —as soon as I've done it
   —while I am doing it
   —as I'm getting ready to start
   —most of the time
   —all of the time

I can list when I have difficulty   _____

   —situations
   —types of listeners
   —feelings
   —time of day
   —physical state

I feel good about my efforts   _____

   —when my teacher praises me
   —as soon as I've done it
   —while I am doing it
   —as I'm getting ready to start
   —most of the time
   —all of the time

PART II
PRACTICE

In Part II we move to a consideration of treatment approaches for children that address a variety of voice problems. Although each child's problem is unique and must be assessed individually, some negative vocal behaviors seem to cluster together. Some are the result of an imperfect mechanism. Others stem from a child's attempts to adjust to short-term or chronic medical conditions or from congenital or acquired structural deviations. Still others may be learned behaviors or manifestations of psychological states.

The approaches presented fall into two categories: Sequential (approaches 1-6) and Gestalt (approaches 7-9). Each approach includes a brief history of the child or children involved, a detailing of the therapeutic goals, and illustrative sample strategies for treatment procedures. These sample strategies are not complete in their presentations; rather, they highlight different aspects of the therapeutic process in each of the plans. They are designed to provide a practical perspective to clinicians engaged in designing individualized programs for children.

Following the treatment approaches are worksheets we have found useful when working with children.

treatment approach 1
Increasing Available Vocal Options

There are many different causes of voice disorders. However, some clusters of symptoms are frequently observed. One such cluster is reduced vocal variety. Cognitive, neurological and affective constraints can limit a child's learning of appropriate suprasegmental features. Children who have sensory deficits, for example, hearing impairment, frequently use limited variation in their voices because their auditory monitoring contributes to imperfect learning. Even children with normal mechanisms sometimes need to be taught how to vary their voices more appropriately. When children habituate only one strategy (such as getting louder) or maladaptive behaviors to get and hold attention, they need help in acquiring a more suitable repertoire of techniques. Thus we can see that learning about the options that are available to vary the voice can be an important aspect of remediation for children exhibiting problems stemming from many different etiologies.

In the case history that follows, we describe three children who were treated together because they exhibited similar negative behaviors. The causative factors, however, were not similar. The group approach proved to be useful since the children enjoyed the interaction and the stimulation, modelling, and evaluation opportunities implicit in the group activities.

KURT, HANS, AND BRENDAN: REDUCED VOCAL VARIETY

The group consisted of three young boys, all approximately 9 years old. Kurt, a vocal abuser, used an excessively loud habitual level, and his attempts to vary his voice consisted of loudness increases. Hans was diagnosed as "speaking in a monotone," a problem that seemed to be a learned behavior, since both of his parents were profoundly deaf.

Although Hans himself had normal hearing, he seemed to have habituated some of the characteristics of his parents' speech patterns. Brendan exhibited a mild to moderate high-frequency hearing loss, bilaterally.

All three boys were stimulable during their initial assessment period. They were intrigued by the visual feedback provided by the Kay Elemetrics Visi-Pitch, which enabled them to see a representation of their voices on the oscilloscope screen. It was decided to use a therapy approach that relied heavily on associating visual patterns with auditory and proprioceptive feedback. In addition, all associations were coded verbally in simple, concrete language. The boys responded well to the idea that they were going to learn how to "make pictures with their voices." They continued as a group for one year, and all made excellent progress on this part of their remediation program. At the end of that time, Hans was dismissed from therapy, and Kurt and Brendan continued to work in individual therapy on additional aspects of their vocal behavior.

GOALS

The clinician noted from diagnostic information, that the three boys exhibited similar negative vocal behaviors. These included:

1. Limited use of pitch variation
2. Limited use of loudness variation
3. Limited use of durational changes
4. Limited ability to describe vocal strategies to express meanings and feelings.

She accordingly decided to address the boys' awareness and use of pitch, loudness, and durational changes in their voices to reflect meanings and feelings. Her three basic goals were to help the boys identify "picture words" in phrases and sentences (nouns, verbs, adjectives, adverbs); to describe vocal techniques to "make pictures" with their voices; and to use vocal techniques to vary pitch, loudness, and duration.

SAMPLE STRATEGIES

Pitch changes We know that we can make pictures with our hands. Watch while I draw a bow and arrow. I'll draw the arrow shooting up into the sky. Now I'll draw the arrow falling down to the ground. But did you know that we can also make pictures with our voices? Watch the Visi-Pitch screen while I say the word "arrow." I'll make it go up.

Now I'll make it go down.

Rate changes Words can be stretched out. Watch while I write "p u l l." Now I'll say it, and you can see how long the word looks on the Visi-Pitch screen. Now I'll say "p u s h"—that was a long push. You put your hands on the edge of the table and give a long, hard push, as if you were pushing a car that wouldn't go, while I say the word. Sometimes a "push" and a "pull" can be quick and short. You give a quick push on the table edge, and I'll say the word quickly.

A group of words can also be said quickly or slowly to help the listener get a picture in their mind. Listen to these:

horses gallop	cars race
worms crawl	the tortoise is slow

We can also stop before or after a word to make it important

Darth Vader . . . arrives!
Ladies and Gentlemen . . . the President of the . . . United States

Loudness changes We know about making our voices loud. That is fairly easy to do, for example, "a loud *bang!*" But some people think that getting louder is the only thing you can do to make interesting voice pictures. Some of the best voice pictures are made when we make our voices soft. Listen to these words. I'll say them loudly and softly.

soft and squishy
stroke the kitten's fur

Now let's talk about how they sound best. Why?

Voice pictures Let's choose some words that make great voice pictures. The best words are those that make us see the picture in our minds. I'll say some words in special ways, and you tell me what you saw in your mind as I said each one. Close your eyes.

fly (upward inflection)	zoom (downward inflection)
creaky (long duration)	purr (softly)
trot (short duration)	out (loudly, as when calling
twitch (short duration)	at a ballgame)

Look at this ladder. I'll draw a boy on top—he's high up—and one on the bottom—he's down low. When I say the word "boy," you point to the one I am thinking of. I'll say "boy" in a high voice and in a low voice.

Now look at these pictures of a giant and a dwarf. They are both called Fred. The giant is big and has a low voice. The dwarf is little and has a high voice. When I say "Fred," you point to the one I am thinking of. My voice picture will let you know which one it is. I could also show you who I am thinking of by making my voice loud for the giant and soft for the dwarf. Listen while I use this different kind of voice picture. Point to the one I am thinking of as I say "Fred" loudly or softly.

Voice pictures can be made lots of different ways. Voice pictures make the words we say more interesting. We can say words high or low, loudly or softly, slowly (stretching them out) or quickly. We can also stop before a word to make the listener know it is important. Here are some cards with pictures of high-low and loud-soft, long-short and a stop sign. Pick the card that matches the word picture I use (loud and soft can be depicted by a large and small drum being struck, or by a listener reacting by cupping an ear or holding both hands over ears; long and short can be shown by lines of contrasting lengths):

giant	quickly	lightning	grab
dwarf	rushing	stretch	reach
fat	lazy	scrunch	twinkle
huge	drop	crash	chirp
little	hole	splash	hiss
sharp	jump	shiver	dark
thick	plop	dive	light
slowly	dungeon		

It's a / spaceship	I hate / oysters
She's / bizarre	No, don't / please
Thank / you	A / new one
A / chocolate egg	A / liar and a cheat

Describe as many different ways as you can how the same word may be said; for example, "The boy jumped." Was it a high jump, a low jump or a broad jump? "The car went by." Was it a racing car or a slow car? Let's try to think of all the different ways that "The car went by" might be said: As a question (Are you sure?), as a fact (Don't argue with me), telling where (It went *by*), telling it's gone (It *went* by), telling it was definitely a car and not a truck (The *car* went by), telling it was special (*The* car went by).

Choosing the word in the sentence to make the picture word is fun. It can change the meaning of the whole sentence. We can also choose more than one picture word sometimes. Or we can let our voices be a picture of our feelings for all of the words in the sentence. Listen while I say some words and tell me if I'm feeling pleased or upset.

"Oh, what a day!"
"I'll come now."
"That's my test."

I have some pictures and words written on these cards. Choose a card and decide whether you want to say it in a high or low voice. Then do it and let me guess which one you tried to do.

Here are some words with arrows beside them. Some of the arrows point down and some point up. Slide your voice on the word. Make it go the same way the arrow goes. Listen while I do one first.

Here is a rebus story. Every time you read a picture you must make a picture of that word with your voice.

Here are some words that are easy to let our feelings out on. Can you think of some more and show us how you say them?

Yuk!	Clever!
devilish	No way!
grody	I forgot
Oh, no	That's mine
You think you're smart.	
I love my hamster.	

We'll be "listening mirrors," and after you say it, we'll tell you what we think you were feeling.

Let's read from your reading book. Use a voice picture in every sentence.

treatment approach 2
Giving Production Goals Initial Priority

Occasionally we encounter a child who has a severely altered mechanism. When these alterations are permanent, we need to teach the child to adapt to the changed state, to avoid acquiring maladaptive compensations and to deal with the interpersonal problems associated with having to adjust to being different from the peer group. We have said earlier that clinicians need to be cognizant of a child's medical history and to coordinate their intervention program with the other professionals involved in the treatment. In the case below, the importance of the child's medical history is especially apparent, since he had a tracheostomy.

The approach in therapy was one that immediately focused on production goals. In our previous discussions we have consistently stressed the importance of beginning therapy with awareness goals. In the case of a child such as Jonathan, however, where an altered mechanism necessitated the learning of very individualized new behaviors, the most pressing need was that he practice new behaviors. Learning theorists might call this approach "behavioristic." As the new behaviors were habituated, the child was then able to gain insight into the reasons why the new behaviors were effective. In cases of a radically and noticeably different mechanism the child comes to therapy aware that he is different and that he has a problem. We need quickly to demonstrate to him that he can be helped. Thus we immediately zero in on showing him what to do and how to do it.

JONATHAN: ADAPTATION TO A PERMANENT TRACHEOSTOMY TUBE

Jonathan was referred to the speech–language clinician by his third grade teacher. He had never received therapy, and had been plagued throughout his life with severe respiratory tract problems. His physician had hoped that as Jonathan grew older his trach tube could be removed. Now, however, it seemed as if Jonathan's breathing difficulties, caused by the excessive production of secretions in the tract, would necessitate the presence of a stoma for many years, since regular suction was needed in order to clear the airway. Until this point, the parents had focused primarily on his health problem, but Jonathan's disruptive behavior in class, the teacher's concern about his communication difficulties, and the physician's assessment that this condition would continue for some years led them to agree that some therapy might be valuable. During the case conference the parents were cooperative; they agreed to work with school personnel to help Jonathan cope in school. The teacher reported that she was anxious about Jonathan's health because she had never before had a child in her class with "a hole in his neck." She said that Jonathan "made strange noises" through his stoma and that she wasn't sure whether or not he did it on purpose. The speech–language clinician evaluated Jonathan, consulted with his physician and the school psychologist, and observed him in class.

It soon became clear that Jonathan was anxious and confused about his altered mechanism; like his parents, he had believed the problem was temporary. Now he was frightened by the prospect of "having the opening forever." He is embarrassed about being "freakish" and he compensated by clowning and making wheezing noises at inappropriate times in order to get his classmates to laugh. Only brief explanations had been given to him about the purpose of the opening, and no one had systematically worked with him to teach him how to coordinate using his finger to close the stoma with exhalation for speech. As a result, he intermittently tried to talk on both inhaled and exhaled air, used hyperfunctional behaviors in order to talk louder, and was inefficient at using his finger to close the stoma and reduce the noise of air leakage through it. His disruptive behavior seemed related partly to his lack of skill in using his altered mechanism and partly to a compensatory attempt to gain attention.

Jonathan needed help in all areas of vocal behavior. Since he was anxious and self-conscious about his vocal efforts, however, the therapist moved quickly to teach him production of more appropriate respiratory, phonatory, and resonance behaviors, in the hope that some initial success at controlling his voice output would help Jonathan develop confidence and would build trust in the therapeutic relationship. This initial targeting of improved production in the areas of respiration, phonation, and resonance proved helpful. Later, as Jonathan developed a sense of control and his random unpredictable phonatory behaviors decreased, the interpersonal aspects of his behavior were emphasized more and more in therapy.

GOALS

The clinician noted that Jonathan's negative vocal behavior could be grouped into four categories:

1. Respiration
   a. Lack of coordination of use of finger to close stoma and exhalation phase for voicing.
2. Phonation
   a. Attempts to phonate on inspiration.
   b. Attempts to phonate when stoma not closed during exhalation.
   c. Voluntary and involuntary stoma noise.
   d. Hyperfunctional muscle tone during phonatory activity (to compensate for inefficient use of airstream).
3. Resonance and Articulation
   a. Minimal use of supraglottal activity to amplify tone.
   b. Minimal articulatory effort.
4. Interpersonal Factors
   a. Attempts to gain attention and bolster self-esteem by maladaptive behaviors.
   b. Attempts to "cover up" embarrassment of involuntary sounds-activity by pretending it was intentional.
   c. Avoidance of talking situations or distracting "acting out" because of fears of ability to control voicing appropriately.
   d. Confusion and fear about nature of handicap, its permanence, and others' reactions to it.

Jonathan needed to achieve a better understanding of the trach tube and of his mechanism. He needed to become aware of his distracting behavior in class and of the effect this had on both himself and his classmates. The clinician felt that if she could show him more appropriate ways of coping with his differences, Jonathan would feel in control of himself and of his effect on others.

The clinician's first goal was to teach Jonathan the key concepts concerning the use of his airstream, and to help him coordinate using his finger to close the stoma with exhaling to speak. It was important to monitor closely his correct and incorrect behaviors.

Once Jonathan understood these basic concepts of *respiration*, the clinician could begin to teach him easy, relaxed *phonation* during exhalation.

The next step would be to teach Jonathan increased *resonance* in supraglottal cavities and improved *articulatory* precision.

As Jonathan became technically more adept, the clinician would begin to address his interpersonal difficulties, helping him to verbalize the effects of his contrasting patterns of behavior on himself and others. She would help him devise strategies to eliminate the "old" behaviors, and adopt more appropriate patterns of interacting.

SAMPLE STRATEGIES

Respiration   Look at these pictures. The air comes from your lungs and can go two ways. It can go straight out of your stoma or it can go up your throat, through your vocal folds, and out of your mouth or nose. When you want to use the air for talking, you must be sure to take a deep breath first. Then, as you let the air out, you cover the stoma with your finger. You must be sure the stoma is completely covered.

On these diagrams I want you to draw lines to show which way the air should go when you breathe in, when you breathe out and don't want to talk, or when you want to use the air for talking. Now tell me where your finger should be when you breathe out and don't want to talk (finger away from stoma), and when you breathe out for talking (finger on stoma).

Let's think of some rules:

Always remember to wash your hands after you go to the bathroom, after recess, or if they get very dirty.
Always talk as the air is going out.
Never talk when you are breathing in.
When you want to talk, cover the stoma with your finger.
When you need more air, open the stoma (move finger).
Make sure your finger completely covers the stoma (no leakage of air).
Keep your neck and shoulders relaxed.

Phonation   When you get ready to talk you must remember to:

Take in plenty of air.
Put your finger on the stoma before you start to breathe out.
Keep your throat relaxed.
Begin the sound gently.

Let's practice some long easy sounds, like this: /ha/. Keep it going as long as your air lasts. I'll say, "Get ready," and then, "Go." When I say, "Get ready," breathe in and have your finger near the stoma. When I say, "Go," close the stoma, breathe out, and make the easy voice as the air vibrates your folds gently. The airstream, your finger, and your vocal folds are a team—they all work together.

Now let's practice stopping and starting the sound during the time the air is coming out. We'll do it in only one breath.

ha—ha—ha (gradually increase number)
Let's see how many you can do in one breath.

Now I want you to use that same easy sound saying, "Hey." Let's practice it. This time I want you to be ready to say it whenever I stop talking. Like this:

"I saw Joe and I called to him, 'Hey.'"
"Cats like milk, but horses like . . . 'hay.' "
"I said [hey!] when the boy knocked into me. He did it again, so I said [hey!] again. Because I said [hey!] he stopped it."

Resonance and Articulation   You can use your lips to do some of the work for you. Let's practice prolonging [h m m m]. Feel the vibrations on your face. Make your lips tickle. "Hum" is a good word because the [h] helps get the air started and the [m] helps you get lots of extra sound vibrating on the bones of your face and teeth. Hear how strong and rich the sound is.

Hum mm my
Hum mm me
Hum mm moo

Keep the sound going as you link the words:

Hum—my name
Hum—my mom
Hum—me me

Let's pretend we are a strange chiming clock:

Hum—bong—bong
bong—bong—bong—bong   [different pitches]
bing—bong—ding—dong   [move lips well]

Let's alternate the chimes, I'll do one and then you do one (match pitch and length).

Interpersonal   Let's think about some reasons why people talk:

To ask for things they want.
To share their feelings or let off steam.
To make friends.
To have fun.
To show how much they know.

Can you think of some reasons why people sometimes choose *not* to talk?

When they don't know something.
When they want to listen.
When they are afraid they'll sound funny or different.
When they are embarrassed.
When they are angry or sulking.
When they don't want to.
When others make fun of them.

Nobody likes to feel embarrassed or to have their feelings hurt. Most people like to feel respected and understood. What are some things that make people feel others understand them?

When others listen to them.
When others don't name-call.
When others don't purposely hurt them, their body, their feelings, their things.
When others notice good things they do or say.

What can people do to help others understand them better?

Tell them about themselves: what they like, what they want, and how they feel.
Tell them to stop doing things they don't like.
Explain things about themselves that are special.
Stop pretending things.

Listen to this story about a boy called Jay. Jay fell off his bike and knocked out his two front teeth. They were not his baby teeth, but his permanent ones. His mother was very upset because now Jay had a big gap in his mouth. Jay was upset too, because the dentist said it would be a long time before he could fix it so that Jay had teeth in front again. He looked funny when he smiled, and when he talked some of the words sounded strange. Jay was embarrassed and tried to keep his mouth closed and not talk much at first. He felt very bad about it but tried to hide his feelings from the other children, who, of course, didn't know how he felt inside. One girl in his class was mean to him and laughed at how he looked. Instead of telling her to quit it or ignoring her until she got tired of it, Jay made a face at her. He stuck his tongue through the gap in his teeth, pulled down his lower eyelids, and screwed up his face like a monster. The girl shrieked and yelled, "The toothless monster!" Jay kept on doing monster faces a lot after that. He always got a reaction of some kind when he did it. But he often felt bad inside. Although he wished people would notice him, being called "monster mouth" all the time didn't help him feel respected. But he kept doing it anyway.

1. What did Jay do to deal with his sadness about the way he looked?
2. What did he do about helping others understand his problem?
3. Did it work?
4. What else could he have done?
5. What would have made him feel better?

Let's redo this story. Let's pretend Jay decided to choose a different way of handling his problem. He could have done some of these things:

1. Tell the teacher about his problem and ask her to tell the class.
2. Explain to his friends that he felt bad about his teeth but was trying not to worry about it too much.
3. Decide not to let other people make him do stupid things.
4. Decide "sticks and stones can break my bones but words can never hurt me."
5. Tell the girl that he had had an accident and it surprised him that she felt like laughing.
6. Ignore the girl (which was what she wouldn't want).

Remember, the way people choose to handle things that happen to them affects how others understand them, and how others act toward them. It also affects how they feel about themselves: if they are hiding their real feelings, or if they can explain. If they can explain their feelings, then others often forget it more quickly.

Some ways that people can explain about things are to say:

1. "Look, this is different but this is how I handle it—it's no big deal."
2. "Would you like me to tell you what happened? It is interesting to learn about things like this."
3. "I know you are giggling because you're embarrassed, but that's okay, I understand your feelings. I used to feel embarrassed about it too."

What other ways are there to cope? Think of what would work best for someone like Jay.

1. Walk away.
2. Look someone right in the eyes and say, "That's a mean thing to do."
3. Talk over the problem with an adult.

I'm asking you for some suggestions because I know you've had a lot of experience in coping with the problem of having the trach tube in your neck. What have been the hardest things for you to deal with? What has worked best for you? What has not worked well? Can you help me make up a list of suggestions for other children who have this problem?

LEARNING NEW COMPENSATORY BEHAVIORS

1. I can demonstrate (at will) the "old" way of using voice-distracting associated behaviors.
2. I can describe how it looks and sounds to others.
3. I can describe how it feels to me.
4. I can describe why it doesn't work well for me.
5. I can demonstrate new ways of talking
   a. with a model, cues, and instructions.
   b. with cues and instructions.
   c. with instructions.
   d. at will some of the time.
   e. at will most of the time.
6. I can eliminate distracting associated behaviors
   a. with a model, cues, and instructions.
   b. with cues and instructions.
   c. with instructions.
   d. sometimes.
   e. often.
   f. always.
7. I can explain the rules of good voice use.
8. I can use my new voice/patterns of behavior
   a. when I'm in the speech room.
   b. when I'm in the classroom.
   c. when I'm on the playground.
   d. when I'm at home.
   e. when I'm calm and think about it.
   f. when I'm excited.
   g. when I want to (usually).
   h. when I want to (always).
9. I can explain the effects of the old and new patterns
   a. on myself.
   b. on others.
   c. on getting what I want.
10. I can analyze a situation (and change what I'm doing)
    a. after it has happened.
    b. while it is occurring.
    c. before it occurs.

treatment approach 3
Associating Semantic Dictates with Respiratory Control

With all children, but with older children especially, it is usually efficacious to present a logical rationale that helps them understand the precise reasons for the needed changes in their behavior. This is particularly so in cases where there are a number of subtle differences that together contribute to an unusual pattern of voice use. At such times, motivation can be enhanced by associating, or making explicit connections, between relevant aspects of the behavior and specific effects on the listener. In many cases we can tie together a group of important supporting behaviors and show their effect on the message that is transmitted. A listener's ability to comprehend what is said is a key concept to which children can readily relate. When we begin with an explicit need (i.e., helping listeners understand our thoughts) and then proceed to demonstrate how what we do helps us achieve this, the therapy seems more relevant to the child. In the case study that follows, the clinician could have merely told the child she needed to improve her breathing. However, the clinician decided to approach treatment by creating an awareness of the way the durational characteristics of the voice pattern shape the way others perceive the meaning. Once this was achieved, the child developed considerable interest in shaping respiratory behavior in response to semantic demands.

DONNA: UNEVEN VOICING RELATED TO RESPIRATORY INEFFICIENCY

Donna was 10 years 7 months and was enrolled in the fifth grade. She had received speech therapy for misarticulation of sibilant consonants and had made good progress with her sounds. Her voice pattern seemed inappropriate, however; it was characterized by poor phrasing and erratic rate changes that seemed unrelated to the meaning. The clinician hypothesized that the inappropriate timing of pauses and the resultant lack of smoothness in voicing during connected utterances were related to inconsistent respiratory support during connected speech. Donna could sustain vowel sounds for approximately 12 seconds on repeated trials. During her reading of a paragraph, however, the clinician noted that phrases were usually approximately two to three words in length and that volume consistently faded at the ends of sentences. Her spontaneous speech sounded sporadic and jerky, and the listener was left with an impression of a pattern of voicing that seemed disorganized. Diadokokinetic rates were within normal limits, and there seemed to be no indication of neurological involvement.

GOALS

Donna was an excellent reader. The clinician designed a therapy to capitalize on this skill and also to coordinate with classroom activities. Her classroom teacher was cooperative and agreed to help Donna practice her new behaviors daily in the course of classroom activities. She also gave Donna opportunities to share with others in her reading group some of the new information she learned in therapy.

The clinician made a list of Donna's negative vocal behaviors:

1. Insufficient depth of initial inhalation.
2. Inadequate "chunking" of exhaled air during connected utterance.
3. Inappropriate use of replenishing breaths.
4. Frequent and inappropriate pauses between word groups.
5. Pauses not used to reflect meaning.
6. Inappropriate variation of rate.
7. Voice faded at end of sentences.

The three general targets during the treatment would be for Donna to verbalize the relationship between durational changes and the transmission of meaning and feeling; to demonstrate appropriate breath support for connected utterances; and to use appropriate durational patterns during voice production. It was important that Donna first learn to identify appropriate and inappropriate durational changes during reading and connected speech, so that she could then use breathing and voicing patterns to convey meaning and feeling more effectively.

SAMPLE STRATEGIES

Let's look at this sentence and find ways that the words can be grouped to suggest different meanings: "Oh George Henry said Mary is not interested." Let's punctuate it.

"Oh, George Henry said Mary is not interested."
"Oh George, Henry said Mary is not interested."
"Oh George Henry," said Mary, "is not interested."

Where we choose to pause changes the meaning.

Sometimes we pause before and after a parenthetical statement, one that is not absolutely essential to the sentence but adds extra information. Make slashes to separate the parenthetical parts of the sentences from the rest of the sentence. After you have marked the page, we'll put my transparency over it and see if our slashes agree.

1. Mary / she is Bill's cousin / was bridesmaid at the wedding.
2. Uncle Dick / who must be at least one hundred years old / is a millionaire.
3. On Tuesday I'll know if I passed the test and hardest one I've ever done.
4. I own my very own horse a bay mare with a white blaze.
5. Last winter Dad and I went ice fishing something I'd certainly like to do again.
6. One day Mom and I visited an art gallery not too far from here in a quaint old building.
7. Betty Josephine and Deborah will live in Washington one of the most interesting cities in the USA.
8. By Tuesday June 30th I'll be told if I'm going to Chicago the windy city capital of Illinois.
9. Glenda an excellent typist loves to ski and is very good at it.
10. Allen and Paul both tall for their age are friends of mine but not really close friends.

As well as using pauses to show the meaning, we sometimes say some parts of sentences faster or slower than other parts. Sometimes we say the essential part of the sentence slower to be sure the listener gets the main idea, then the extra information is said faster because it's not as critical.

Let's take two colored magic markers and underline parts of the sentences above. Use one color for important parts to be said slowly and the other color for extra pieces of information that can be said more quickly.

The meaning of the words also helps us decide whether to say them fast or slow. Underline word groups in the following sentences that could be lengthened or shortened to suggest the meaning.

1. Jill is as slow as molasses.
2. My new Trans Am can go ninety miles an hour.
3. The farmer plodded behind his oxen.
4. Mom said that getting my brother to do the dishes is like pulling teeth.
5. "I'll get you for that," said the boy, suddenly darting across the room.
6. The car sped by, and then all was still.

Feelings also can be expressed by using pauses and rate changes. Think of different feelings for these words. Say how a rate change, a pause, or both could change the feeling.

"Oh it's you is it."
"No I won't and you can't make me."
"I wonder if she knows we saw her do it."

Listen while I read these sentences from your reading book, and you tell me where I used pauses and rate changes and why I said them the way I did. How could I have said them differently?

Sometimes groups of words have to be said together to make the meaning clear. Take, for example, "Rae, she is my best friend, is very pretty." There are five words together that must be said in one breath. Let's practice taking in plenty of air and counting to five so we get used to making the breath last for five words. Don't run out before the end. Now say a b c d e in one breath. Now, "She is my best friend." Do you think you could stretch the breath long enough to say, "Rae, she is my best friend"?

Sometimes we can add to our air supply as we go along. We take a deep breath to start and then little "catch breaths" at pauses. Let's try taking a "catch breath" after "friend" and then finishing the whole sentence. Remember "catch breaths" must be quick so that the smoothness of the sentence is not interrupted. Mark places for "catch breaths" in the sentences in this book.

Smoothness, also, is very important, especially if a mood or feeling would be changed if our speech was jerky. Practice smooth pauses and phrases in the sentences that follow. Mark the pauses first.

1. Slowly and silently the river flows to the deep blue ocean.
2. Without a sound or even a flicker of recognition the man glided by them all.
3. In her dreams she floated gently away up up and over the tree tops to be gone forever from the earth.

Quotation marks show us the direct speech, and after it we must pause long enough so the listener knows where the quote ends. Sometimes it helps to change our voice after a pause to signal to the listener that a different person is speaking. Mark the breath pauses in the passage in this book and practice reading the paragraph so the meaning and feeling comes through clearly. Let's record your reading and play it back.

Did you take in plenty of air to start?
Did you make the air last for the whole group of words?
Did you let your voice fade at the end of words?
Did you pause after important thoughts so the listener could digest the meaning?
Did you use enough catch breaths?
Did you use catch breaths in the right places?
Did you use catch breaths without interrupting the flow?
Did you vary the rate?
Did you sound jerky at any time?

It is harder to remember to ration our air when we are talking instead of reading from a page. Let's gradually increase the number of words per breath as we take turns saying the following, adding only words that start with /b/.

"I went on a picnic."
"I went on a picnic and I took bread."
"I went on a picnic and I took bread, butter, etc."

Now I want you to think about using your air supply correctly as you explain some things to me. Pause and take catch breaths as you need them.

1. Name all the children in your class.
2. Name all the families who live on your street.
3. Name all the months of the year, making one parenthetical statement about each, e.g., "The first month is January—usually it's snowy. The second month is February—Valetine's Day comes then." And so on.
4. Describe the plan of your house, going through each room in order and stating one piece of information about each. Remember the breath! For example, "You go into the hall, and the coats are kept there. Then there's the kitchen, and we cook in there." And so on.
5. I'll give you some riddles and jokes. Then you tell them to me, making sure the pauses illustrate the punchlines. For homework, practice a new joke to tell me next time.

treatment approach 4
Treating Hypernasality

Because of the complex pattern of voicing during speech production, children with resonance problems are often unaware of the specific aspect of their behavior that warrants attention. When we deal with a hypernasal child who has a functioning velopharyngeal mechanism, it is important to teach the behavioral characteristics of orality and nasality. Andrews et al. (1984) have suggested that this can be accomplished during the awareness phase of a treatment program by grouping all the speech sounds into two basic categories. In this way, commonalities in the observable cues and feeling states can be related to the auditorially perceived resonance patterns. It is also important to teach the associations between the auditory targets and the obligatory modifications in the vocal tract. Self-regulatory speech, in the form of concrete verbal descriptions, should be modeled for the child. These verbal patterns become an integral part of self-monitoring and self-evaluation in the production phase of therapy.

The oral–nasal dichotomy in voice resonance is difficult for a child to perceive, since in running speech the modifications of the vocal tract occur in rapid succession and the resonance characteristics are only part of the fleeting auditory events. Before any awareness of the appropriate sequencing and interplay of oral and nasal voicing can be learned, the behaviors have to be reduced to static states. Later, the transitions between the two states can be taught in slow motion and then, gradually, production of dynamic movements and sequences can be habituated.

The case study that follows illustrates ways of teaching a child the basic distinction between orality and nasality during the awareness phase. During the production phase, ideas from sources such as Hanley and Thurman, 1970; Fisher, 1975; Cooper, 1973; and Moncur and Brackett, 1974 are verbalized in language consistent with the child's developmental stage. Some techniques are described as "tricks" the child can use to facilitate oral resonance. Since some children who have, or have had, velopharyngeal valving difficulties use hard glottal attacks (Wilson, 1979), /h/ was frequently used to precede vowel sounds during early production tasks.

VIRGINIA: HYPERNASALITY THAT REMAINED AFTER AN ADEQUATE VELOPHARYNGEAL CLOSURE MECHANISM WAS ACHIEVED

Virginia was 7 years 11 months, was in the second grade, and was above average in her classroom work. She had been treated at a university medical center for a congenitally short palate. A year earlier she had undergone pharyngeal flap surgery. When she was referred to her school's speech–language clinician, the report indicated that she had had two years of articulation therapy, and it was recommended that she now receive therapy at school, while continuing regular six-monthly evaluations by the Medical Center Cleft Palate team. Testing revealed that Virginia produced all speech sounds correctly with the exception of the /r/ phoneme, which was inconsistently correct in connected speech. Her voice quality, however, was still hypernasal in connected utterances, although she could produce sustained vowels with appropriate resonance when cued.

The clinician decided that she would continue therapy to habituate correct production of the /r/ phoneme in reading and spontaneous speech. In addition, she planned a treatment approach that would capitalize on Virginia's academic strengths. Since Virginia could read and knew the letters of the alphabet and the sounds those symbols represented, the sounds were divided into two categories: the sounds made with the mouth voice and the sounds made with the nose voice. Once the child learned to categorize the nasal sounds (e.g., m n ŋ) contrasted with vowels and all nonnasal consonants, the clinician would then teach the specific behavioral characteristics of the two categories. For example, "How do you know it is a sound where the voice comes out of my nose or mouth?"

Mouth Sounds

1. The mouth is open.
2. The air comes out of my mouth.
3. It is a vowel, and all vowels come out of my mouth.
4. I can make it, even if I hold my nose.

Nose Sounds

1. I can feel the vibrations in my nose.
2. My mouth is closed or blocked in some way.
3. I can't make it if I hold my nose.
4. Some air comes out of my nose.

Since Virginia needed to learn to associate proprioceptive feedback from the velopharyngeal area with the auditory characteristics of orality and nasality, the therapist decided to use the concept of a "door" at the back of her mouth. When the door is open, the air comes out of the nose. When it is closed, the air comes out of the mouth. The See-Scape, a piece of equipment that provides visual feedback when air is emitted nasally, would be used to operationalize this concept. The See-Scape is available from C.C. Publications, P.O. Box 23699, Tigard, OR 97223. A tube is placed in the nostril, and when nasal emission occurs, a small balloon rises in a plastic tube on the table in front of the child. When working with Virginia, the clinician decided to describe the velopharyngeal closure mechanism as similar to a door. However, in order to emphasize the part played by the pharyngeal muscles in closing the apertures on either side of the pharyngeal flap, the clinician would also use a drawstring and show how an opening can be closed when the drawstring is tightened. The clinician would link these demonstrations of tightening to the feeling at the back of the throat when the muscles help close off the opening (or door).

GOALS

Because Virginia used a hypernasal voice in connected speech, she needed to learn to produce appropriate oral–nasal resonance in simple, self-generated sentences. The clinician would achieve this by first making Virginia aware of the two categories of sounds: sounds made with the "mouth voice" and sounds made with the "nose voice." She would work with Virginia to verbalize the connection between pharyngeal movement, air emission, and type of voicing, and to identify sound sequences coded as "mouth, mouth, nose" or "door closed, door closed, door open." Virginia would then be ready to learn production of sequences of all oral sounds (syllables, words, sentences); production of transitions between oral–nasal and nasal–oral sound sequences in "slow motion"; and production and evaluations of strategies used (e.g., "I opened the door too soon/too late"). Virginia would then be able to verbalize and apply "rules" to increase perception of orality.

SAMPLE STRATEGIES

Let's work with these cards. I'll say the sound of the letter printed on each card. If the sound comes out of my nose, then it's a "nose sound" and it goes in this box. Remember, m, n, and ŋ are the only nose sounds. All of the other consonants and all of the vowels are "mouth sounds" and they go in the other "mouth box." Let's begin. I'll pick up the card and say the sound. Then you decide if it's a nose or a mouth sound and put the card in the correct box.

Here is a picture of a side view of the top half of the human body and head. It looks as if the poor person has been sliced in half! We can see from this drawing how air travels from the lungs, through the vocal folds into the pharynx, and then goes out of either the mouth *or* the nose. Trace with your finger the direction of the airstream as I make some different mouth and nose sounds.

Remember we can use muscles at the back of our mouth (in the pharynx) to close off the door to the nose. When I make a mouth sound such as /a/ I close the door to the nose and send the air and the sound out of my mouth. When I say /m/, though, it is a nose sound, so I leave the door open. Describe the next sound I make and tell me whether the door is open or closed. (Clinician says ŋ; child says, "It's a nose sound, so the door is open.")

Now I'm going to say a series of sounds slowly (e.g., /p/, /æ/, /m/). They are mouth sound, mouth sound, nose sound, or, if I describe the position of the door I could say, "door closed, door closed, door opened." Are you ready to try one?

Sometimes we make mistakes and send mouth sounds out the nose because we forget to close the door properly. If air leaks out of the nose during a mouth sound, that's a sure sign that we forgot to close the door tightly enough. Today I brought the See-Scape. I'll say a vowel and you watch to see if any air comes out of my nose. The balloon will move up if it does. Tell me how you know that was a correct mouth sound? Did the balloon stay down? (If the See-Scape is not available, simpler materials, such as feathers and Kleenex can be used to illustrate direction of air emission [Wilson, 1979].)

Now you make some mouth sounds. Watch and listen and say them after me. We'll make them long (vowels and continuant consonants). Feel the door squeezing shut at the back of your mouth. Feel the sound vibrating on your teeth and in your mouth. Be sure no air comes out of your nose. We'll check with the See-Scape if we think we hear some air coming through the nose.

Now let's try some strings of sounds in slow motion. We'll use both mouth and nose sounds this time. (Clinician contrasts and produces the sounds and the child imitates.)

	(h)	æ	m
Prolong the sound	(h)	ɪ	m
Feel the vibrations	(h)	eɪ	ŋ

Here are some more strings of sounds to try. We'll read from the letters printed on these cards. These are all mouth sounds, so I've drawn a mouth on the card. I'll do each one and then hand the card to you and you have a turn. (Child imitates CV's and is encouraged to describe the characteristics and to self-monitor. Visual, auditory, and graphic cues are provided throughout.)

Now we'll play a card game. We'll take turns taking a card. If we say the sounds correctly we keep the card. We'll see who ends up with the biggest pile. (Child produces CVV syllables and then CVC syllables, first with a model and cues and then spontaneously.)

Here's a word list:

book	baby
take	hot
set	fat
say	doll
lady	bug

Let's say these words in a sentence: "I have a _____."

Now pick an object from this secret box and say its name. (Box can include a toy horse, a toy truck, a toy car, a doll, a ruler, a vase, a shoelace, a book, a feather, a leaf, a piece of chalk, etc.)

Here are some pictures of words with all mouth sounds. Make a sentence, for example, "At the store I bought _____," with the words:

eggs	peppers	bread
juice	radishes	butter
apples	peaches	chocolate
pears	cottage cheese	

Use your lips, and open your mouth well to send *all* of the mouth sounds through your mouth. Say these sentences after me. Then we'll play them back and you tell me any words that sounded as if they came out of your nose.

1. Peter picked peppers quickly.
2. Charley Chadwick liked the toys.
3. Here, Harry, that's a good dog.
4. There are pretty leaves in October.
5. March is cold and gray.
6. The lovely doll has clothes to wear.

I'll say some sounds slowly, and you say whether they are mouth or nose sounds. Then we'll switch, and you say them in slow motion. Remember to separate each sound.

(oral–oral–nasal):

same	hem	ham	pan
fang	song	Sam	fame

(nasal–oral–oral):

meat	nose	news
moat	neat	knees

(oral–nasal–oral):

Amy	ant	end
any	ink	eeny

Now instead of separating all the sounds in the words, let's make the vowel sound long and end with a short nose sound.

(prolonged vowel–pause–short nasal):

Ben	hem
sang	pan
fine	Tim

Now let's make a short nose sound to start and then stretch out the rest of the mouth sounds in these words:

Maze	niece	Noddy
Neal	mess	meaty

Color all the nose sounds red in the words on these cards. Then say them after the phrase, "I have a." Don't open the door before you get to the red letter.

I have a balloon.
I have a pen.
I have a song.
I have a ring.
I have a ham.

Did you send all the sounds through your mouth except the red letters? Let's play the tape recording of those sentences and listen. Circle any words you think you could do better.

Let's practice these pairs of words:

hat	ham
fad	fan
seed	seen
oat	own

Did you open the door too soon?

Me	he
meal	seal

neat   feet
no   toe

Did you close the door too late?

Can we think of some tricks to help us?

1. Find the nose sounds before starting to read the words.
2. Make the nose sounds shorter.
3. Make the vowel sounds longer.
4. Make sure the door doesn't open too soon or close too late.
5. Feel a "squeeze" as the door closes well.
6. Open mouth well.
7. Use lips and tongue well.
8. Read slowly at first.

Read these sentences and then we'll play them back and see if you used some of those tricks.

I need a pen.
I need a gong.
I need a dress.
I need a book.
I need a pear.
I need a fan.

Now you think of some ways to finish this sentence. Say the whole sentence. We'll take turns.

"I know _____."

Here are some things in a bag. Put your hand into the bag and feel one of them. Then describe how it feels.

"It feels small and has wheels."
"It feels thin and long."

treatment approach 5
Improving Supraglottal Behaviors

We have noted that all children do not always need to exhibit optimal behaviors in every area relating to voice production. Adequate skills and the absence of maladaptive behavior are realistic in most instances. When there are limitations in one area, however, the overall vocal effect can usually be improved by enhancing activity in other areas. If, for example, a child has a permanent structural constraint in the phonatory system, improved respiratory activity, better resonance, and more precise articulation may help the child compensate for the laryngeal defect. In fact, teaching the child to use other parts of the vocal mechanism optimally may also be a way of preventing the development of less appropriate compensatory behaviors.

In our next case study we describe a treatment plan devised to optimize supraglottal activity. During our discussion we shall be using the term *forward tone focus*, meaning a concentration of attention, energy, and activity in the front of the oral cavity. With young children it may sometimes be helpful to contrast "front of the mouth" voice with "neck voice." We can then link the sound and the feel of the voice to specific anatomical sites.

ROBBIE: PHONATORY BEHAVIOR LIMITED BY STRUCTURAL DEVIATION

Robbie, age 10 years, had a paralyzed right vocal fold, fixed in the abducted position. He had previously been enrolled in therapy in another school district and had worked on techniques to encourage compensatory movement of the left vocal fold during adduction. Strategies, such as pushing while phonating, in order to achieve closure had been used with some success. Robbie's vocal quality during cued and prolonged phonation of vowels was appropriate, but in his connected speech there was reduced loudness and considerable breathiness. Robbie's voice was weak and did not carry well, and he had difficulty being heard in noisy environments. It was noted that while Robbie did not exhibit any negative behaviors in terms of resonance, neither was he maximizing his full potential in that area in order to compensate for his reduced phonatory power. Robbie demonstrated appropriate respiratory behavior and had hearing sensitivity that was within the normal range bilaterally. His interpersonal skills also seemed to be within normal limits.

The speech–language clinician hypothesized that Robbie needed to develop more optimal use of resonance and improved mouth-opening and articulatory precision in order to enhance his vocal effectiveness. She felt that Robbie needed to improve the carrying power of his voice, particularly during projected speech. She decided that she would continue to work on improving Robbie's phonatory adjustment, moving systematically from sustained vowels, CV's and VC's and CVC's (voiced continuant consonants) to words, phrases and sentences. However, she decided to add some new objectives.

GOALS

Robbie's negative vocal behaviors included:

1. Reduced loudness in connected speech.
2. Breathy quality.
3. Lack of projection.

The clinician's target areas during treatment would be to improve Robbie's use of resonance to compensate for weak and breathy laryngeal tone during connected utterances and conversational levels, and to improve his vocal power during projected speech. She established six goals for the therapy:

1. Identification of techniques to enhance audibility during connected speech
2. Increased mouth opening
3. Improved forward tone focus
4. Increased durations of vowels and voiced continuants
5. Increased reverberation in supraglottal cavities
6. Increased precision of articulatory contacts to maximize intelligibility

SAMPLE STRATEGIES

Listen to the following sounds. Some carry more sound than do others. In fact, some (like f, θ, and s) are just breath. The sounds that carry the vibrations (like v, ð, and z) can help us get more power in our voice if we make the most of them. Listen while I prolong some sound-carrying consonants. Feel the vibrations on the front of my face as I make them [m n v ð z ʒ]. These consonants can help put more "oomph" and "carrying power" in our voice. Let's look at this list of consonants, and we'll circle all the ones that are the best "sound carriers."

The vowel sounds can be a great help to us also, since all vowel sounds are voiced. When we open our mouths well and linger on the vowels, we can help to make our voice carry better. You underline the vowel sounds in the following words, and then I'll say each word, making sure I open my mouth well so that the sound waves vibrate on the bones of my face. Which ones sounded richest? Which ones sounded muffled? Why? Sometimes people say vowels too far back in their mouth. The back of the mouth is soft tissue. The front of the mouth has more hard surfaces. Listen while I make the /a/ sound in the back of my mouth. Now listen while I throw the sound /a/ forward so that it "rings" against the hard roof of my mouth and my teeth. Listen, too, while I say it just in my throat, with not much mouth opening for it to come out. The vowel had a muffled, "deadened" sound with no "ring" to it.

Using "sound carrying" consonants well and opening the mouth and throwing the sound forward is sometimes called "focusing" the voice in the front of the mouth. A lot of our voice energy is then at the front. I will say some words, and you tell me whether the voice was a "front of the mouth" voice or a "muffled" voice (e.g., too much in the throat only or stuck in the back of the mouth).

Bobby	arrive
little	brave
lazy	pleasure
vase	range

When we take photographs, the picture is sometimes blurred if our camera is not focused well. Our voices can sound blurred and fuzzy too if we don't focus the voice forward in our mouth. Tell me which of these words are focused forward and which are not. (*Hint*: Watch to see if I am using my lips and tongue well to help the focus.)

Tell me what I did wrong, and I'll do it again; for example: Was my mouth open enough? Did I make the bones of my face vibrate? Did I use the sound-carrying consonants?

Let's look at the words that follow and decide some things we could do to help focus them forward. Underline the sounds that could help.

able	Maisie	easy
tunnel	dime	revise

Some ways we can focus forward on the above words are:

1. Prolong the vowels.
2. Prolong the voiced continuants.
3. Use lips and tongue well.
4 Open mouth well.

I'll use some of the hints, and you guess which ones I'm using. (Chant letters of the alphabet prolonging vowels; count using emphasized mouth opening; say "Bob, Bill, Ben, Boris" using vigorous lip movement; say "running, jumping, going, coming" prolonging voiced continuants, etc.)

In the words that follow, underline the vowels in red and the helpful sound-carrying consonants in green and then say the words, prolonging the red and green sounds.

Come on	Mommy	lizards
go now	lazy boys	ending

Pretend you are chanting in a big cathedral. Throw the sound to hit the back walls of the church.

Sing a new song.
Away in a manger.
Monday morning.
Have some more honey.

Let's listen to a tape recording and note which words sounded strongest. Why? Redo the ones that could be made to sound better.

I am going to tell you a short story. Every time I pause I want you to say, "*Tell me more*" or "*maybe*" or "*never mind*." (Make sure your voice is well focused and that the "sound carriers" vibrate.)

M is a good sound carrier because the bones of the face (and nose) vibrate when *m* is prolonged with forward tone focus. Let's make up as many words as we can with *m* in them. Make sentences with those words (e.g., Mary Manning made Mervyn mad). Let's play a game where we add *m* words, e.g., May motored to Maine and met _____ (Mabel; Mabel and Mary; Mabel, Mary and Millie; Mabel, Mary, Millie and Mort; Mabel, Mary,

Millie, Mort and Melissa; etc.) Think of all the foods (cities, games, movies, etc.) that have *m* in their names.

A good way to practice prolonging the vowel sounds in words is to play a rhyming game. (Make sure you prolong the vowels.) For example, "I'm thinking of a word that rhymes with 'tree.'" Take turns rhyming until you run out of ideas.

Sea rhymes with tree.
Bee rhymes with tree.

Now that you are really good at focusing the sounds, let's make the rhyming game harder.

Person 1: I'm thinking of a word that rhymes with hole.
      2: Is it a horse's baby?
      1: No, it's not foal.
      2: Is it something you eat cereal in?
      1: No, it's not bowl.
      2: Is it a small animal?
      1: No, it's not mole.

Mark all the sound-carrying consonants in the following readings. Hum *m* before you start each line to get your tone focus. Whenever your tone focus slips as you are reading, hum m again to get it back.

In this poem there are lots of sounds at the ends of words that can be prolonged. Circle them. Now chant the poem. When you are good at chanting it, then try to say it in a normal conversational way, keeping the tone focused forward throughout.

treatment approach 6
Modifying Pitch

In this plan we focus on some strategies that are useful for children with pitch problems. When a child exhibits an habitual pitch that is inappropriate for age and sex, the clinician's first task is to obtain information concerning the condition of the folds. Congenital anatomical constraints, such as the presence of a laryngeal web, can limit a child's laryngeal function. Additive lesions, such as nodules, also may result in a pitch level that is inappropriate. If there is no anatomical constraint present, and if there is no medical condition that causes swelling of the folds (consistently or intermittently), it may be that the child has habituated a pattern of misuse. Wilson (1979) has noted that faulty learning may be a factor in the inappropriate use of pitch. It is important for the clinician to consider relevant case history information carefully, including the possible influence of vocal models in the child's family and peer group.

Before treatment was planned for Cynthia, the child to be discussed in the case history that follows, the clinician ascertained that the problem was functional and that no laryngeal pathology existed.

CYNTHIA: A CONVERSATIONAL PITCH RANGE THAT WAS INAPPROPRIATELY LOW

Cynthia, age 10 years, was referred by her fifth grade teacher because her voice sounded "too low and gravelly for a female student of her age." Reports indicated that Cynthia had hearing thresholds in the normal range bilaterally and had no indications of laryngeal pathology or allergic or infectious conditions. Cynthia's mother reported that the girl had always been a tomboy, who had tried to emulate her older brothers in the past but now became upset when she was mistaken for her brothers on the telephone. Cynthia told the speech clinician that she would like to sound "more like a girl" at times when she was not trying to "clown around" with the boys. She said, "I used to try to talk in a gruff voice, but now I don't seem to be able to talk any other way, even when I want to."

Cynthia seemed to be at a stage in her life where she wanted to increase her vocal options. After years of trying to be "one of the boys," she had habituated a pattern of pitch use that now made her feel different from the girls in her peer group. She had habituated a conversational pitch range that was limited to the lower end of her available pitch range. Vocal testing revealed that she spoke at a pitch level that was so close to her basal pitch level that she frequently lapsed into vocal fry. She used few rising intonation patterns, with the result that her variability was minimal. Most often, when her pitch changed, the movement was downward. The perception of her voice as "gravelly" was related to the frequent episodes of vocal fry during connected speech. Cynthia was stimulable and could produce more appropriate pitch levels when she was cued. The most useful cues seemed to be words and phrases that evoked an upward movement of the voice. The clinician decided to present visual cues (diagrams and patterns depicting the desired range of pitches and sequences of inflections) and words and phrases whose meaning evoked rising inflections. Cynthia was quick to see the relationship between meaning and voice patterns. The selection of materials for Cynthia seemed a critical component of the treatment plan. It made sense to her to explore different methods of varying her voice in response to specific word images.

GOALS

Cynthia's negative vocal behaviors included:

1. An inappropriately low habitual pitch level.
2. Restricted conversational pitch range.
3. Limited use of upward inflections.
4. Frequent episodes of vocal fry.

The clinician decided to target in on developing in Cynthia an appropriate habitual pitch level and an increased use of inflection. Her goals were:

1. To orient the child to the area to be addressed in therapy.
2. To develop concepts that are basic to learning in the area.
3. To elicit the target behaviors
   a. in isolation.
   b. in simple linguistic contexts.

c. in complex linguistic contexts.
4. To describe the child's responses in terms meaningful to the child:
   a. how.
   b. why.
   c. when.
5. To provide techniques to shape consistency and accuracy of responses:
   a. imitation.
   b. extensive cuing.
   c. minimal cuing.
6. To encourage the child's self-monitoring of responses.

SAMPLE STRATEGIES

Think of your voice as similar to a multilevel house or apartment building (show diagram). The basement voice sounds like this (demonstrate and explain vocal fry). The first floor contains a number of different and useful clear pitches, as does the second floor. Then there is an attic, which contains high notes that we use mainly for singing . When we talk, the best notes to use are the ones from the first and second floors. The voice moves around most effectively in the main part of the house. Your conversational pitch range is located in the "main living areas" of the house. If you begin to talk on a note that is too low, it's far too easy to slide on down into the basement. But if you try to aim for a level somewhere in between the first and second floors, you'll find that you can vary your voice quite comfortably. It would be helpful if you'd try to keep your voice away from the basement. On this diagram mark an X every time you hear me use my "basement" voice. Describe the way it sounds.

Now take the pencil and mark the X's in the "living areas" of the house. Mark the X on the first floor when I use a low, clear pitch and on the second floor when I use a higher, clear pitch. Now draw arrows down and up between floors as I slide my voice in different directions.

There's a word that is sometimes used to describe words that sound like the idea they are expressing. That word is *onomatopoeia*. For example, "squeak" can be said so it reminds one of a "squeak." "Shush" is another—it makes one feel like being quiet. Here are some words that make us think of high and low sounds:

shriek–growl
eek–groan
shrill–grovel
creak–thump
meow–moo

Below is a list of words. Which of these would be easy to say in a high-pitched voice? Which would be hard to say in a high voice? Thinking of the meaning of the words helps us decide.

shriek	bump
whine	crash
valley	kite
thin	cave
down	fly
zip	peak
eek	sad
bang	glum
tip	glee

Sometimes the sounds the letters make (especially the vowels) suggest the pitch level. For example [i] vowels in words are easier to say in a high voice that are [ʌ] vowels. Some of the letters in words can be helpful as we practice different pitches.

Sometimes what the words stand for suggests something high in space; for example, "peak" is easier to say on a high note than "cave."

A movement or action suggested by a word, for example, "fly," or "zip," sometimes helps the voice move in the same direction. Of course you can "zip" a "zipper" in two directions. Listen to me say the word and tell me which direction I am "zipping." Feelings can also suggest the way a voice can move. Generally, happy excited feelings are said with an upward movement of the voice; unpleasant feelings (and the words that express them) tend to drag the pitch of the voice down. Consider "sad," "excited," "laugh" and "cry."

Not only single words but also groups of words can be said at different pitches. Look at the sentences that follow and start them in the voice you normally use, and then let your voice go up as the meaning suggests.

The rainbow in the sky.
The chairlift on the top.
The balloon floated up.
The bird soared away.
The plane flew off.
The hawk circling.
That girl stand up.
The arrow shot up.
Oh, a surprise.
Gee whiz.
Oh gosh.
The fish jumped.

Oh no.
The siren shrieked.

Now let's reverse some of these sentences. We'll start off with the high part and then say the low part. But start high enough so that the low part is low and clear. Let's not dip down into the basement if at all possible.

In the sky, the rainbow.
On the top, the chairlift.
A surprise, oh!
Circling, the hawk.
Stand up, that girl.

This time I'll ask you a question, and you reply with just the high part of each of our word groups.

Where is the rainbow?
Where is the chairlift?
Where is the hawk?
What did the girl do?

Here are some words and phrases that have "up" feelings. See if you can use pitch changes to show those feelings.

"Oh boy"
"Right on"
"Yes, sir"
"Happy day"
"Good morning"
"Fun time"

When we are uncertain or questioning, we let a word drift or slide upwards: Who? What? When? Sometimes the same words can be said with different meanings depending on the direction of our voice. Read the following words that can sound as if we mean "Yes, for sure" or "Yes, maybe." As you say them, I'll try to describe what I think you mean.

yes	me	Dad	you're kidding
good	mine	food	for sure
tomorrow	yours	dirty	right now

Here is a short reading passage. Underline any words or phrases that may be helpful in varying your pitch. A good rule is to remember that new ideas often need a new pitch.

The siren shrieked, and the girls exclaimed, "Yippee." The adults laughed at the young people's joy. The air raid was over. Mary looked up in the sky. Some white clouds floated by. The bombers were gone. "Oh, happy day," she said. All over London people came up out of bomb shelters, happy that the danger was past.

Now we'll replay our tape recording of your reading. Use this red pencil and mark the places where your voice goes into the basement (fry). Circle words that you think you can do better when we try it again.

treatment approach 7
Using a Hero and
an Antihero

It is traditional in voice therapy to focus on individual maladaptive behaviors in a sequential fashion. This case study, however, illustrates a Gestalt approach. In a Gestalt approach, desirable and undersirable behaviors are presented as sets associated with characters in a narrative framework; there is a storybook hero and an antihero. The child's identification with the hero character enhances his motivation to change his abusive practices and negative behaviors. During the General Awareness phase of therapy, the child gains an understanding of the effects of certain patterns of behavior first and then is more willing to focus on individual perceptual attributes. The meaningful context facilitates discussion of intangible vocal events. This use of a meaningful context is one way of organizing a program so that it meshes with a young child's developmental stage.

To begin our discussion we shall look at a treatment approach that was designed for Freddie, a kindergarten child who was demonstrating a pattern of excessive muscular tension but who did not exhibit any tissue change in the larynx. Freddie is a dramatic example of a hyperfunctional voice user, yet many of his negative behaviors are typical of vocal abusers. The severity of his problem was somewhat unusual for his age.

Some young children gain attention from their peers because of their ability to produce atypical voice patterns. Freddie's entry behaviors included maladaptive voice use as a way to seek and hold attention. Because of his age, the satisfactions he was deriving from his behavior, and the difficulty in focusing his attention on individual vocal parameters, the storybook approach was adopted.

FREDDIE: HYPERFUNCTIONAL VOICE USE

Freddie, aged 5 years, 6 months, was referred by his kindergarten teacher because the other children in his class told him he sounded like a frog when he talked. The otolaryngological report noted that the child had a normal larynx but that there was observable tension in the vocal tract during phonation and some intermittent dysphonia plicae verticularis.

During the initial diagnostic interview the parents reported that their son had begun using his "frog voice" following recurrent episodes of laryngitis during his preschool years. His general health at the time of the interview was described as "excellent." The parents were concerned about the excessive amount of loud strained talking that the child engaged in and his attempts to gain attention and amuse his peers by using his strange voice. They described him as "a bit of a clown" and said he "got very uptight if he wasn't the center of attention." They had attempted to modify his behavior by telling him not to talk so much. They said he was aggressive at play and that he tried very hard to make friends.

Voice testing revealed that when Freddie was asked to prolong vowel sounds he had difficulty sustaining phonation for longer than four seconds. He prolonged the consonant sounds /s/ and /z/ for approximately five seconds each (Eckel & Boone, 1981). When he counted to 10 loudly he demonstrated hard glottal attack on 8, and his voice sounded strained and diplophonic. When he was asked to count to 10 softly, he demonstrated no observable tension in the neck, jaw, and shoulder areas and improved vocal quality up to the number 5; thereafter he appeared to have run out of air and attempted to complete the sequence using residual air with a recurrence of observable tension. Inspiration appeared to be shallow with no lower chest movements, and he appeared to have little control over the expiration phase. Replenishing breaths were rarely used during connected speech. An analysis of his pitch level and range, using the Kay Elemetrics Visipitch, resulted in findings that were within normal limits for age and sex. In order to analyze his pattern of usage of hard glottal attacks on words beginning with vowels, the clinician asked Freddie to repeat the sentence "Uncle Eddie eats eggs" at varying loudness levels as she moved farther away from him across the room. He consistently initiated phonation with hard attacks on every word during every trial. However, the consistency of the diplophonic production seemed related to the increase in loudness. During conversational speech the child spoke rapidly and eagerly and seemed anxious to maintain the clinician's attention on him at all times. When the clinician looked down at her notes, the child responded immediately by interjecting a loud statement or by suddenly becoming diplophonic. His attempts at vocal variety during conversation were restricted to increasing the loudness level or increasing the amount of diplophonia. In order to see if the child was aware of other, less abusive methods of varying his voice, the clinician asked him to make "pictures" with his voice. She presented him with nouns and adjectives selected for the purpose of eliciting pitch and duration changes. Visual and auditory stimuli were provided, and the child was stimulable when given a model (e.g., worms *crawl*; reach *high*; a *deep* hole; a *fat* man; warm and *snuggly*). Audiological testing revealed that hearing sensitivity was within normal limits bilaterally.

Freddie was enrolled in therapy for two 20-minute sessions each week for individual voice therapy. In addition, his parents agreed to participate in a parent program designed to help them provide additional modification of the vocal behavior in the home environment. Conferences were arranged with Freddie's classroom teacher and a school psychologist in order to gather information and ensure cooperation and understanding of therapy strategies.

The parents, teacher, and voice clinician agreed to coordinate their efforts to find ways in which Freddie could be rewarded for using an easy phonatory pattern. They decided to ignore the boy's attempts to gain attention by using the diplophonic voice and to give him a great deal of attention whenever he was *not* using a forced production. They identified methods of describing the characteristics of the vocal behavior and the general behavior that was targeted. For example, they described their own reactions to the sound of his voice when he spoke at an optimal loudness level or with an absence of diplophonia by saying, "You make me feel so calm when you use your easy voice"; I like to sit and talk with you—your smooth voice sounds so good to me"; "I love the feeling of sitting close to you and talking quietly together"; "When you talk to me like that, my ears feel so good"; "Children know you are a friendly boy when you use that voice to talk to them."

The clinician adopted two characters to personify the behavioral characteristics associated with the "old" vocal pattern and the "new" vocal behavior. In order to achieve worthwhile results, since Freddie was an energetic, assertive boy, the character chosen to personify the easy laryngeal production needed to be a high-status, masculine figure who illustrated efficient and economical use of vocal power. Superman was selected to fulfill those expectations. It was essential that the character personifying the less acceptable vocal behaviors be a less enviable personage and one with whom the child might be less inclined to identify. This character needed to be noisy yet inefficient in the use of his vocal energy, and unsuccessful in achieving meaningful relationships and personal goals. The Tin Soldier was chosen for this role.

In the awareness sessions the clinician told Freddie stories about the exploits of the two central characters, emphasizing the consequences of their total behaviors. Later, specific behaviors were discussed, and Freddie was encouraged to predict possible outcomes. This nonthreatening framework offered frequent opportunities for him to practice identifying appropriate and inappropriate behaviors at the interpersonal level. Later, behavioral objectives were decided on by the clinician and Freddie together. They agreed that certain behaviors were worth copying because they worked. Freddie discovered that both Superman and the Tin Soldier had similar personal needs but used different strategies to try to meet those needs. He verbalized insights such as, "The Tin Soldier wants people to like him but he makes too much noise. His friends get tired of listening to him" "Superman helps people. They listen to him when he talks. The baddies are scared of him, too." The child was especially impressed by one situation in a story, which he paraphrased by saying, "That Tin Soldier just yelled and screamed at the bad guy, but he wasn't even scared. Then Superman talked in a deadly voice—real quiet but it sure scared that guy."

The following reasons for talking and listening emerged and were summarized on a chart in the therapy room.

Why People Talk
To tell others what they want
To share feelings
To find out things
To get adults to help them
To make friends
To scare enemies
To show off
To make people laugh
To hear how good they sound

Why People Listen
To find out things
To show they like you
To think what they'll say next
To share with you
To rest their voice
To get clues to mysteries

It seemed unrealistic to tell Freddie that he could never talk loudly. The environmental and emotional demands relating to loudness were discussed and some conclusions were drawn.

Times People Talk Loudly
When playing outdoors
When listeners are a long way away
When lots of people are making a noise
When they are talking to lots of people
When grandparents can't hear you
When they are in a big place
When cheering at a game
When they are angry

As therapy progressed, the stories focused more on specific vocal strategies that were productive and nonstressful. It became possible to help the boy state his own goals for changing his behavior.

Superman's Super Voice Rules

1. Always take plenty of air deep into your lungs before you start to talk (use lower chest breathing).
2. Make sure you have a lot of air before you talk loudly (use deeper inspiration for projected speech).
3. Always "top off" your air supply before you start to run out of air (use replenishing breaths.)
4. Start your voice motor gently (use easy initiation of phonation).
5. Use a smooth voice to talk (elimination of diplophonia).
6. Never talk with a tight neck (avoid tension in laryngeal area).
7. Let your mouth and tongue do more work when you throw your voice a long way (use improved resonance and articulation to help voice carry).
8. Think of ways to save your voice so that it doesn't get tired (use alternative nonvocal behaviors).

By the end of the first semester Freddie was able to use appropriate respiratory patterns in the therapy situation during the production of prolonged vowels and consonants. His respiratory behavior on both an inter- and intrapersonal level was advanced to the stage that it was possible for him to give a presentation during Show and Tell in his kindergarten classroom about the best way to breathe. During the second semester of therapy he extended his skills in the appropriate use of speech breathing so that he was able to use the correct methods most of the time. After approximately two years of therapy, there was complete habituation of the use of the target vocal production. Intermittent diplophonia still occurred occasionally during the second year, when he was excited or anxious about maintaining the clinician's attention. Dismissal with periodic follow-up checks occurred when the parents reported that they were no longer hearing the "old" voice used at home during animated play sessions with peers.

The initial grouping of the behaviors as constellations associated with the hero and antihero, reduced the level of abstraction and enhanced the child's motivation throughout the course of therapy. This approach appears to be a fruitful one to use with young children with limited motivation to change their abusive vocal behaviors. The selection of the two major characters is, of course, a key factor in the process. The characters need to be chosen with care and developed in a manner consistent with the child's interests and needs.

GOALS

The clinician grouped Freddie's negative vocal behaviors into three categories:

1. Respiration
   a. Shallow inspiration.
   b. Tension in shoulders, neck, and jaw.
   c. Short, inefficient exhalation.
   d. Inefficient use of replenishing breaths.
2. Phonation
   a. Hard initiation of phonation.
   b. Inefficient coordination of respiration and phonation.
   c. Diplophonia.
   d. Weak resonance on voiced continuants.
   e. Little mouth opening or articulatory movement.
   f. Effortful laryngeal tone.
3. Interpersonal
   a. Excessive bids for attention, and excessive talking.
   b. Poor listening skills.
   c. Lack of awareness of other's feedback and needs.
   d. Little adaptation to situational constraints.

The targets for treatment would be Freddie's use of appropriate respiratory patterns for sustained voicing; use of easy laryngeal tone; use of appropriate attention-getting behaviors. The clinician decided to structure the therapy goals in three general areas.

1. Respiration
   a. Describe appropriate respiratory patterns.
   b. Achieve deep, quick inhalation.
   c. Sustain long controlled exhalation (15 seconds).
   d. Use replenishing breaths.
2. Phonation
   a. Describe appropriate phonatory patterns.
   b. Initiate easy phonation.
   c. Use appropriate loudness level during phonation in conversational and projected speech.
   d. Use vocal variety through pitch and duration changes.
   e. Maintain a "smooth" quality during phonation.
3. Interpersonal
   a. Describe purposes of talking.
   b. Discuss or role play varied communication strategies.
   c. Improve ratio of talking and listening time.
   d. Improve question-asking skills.

SAMPLE STRATEGIES

The Story of Superman and the Tin Soldier   Superman came out of the phone booth and looked at the crowd. He stood with his head high; his cape floated behind him in the wind. He took a deep breath and his lower chest and rib cage swelled with air. Suddenly he swirled around, called, "I'm off and away," in a strong clear voice, and flew off as the startled crowd watched.

The Tin Soldier rattled around yelling, "Did you see that? That was Superman. He can fly. I can fly, but I won't do it now. I'll do it later. I am as strong as he is, you know. I can do anything I want to."

Someone in the crowd said, "Oh, shut up, you stupid soldier. Stop making such a fool of yourself. We're sick of listening to you. Your voice is so creaky and rough it hurts our ears!"

The Tin Soldier shook with embarrassment and anger, and so he tried even harder to be important. "Look at me, look at me," he screeched. "Watch me fly." He tried to take a deep breath and jerked his arms, but he couldn't move his chest at all because he was so stiff and rusty. Instead he pushed his shoulders up, tightened his neck and tensed his creaky jaw. He screeched, "Look at me fly." He twirled around, tripped over his feet, and fell with a crash in a heap on the sidewalk.

The crowd roared with laughter. "What a jerk," someone said. "He thinks he can fly like Superman, and all he can do is fall on his face!!"

"*I* can so, too—fly," said the Tin Soldier. But no one heard him, because he ran out of air before he could say all the words.

Later that day Superman came back to see some of the boys on the block. He asked them all about themselves and listened to their answers. The Tin Soldier rushed up to the group later on while they were playing ball. "I want to show you how good I am," he said, grabbing the ball. "Look at me, I'm really something. Watch me, watch me, I can do it better."

"Oh, get out of here," the boys said. "You butt in all the time and we're sick of the sight of you."

Guess whether I am breathing like Superman or the Tin Soldier.
Tell me what the Tin Soldier is doing.

His shoulders are raised.
His neck is tight.
His arms are tight.
His jaw is clenched.
His chest isn't full of air.
He runs out of air before he's finished.
He doesn't top off his air tank.
He looks uncomfortable.

Tell me how Superman gets his air supply.

He fills the bottom of his chest.
He holds lots of air in his air tank.

Simple props help the Tin Soldier demonstrate overall tension.

He lets it out slowly (15 seconds).
His shoulders are down.
His neck is relaxed.
His jaw is not stiff.

Guess who is talking—Superman or the Tin Soldier.

Superman starts his voice motor easily. Describe how he does this.

He first takes in plenty of air.
He begins with /h/.
He doesn't jerk or click.
His neck is relaxed.

What are the Tin Soldier's mistakes? Tell him what he is doing wrong.

He doesn't take in enough air.
He is too tight all over.

He grunts as he starts.
He is jerky and creaky.

Let's analyze people's reactions to Superman and the Tin Soldier. Why does the Tin Soldier talk all the time? Do people like him? Describe how they feel when he makes so much noise.

Why do people like Superman?

He listens to them.
He asks good questions to find clues.
He praises others when they help him.
He sounds good—easy and relaxed.

What could the Tin Soldier do to get what he wants? Think of another ending the story, for example: The Tin Soldier could play quietly with the boys and then ask them about their game. Before, when he just butted in and kept talking about himself, it made the other boys angry with him.

Let's copy the way Superman breathes in. How long can he make his air last? (Prolong continuant consonant 15 seconds.) Let's both count to ten in one breath. Now let's both count to ten, take in air, and count to ten again. I'll go first, then you do it.

See if you can be Superman saying /ha/. Walk around the room saying /ha/ like Superman. Now say /ha/ like the Tin Soldier. Who lasted the longest? Describe how you felt.

Superman has some tricks to get extra power without tiring himself. Copy the ways he gets extra power by working his mouth not his neck. Feel the vibration (*m, n, z, z*, etc.; CV's; Chant phrases loaded with vowels and voiced continuants). Stretch out the words—give them Superman's easy power. (Prolong vowels and voiced continuants.)

I'm Superman.
I'm flying high.
My, oh my, I'm so high.
Baddies, beware—if you're there!

How do you know you sound like Superman?

smooth
easy
not tight
can go on longer
not ever jerky
easy to listen to

Show the Tin Soldier how Superman would do it. Let's go through our Tin Soldier story again and find the places where he could have paused to be sure he was understood. Now speak the words he said, showing him how Superman would have done it. What does he do instead of shouting? When he uses a quiet but "deadly" voice, the baddies know he means it all right! Why did the pauses help?

He could use them to get more air.
He made the pauses before important words.
During pauses he could receive feedback from his listeners.

treatment approach 8
Using a Storybook Character

Our text case history illustrates a different symptom pattern. The otolaryngology report noted the presence of bilateral voice nodules, which meant we were dealing with a child who has an altered mechanism. In such cases, until the nodules subside, it is unrealistic to suggest that the child use a normally smooth and clear tone. Thus the target voice, at first, is an easy breathy voice that allows the child to learn a less forceful adduction pattern.

AMANDA: REPETITIVE ABUSIVE PRACTICES

Amanda, age 6 years, 4 months, was referred by the school nurse, who noticed that she sounded "more like a man than a young girl." According to the medical report, Amanda had a history of severe allergic reactions of the upper respiratory tract, but the situation was now controlled by desensitization shots. Bilateral nodules were observed under direct laryngoscopy; redness and edema of the laryngeal mucosa were also noted. The parents reported that Amanda had always had a "low-pitched, gruff-sounding voice" and that people used to think it was "cute" that she had such a deep voice when she was a little girl. Lately, however, they had become concerned because they felt her voice made her self-conscious and prohibited her from joining a children's choir. She took ballet lessons but had not been given a speaking part in a recent recital because the teacher said, "She dances like a fairy but doesn't sound like one." They said Amanda coughed and cleared her throat a lot, even though she no longer seemed to have problems with excessive mucus.

Voice testing revealed that Amanada demonstrated adequate respiratory support: She could prolong /s/ for 25 seconds on repeated trials. Amanda said her dancing teacher stressed good breathing habits.

Sustained phonation of /z/ was approximately 11 seconds and was characterized by low-pitch, uneven voicing, breaks, and severe hoarseness. The quality improved when she phonated loudly. During sentences there were frequent episodes of aphonia on unstressed syllables and some hard glottal attacks. Audiological testing revealed that hearing sensitivity was within normal limits bilaterally. Frequent nonproductive coughing and throat clearing were observed; Amanda also filled pauses ("ahs," "ers") with hard glottal attacks while she appeared to be thinking of what to say next. She listened attentively, used appropriate eye contact and facial expression, and appeared to be eager to have help with her voice. She said, "My granny says I should sound more like a lady."

Amanda was enrolled in therapy for two, 20-minute sessions each week. In addition, the parents agreed to help Amanda at home. It seemed that Amanda's frequent use of abusive behaviors (e.g., throat clearing and coughing) stemmed from earlier attempts to deal with excessive mucus in the vocal tract. Now that her allergies were under control she continued to habituate behaviors that were irrelevant and irritating. The use of hard glottal attacks had probably also developed as a compensatory device.

The clinician adopted two characters to personify the behavioral characteristics associated with the clusters of inappropriate and appropriate behaviors. Since Amanda was interested in pretty visual effects, ballet, and fairies, the clinician decided that the heroine character would be "Princess Amanda"—a feminine and beautiful woman who spoke in a gentle, easy voice and sighed (a breathy, easy sigh!) happily every time the Prince rode by her castle window. The inappropriate behaviors were assoicated with "Wendy the Witch," a most unenviable character, who could not dance or sing or use an easy breathy voice at all! The noises Wendy made in her throat were irritating to everyone, and the Prince even said that they gave him a headache and startled his white charger.

Amanda eagerly identified with the beautiful princess. During the awareness phase of therapy, stories about the Princess and the Witch focused on the effects their behaviors had on others (especially the Prince). Amanda quickly identified the distracting mannerisms exhibited by the Witch and described the specific characteristics of her behavior. She also analyzed why the Witch was making so many noises and identified some things that the Witch could do instead.

Why Wendy the Witch Makes Noises in Her Throat	What Wendy Could Do Instead
To scare people.	Be more pleasant.
Because she doesn't realize she's doing it.	Try to relax.
	Notice what she's doing.

To be silly.

To stop other people from talking.

To show she is thinking of what to say next.

Because her throat tickles.

To try to clear her voice.

Use more quiet pauses.

Swallow when her throat tickles.

Drink more water.

Use a gentle voice.

Copy the beautiful princess.

As therapy progressed, the stories focused more on specific vocal strategies that were nonstressful to the mechanism. Amanda stated some goals in her own words to describe how the Princess behaved.

Princess Amanda's Beautiful Voice Hints

1. Always sound relaxed and easy.
2. An "airy," gentle voice is nice.
3. Start each word gently.
4. "Mmm" is better than "ah," "er" or "um" (because your lips work, not your throat).
5. Don't make noises during pauses if you can help it. Just listen and nod or smile.
6. Think of ways to save your throat from getting tired (use alternative nonvocal behaviors).

Amanda quickly adapted her behavior and was dismissed after one year in therapy. Her voice notebook included pictures of her characters and lists of their "special" habits. She also kept lists of actresses on television who did not use their voices well and became expert at describing what they were doing incorrectly.

GOALS

The clinician noted the following negative vocal behaviors, all having to do with phonation:

1. Hard initiation of phonation.
2. Weak resonance.
3. Laryngeal tone focus.
4. Habituated nonproductive coughing.
5. Habituated nonproductive throat clearing.
6. Filled pauses (hard glottal attacks on fillers).
7. Low pitch level (related to size and mass of folds, i.e., nodules, edema).
8. Limited pitch variability (related to size and mass).
9. Restricted pitch range (related to size and mass).

10. Hoarseness (related to size and mass).
11. Intermittent aphonia (related to size and mass).

The target areas for treatment would be to teach Amanda to use easy breathy phonation, and to reduce her abusive practices.

The clinician established the following goals:

1. Easy initiation of phonation.
2. Gentle, easy approximation of folds.
3. Substitution of alternative behaviors (e.g., swallowing, quiet pauses, nonvocal signals).
4. Verbalization of key concepts of voice conservation.
5. Verbalization of key concepts of effects of negative behaviors on others.
6. Increased resonance and forward focus to improve tone.

SAMPLE STRATEGIES

Story of Princess Amanda and Wendy the Witch   Wendy the Witch got very excited every time she saw the handsome prince. She was so excited, she talked all the time. When she didn't know what to say next, she said "ah" or "um" or "er" very loudly so that no one else would start to talk until she thought of what to say. The Prince never seemed to notice her, because he was too busy smiling at Princess Amanda. The Witch tried dancing and hopping and skipping. She tried coughing and throat-clearing and cackling. She tried talking and singing louder and louder. But the harder she tried, the worse she sounded and the more the Prince frowned and ignored her. All her noises made his head hurt. And the more anxious Wendy got, and the more she tried to impress the Prince, the more awful her screeching voice sounded. She even tried hiding behind a curtain in the Prince's palace, just so she could be near him. But nothing she did seemed to work. He only wanted to talk to Princess Amanda. Poor Wendy felt terrible. She so much wanted him to notice her.

How do you know Wendy is behind that curtain?
What exactly did she do to make that noise in her throat? (sensory awareness)
What else made the Prince annoyed with Wendy?
What did the Princess tell Wendy to do to help her voice?
How does the Princess start to say her name? (*A*manda); the Prince's name? (*A*lbert); the horse's name? (*A*lphonse). How is that different from the way Wendy says those names?

Listen to the poem Wendy says and count her mistakes and tell me what they are:

I'm angry and anxious
Because everyone's aware
that my voice is awful
and at me they stare
(cough, throat clearing, cough!)

Tell poor Wendy about the Princess's beautiful voice hints. How could they help her?

You copy the princess and say her words after me as I read the story:

The Princess was at her window as the Prince rode by. She waved her scarf at him and called happily, "Hello, Albert."

"How gentle and soft and pretty your voice is, Princess," said the Prince.

Suggested Characters	Possible Sets of Vocal Characteristics
Inspector Clear Tone	1. Adequate respiration for speech 2. Appropriate loudness level for varied situations 3. Use of vocal variety 4. Appropriate listening skills 5. Easy initiation of phonation
Sergeant Sore Throat	1. Inadequate respiration for speech 2. Inappropriate use of loudness levels for varied situations 3. Limited vocal variety 4. Underdeveloped listening skills 5. Strained quality 6. Hard glottal attacks
Raggedy Anne or Andy	1. Relaxed posture 2. Flexible jaw and neck 3. Lower chest expansion during speech breathing 4. Relaxed vocal production
Rusty Ruth or Randy	1. Tense posture 2. Tight jaw and neck 3. Clavicular breathing 4. "Creaky" strained vocal production

Suggested Characters	Possible Sets of Vocal Characteristics
Luke Skywalker	1. Smooth, easy quality 2. Direct eye contact and facial expressions 3. Honest expression of feelings 4. Effective results
Jabba the Hutt	1. Rough, "crackly" quality 2. Erratic eye movements and facial expressions 3. Manipulative, angry, or unpleasant feelings 4. Ineffective results
Batman	1. Appropriate tone focus (opens mouth well) 2. Appropriate breath support for projected speech 3. Maximizes loudness by increasing articulatory contacts 4. Appropriate balance of oral and nasal resonance
Mumbles Morgan	1. Pharyngeal tone focus 2. Inappropriate breath support for projected speech 3. Increasing loudness with laryngeal effort 4. Cul-de-sac resonance
Wonder Woman	1. Appropriate posture during inhalation 2. Use of mouth opening and tone focus 3. Clear articulation 4. Clear, pleasant vocal quality 5. Authoritative inflectional patterns
Shy Sue	1. Inappropriate posture during inhalation 2. Minimal mouth opening 3. Slurred articulation 4. Soft, breathy vocal quality 5. Timid, questioning inflectional patterns

"Oh, Albert," said the Princess in an excited (but gentle) voice. *"May I ride your horse later today?"*

Let's listen to the tape recording of the Princess reading words. We'll put a purple tiara over every word that sounds just right. Did we both put tiaras over the same words, I wonder? Why do you think I didn't have one on that word?

Our case studies of Freddie and Amanda illustrate a Gestalt approach and how to use storybook characters to establish behavioral associations. This approach is useful because it allows liberal opportunity to use visual cues and images that are so necessary in therapy with very young children. In both cases the purposes and effects of voice use were defined in simple, direct language in order to help the children develop personal rationales for change. In both cases the children created dialogue for their characters and adopted appropriate vocal behaviors when speaking as the person with whom they identified. Since reading Kolbenschlag (1981), we are careful to encourage "princesses" to be action-oriented rather than submissive when they talk to "princes." While the princess character appealed to Amanda, we advocate the use of strong female characters, such as Wonder Woman, and the avoidance of characters that suggest stereotypical nonassertive feminine characteristics.

Before we conclude our section on the use of behavioral Gestalts associated with storybook characters, here is a list of some additional examples that may be useful in therapy with very young children.

Star Wars Characters are appealing as hero figures for many children; however, it is sometimes difficult to identify an antihero who is not perceived as powerful. Other characters suitable for older children are Arthur Ashe (other locally and nationally well-known sports figures), Bryant Gumbel (other locally and nationally well-known television or radio personalities), and Susan (from "Sesame Street").

treatment approach 9
Addressing Interpersonal Behavior

Before adopting a particular approach to treatment, it is helpful to review all the negative behaviors and decide which should be translated into therapy objectives. In the cases of Freddie and Amanda, objectives were selected from more than one area of behavior, and sets of negative behaviors were contrasted with sets of positive behaviors. Thus the approach involved a substitution of a whole new set of respiratory, phonatory, and interpersonal behaviors.

Although this approach worked well with Freddie and Amanda, other approaches need to be considered. In this section we describe a treatment plan designed to meet the needs of children who were exhibiting severe problems in interpersonal behavior. Their negative vocal behaviors were only one aspect of a general pattern of aggression. Thus, although negative behaviors in the areas of respiration and phonation were observed, the area of interpersonal behavior was targeted as the priority area for treatment. This case study, therefore, demonstrates an approach predicated on the assumption that improvement in interpersonal behavior is a prerequisite in some cases to improvement in other areas.

JOE, BILL AND HOWIE: AGGRESSIVE VOCAL BEHAVIOR RELATED TO REDUCED EMOTIONAL CONTROL

Children who habitually respond by shouting and yelling and acting aggressively rarely get what they want. Sometimes, as they become more frustrated in achieving their needs, they may increase the frequency of unproductive vocal strategies and act out more belligerent physical behaviors.

Clinical psychologists, such as Spivack and Shure (1974), have shown that there is a relationship between the cognitive ability to generate a variety of solutions to interpersonal problems and behavioral deviance in young children. In particular, deficiencies in cognitive skills, such as role-taking, have been identified by some (see Chandler, 1973) as possible explanations of aggressive behavior. Dodge (May, 1981) believes that, since an aggressive child does not always behave aggressively, the relationship between cognitive skills and social behavior must be assessed within situations. To perform competently in a social situation a child may need to process cues in an orderly manner. Dodge (May, 1981) suggests that aggressive boys carry in their memory an expectancy that peers will be hostile; then they act aggressively and encounter more retaliatory aggression which confirms their expectations. It is possible that training them to attend to a greater number of social cues and to process social information more carefully may improve their social interactions. Richard and Dodge (1982) have shown that the deviant boys in their study had particular deficits in the ability to generate alternative solutions during problem-solving tasks.

Aggression is an acquired strategy for dealing with strong feelings such as anger and anxiety. In an interesting study done by Seymour Feshback (in Mallick and McCandless, 1966), third grade children were presented with three alternative strategies for handling their anger, frustration, and irritation caused by the behavior of another child. The three strategies presented were:

1. Talking out the anger with an adult.
2. Getting even with the other child, or releasing the feelings by playing with toy guns.
3. Receiving reasonable explanations from an adult for the child's annoying behavior (i.e., the child was not feeling well, was upset).

The most effective strategy was found to be the reasonable explanation of the classmate's behavior.

Fixsen *et al.*, (1978), in a discussion of strategies for teaching the peaceful settlement of disputes and the nonviolent resolution of angry feelings in a program that was successful at Boys Town, highlighted the importance of teaching problem solving. They maintained that more effective problem-solving techniques than aggressive and abusive behavior could be learned. They stressed the importance of differentiating between aggressive actions and controlled, understood anger.

Some children need to learn about their emotions, how those emotions are reflected in actions and voices, and how one assumes responsibility for one's actions. When an awareness of the effects of one's behavior is created, it becomes easier to develop a rationale to promote change.

Joe, Bill, and Howie were all in different fourth-grade rooms in a large elementary school, and the clinician decided to work with them as a group for 30 minutes once a week. All three boys used combative styles of interaction, were of average intelligence, and had normal hearing. They were referred by their teachers, who complained about loud and constant talking, strain and effort in speech, and difficulties with peer interactions. Bill had been labeled a "behavior problem" for some years and had a long history of visits to the principal's office because of fighting on the playground. His mother described him as "difficult to manage, mouthy, and destructive." Joe was heavy for his age and talked in a low-pitched, "gruff" voice; he was described by his parents as "belligerent, sullen, and moody at times." Howie was small and wiry in appearance and his mother reported that he was "always wound up and tense" and that he teased his younger siblings constantly. The medical reports indicated that Bill and Howie had vocal nodules and that Joe's folds were edematous and red. Joe's physician suspected "chronic nonspecific laryngitis" related to hyperfunctional use. The speech–language clinician observed that all the boys used too much effort and tension when talking, seemed unaware of the effect of their behavior on others, and exhibited poor impulse control in dealing with aggressive feelings. He suspected that the frustrations and tensions of their interpersonal relationships precipitated and maintained the loud and strained patterns of their voice use.

During the initial case conferences, the school psychologist and the speech–language clinician explained to the parents that the priority objective in therapy should be to demonstrate the effects of aggressive behaviors on self and others. All participants in the conferences agreed that the current strategies used by the boys were not helping them achieve acceptance by their peers, positive recognition from teachers and family members, or solutions to their everyday problems. It did not seem likely that the boys could change their abusive vocal patterns until some amelioration of the maintaining factors was achieved. The classroom teacher, the parents, the psychologist, and the speech–language clinician decided to give consistent rewards for desirable interpersonal behaviors. The parents agreed to cooperate with the school personnel by implementing a home program. They observed therapy periodically, met with the psychologist to discuss strategies to manage the aggressive behavior at home, and helped the boys with worksheet assignments.

The boys attended group therapy for two and a half years. During that time they developed insight concerning their emotions (specifically their anger, anxieties, fears, and satisfactions), their available options to express or inhibit emotional reactions, and the effects of a variety of their interpersonal strategies. A framework of analysis and evaluation was initially applied to general interpersonal behaviors (e.g., fighting) and then was applied to specific vocal practices.

In the treatment plan that follows, only the therapist's work on the boys' interpersonal behavior is outlined in detail. The clinician drew on previously published materials to formulate strategies specifically designed to eliminate vocal abuses and substitute improved phonatory behaviors. (For example, the Drudge & Philips [1976] program, originally designed for college students, was adapted to eliminate hard glottal attacks. Ideas for elimination of phonatory abuses and the substitution of alternative behaviors were drawn from Blonigen's 1978 excellent article; Deal, McClain, & Sudderth's 1976 comprehensive approach to the rehabilitation of children with vocal nodules also provided valuable suggestions that were implemented.)

GOALS

The clinician grouped the boys' negative behaviors into three categories:

1. Immature Understanding of Feelings
    a. How to describe them.
    b. Ways they are communicated.
    c. Effects on others.
    d. How feelings are controlled.
    e. Relationship to goal achievement.
    f. Effect on physical and psychological state.
2. Poor Self-esteem
    a. How actions affect self-concept.
    b. How others see us.
    c. How we decide what we want and why.
    d. How we can choose how to react.
3. Ineffective Vocal Practices to Satisfy Needs
    a. Level of tension.
    b. Amount of listening.
    c. Adaptation to feedback.
    d. Limited, unproductive strategies to gain attention (e.g., talking too much, too loudly).

The targets in treatment would be for the children to describe their emotional expression and response patterns, and to analyze the effects of their behaviors on themselves and others. The clinician also needed to help them adopt more productive interpersonal strategies. Specifically, the goals would include:

1. Defining emotional states (e.g., anger, anxiety, fear and satisfaction).
2. Expressing anger, anxiety, fear and satisfaction appropriately.
3. Deciding when and how to deal with anger, anxiety, fear, and satisfaction.
4. Practicing methods of dealing with the emotions of anger, anxiety, fear, and satisfaction.
5. Evaluating effects (on self and others) of these new methods.

SAMPLE STRATEGIES

Guess how everyone feels in the following three stories. Are the feelings the same or different? Why?

1. Henry was sitting next to George during a math lesson. George kept trying to see Henry's paper. Finally, Henry yelled, "Don't look at my paper or I'll break your face." The teacher, seeing Henry talking, came over and said, "You'll stay in during recess, Henry. I told you not to talk during math." Henry was upset and said, "It's not my fault. George is the one that was cheating." The teacher said, "I've had enough of this. See me at recess, both of you."

How did Henry feel? Why?
How did George feel? Why?
How did the teacher feel? Why?

2. Blair was drinking at the water fountain when Jack and Greg ran by. Greg accidentally knocked Blair's elbow, and the jolt caused water to spray over Blair's shirt. Blair immediately grabbed Greg and hit him. Jack, turning, saw Blair hit Greg and screamed at him, "Hey—leave Greg alone or I'll smash your face in."

How did Blair feel? Why?
How did Greg feel? Why?
How did Jack feel? Why?

3. Mario's young brother, Ramon, was doing his homework at the kitchen table. Mario passed by and said to him, "Mom said I can go to the pool for an hour before we eat, but you can't come." Ramon let out a yell and screamed, "I *can* go. Mom said I could go as soon as I finish." Mario laughed and yelled, "But you're *not* finished, and I'm not waiting for you anyway—so there!" Mario ran out the door laughing as Ramon started crying loudly. Their mother, hearing the noise, came in and said to Ramon, "Why are you crying? I thought you'd be pleased that I told Mario to tell you that

you both could go to the pool now and that you could finish that work later."

How did Ramon feel—why?
How did Mario feel—why?
How did their Mom feel—why?

How can a person tell when someone else is angry? What does he or she do (e.g., yell, scream, punch, kick, scowl, bite, sulk, get red in the face, fight, pout, clench teeth, curse, bully, frown, complain)?

How can people hide their feelings when they are angry (e.g., clench fists under table, choke back angry words, take deep breaths, think of something else, pretend not to be angry, walk away, ignore the cause, it's not possible to hide it if you're really angry)?

What makes people feel angry?

When something isn't fair.
When people get in their way.
When someone hurts them on purpose.
When someone takes their things without asking.
When someone damages their possessions.
When they are teased.
When someone puts them down.
When someone ignores them.
When someone insults them.
When they do something "stupid" themselves.
When something won't work properly.
When someone is mean or cruel.
When a lot of things go wrong at once.
When they think someone is out to get them.

What do people want when they act out anger?

They want to feel better.
They want to let off steam.
They want to get what they want.
They want to punish someone or get even.
They want to tell their side of it.
They want an apology.
They want another person to stop doing something.
They want another person to change.
They want to hurt or get back.
They want attention.

They want their rights.
They want to stop an injustice or a meanness.

Do people always get what they want when they act out their anger? Listen to the following two stories.

1. David saw Kevin working on a science project during a free period in class the week before the science fair. David walked up to Kevin's table, stumbled, and knocked Kevin's project onto the floor. Kevin was angry because . . . Think of some reasons why Kevin was angry.

He thought David did it on purpose.
He thought David was clumsy.
He thought his project was ruined.
He thought David didn't like him.
He thought the teacher would be mad at him.
He thought David should help him pick it up.
He thought David should apologize.

David felt _____ because . . .

He wanted to ruin Kevin's project.
He accidentally knocked the project.
He was clumsy and he felt foolish.
He was afraid of what the teacher would say.
He wanted to be friends with Kevin.
He tried to get even with Kevin for something that happened earlier.
He wanted to make sure his project was the best in the class.
He wanted the other children to notice him.
He didn't know why he had done it.

2. Bob saw Hugh had a new bike. He watched Hugh ride up and down the street for a while but pretended not to be looking. Then he yelled out to Hugh, "Hey, you stupid idiot, you're going to get run over."

Bob felt _____ because . . .

He thought Hugh was showing off.
He was concerned about Hugh's safety.
He wished he had a new bike, too.
He was thinking of something Hugh did earlier.
He wanted Hugh to let him ride it.
He felt bad about himself.
He wanted to hurt Hugh's feelings.
He wanted to be friends with Hugh.
He was afraid Hugh didn't like him.

He knew Hugh wanted him to be impressed.
He wanted to show he didn't care.

Hugh felt _____ because . . .

He thought Bob was putting him down.
He was sensitive about his safety skills.
He wanted Bob to be impressed.
He wanted Bob to like him.
He thought he was stupid to ride by Bob's house.
He thought his new bike was just great.
He thought Bob was jealous.
He thought Bob was just kidding him.

Feelings are messages. Sometimes people misunderstand the messages they are sending and receiving. Sometimes they send messages that don't help them get what they want. Describe some of the messages sent in the previous examples. Then describe another way those messages could have been sent.

Different people sometimes feel differently about the same situation or event. The way they feel depends on:

1. What they want to get.
2. What they think should happen.
3. How they feel generally about themselves.
4. What happens before an event.

Describe how the boys in the following three stories deal with their feelings.

1. Kenneth broke the point on his pencil just before the spelling test. He wanted to do well on the test because he'd have to stay in at recess if the words weren't well written. He had done badly on the test the week before because his writing was messy. He knew he was a bad writer and the teacher was always telling him he was careless. He was sure the broken point on the pencil would ruin his chances on the test. He swore loudly and felt himself get tense all over. He kept thinking how unlucky he was and how everything was against him. He sat at his desk brooding until the test began.

How could Kenneth have dealt with his feelings in a different way? What actions or thoughts might have helped? Do you think he did well on the test?

2. Russ saw Ed knock some papers off the teacher's desk. He wanted to feel important so:

He told the teacher quietly that Ed did it.
He told Ed he saw him but wouldn't tell.

He told Ed he'd help him pick them up.
He told Ed he was always doing stupid things.
He told the other boys Ed was in trouble again.
He waited until recess and made fun of Ed.
He minded his own business and got on with his work.
He yelled out loudly, "Look what Ed's done!"

3. Isaiah was playing ball with James. Isaiah accidentally knocked James over, and James was angry. James had a difficult choice to make. He could choose to interpret the event a number of different ways. Which ways would make him feel best? Which ways would make Isaiah feel best? Why? What penalties are there for himself and others?

James retaliates
He yells, "I'll get you for this!"
He screams, "I'll never play with you again."
He punches Isaiah.
He insults Isaiah.
He complains to the teacher.
He sulks and broods.

James denies his anger
He pretends it's ok.
He blames Isaiah.
He swears at the "dumb ball."
He blames himself for his clumsiness.

James acknowledges his feelings but keeps them specific to situation
He says, "That hurt, you know."
He asks Isaiah to be more careful.
He cries for a while but then tries to forget it.
He says, "I know it was an accident, but it really hurt me."
He asks Isaiah to apologize.
He says he's "had enough" for now.
He suggests they both go and get a drink.

Discuss penalties with respect to self-esteem and the relationship.
    List some ways feelings are redirected or transformed.

By describing them.
By taking them out on inanimate objects.
Through physical exercise.
By writing them down.

By thinking about something pleasant.
By counting to ten.
By breathing deeply.

Discuss some situations when you might choose not to reveal the full force of your feelings.

When the penalty is too great.
When it makes you feel worse.
When the person couldn't help hurting you.
When you can understand why the person behaved badly.
When you're angry with someone in authority over you.

People make choices about what they do. Things don't always just happen to them. Think about some of the ways people make choices.

1. How to act.
2. When and how to talk.
3. Whether to show real feelings.
4. Whether to let a tense situation get worse.
5. Whether a relationship with a friend over the long term is more important than a specific incident.

Let's talk about each of these choices.
Sometimes when we are upset we just blurt out things. Sometimes expressing strong feelings without thinking much about it is helpful to us and sometimes it isn't. Think of as many reasons as you can why people yell at others when they are angry. I'll write them on the blackboard.

1. To get even.
2. To get revenge.
3. To improve things.
4. To make someone stop or change.
5. To get fair treatment.
6. To blow off steam.

Let's role-play as many different endings to this story as we can:

Lamont came out of school to discover his bike had a flat tire. He saw Pete and Mike not far off, grinning. . . .
Describe the effect of what Lamont said. How did it make him feel? How did it make the other boys feel? Did Lamont act in a hostile way? Do you think the flat tire was an accident? Did Lamont? Could it have been? Do you think that if Lamont immediately felt someone had done something to him on

purpose, he might have overlooked other possibilities? Solving problems involves thinking about all of the possible alternatives—not jumping to just one conclusion. Let's make up some rules for solving problems. A solution to a problem should make us feel better, not get us into a worse mess.

1. Take time to think about all the possibilities.
2. Don't automatically suspect the worst possible outcome.
3. Don't try to get even without thinking first. You might attack an innocent person.
4. Assert your rights in a way that does not violate the rights of others.
5. Don't do anything that will later make you feel bad about yourself.
6. Never hurt someone else's feelings, body, or property.
7. Remember that if you lose control you often feel worse.
8. Remember that yelling, screaming, and fighting cause tension in your body.
9. Choose the best thing for you and not just the easiest.

Look in the mirror and say the following sentences with both an angry feeling and a good, satisfied feeling.

I knew that all the time.
My mom saw me do it.
My father is a policeman.

Now look in the mirror and say the following sentences with both a scared, anxious feeling and a satisfied, confident feeling.

Is anyone coming with me?
I think I can do that!
It wasn't me, Mr. Anderson.

Note what your face and body looked like and how your voice sounded when you expressed anger. Think of some alternative ways to tell people how you feel and how to avoid problems in the next stories.

> Jason was playing with his Legos and left them on the floor of the family room. His young brother, Jeremy, messed up the space station Jason had made and scattered all the pieces. When Jason came back, he grabbed Jeremy and shoved him aside. He yelled, "I hate you! You're always messing up my things, you brat!" Jeremy cried, and their mom was angry at Jason for hurting his brother.

What did Jason want? Let's see how many we can think of:

1. He wanted his brother not to touch his things.
2. He wanted to punish his brother for ruining the space station.
3. He wanted to make sure his brother never did it again.

Do you think he got what he wanted? What effects did his actions have? What could he have done differently?

1. Put his Legos away in a safe place.
2. Told his brother, in advance, not to touch his things without asking.
3. Asked his mom, in advance, if it was ok to leave the Legos on the floor, and if so, if she'd tell Jeremy to leave them alone.
4. Told Jeremy he was angry because he'd worked a long time on that space station.
5. Told Jeremy he had to help pick up the pieces.
6. Avoided name calling and "put downs."
7. Told Jeremy he'd let him play with the Legos if only he'd ask first.
8. Told their mom that Jeremy had done it.
9. Remembered not ever to hurt another person's body or feelings.
10. Tried to think why Jeremy might have done it (e.g., to get attention, to make Jason mad, to get Jason into trouble, to get back at Jason for not letting him play, because he felt upset or angry about something else).

Discuss the effects of the following ways of expressing anger:

1. Name calling
2. Put-downs
3. Yelling and screaming
4. Talking quietly
5. Tenseness and strain
6. Calm discussion
7. Repeating oneself
8. Saying something once and waiting for an answer

For homework, find some definitions of the following words:

proof	circumstantial
evidence	suspect
hearsay	victim
retaliation	rights

Imagine you are a detective assigned to the following case. Read the facts and decide a) how to proceed, b) whose rights need to be protected, and c) what advice you would give.

Tony's grandmother was mugged. Her purse was later found in a trash can and her money and credit cards were missing. Two teenagers had been seen loitering on a nearby corner after the incident. The grandmother reported that she did not see the assailants who came up behind her and knocked her to the ground as her purse was grabbed. She was hospitalized for a broken hip. Tony says he won't rest until he finds those two teenagers and breaks *their* hips!

Note that emphasis is placed on the universality of the feelings before specific discussion of an individual child's own feelings is attempted. The task sequence that follows is a useful guide for clinicians. It shows a progression of steps in which feelings are first described and then related to specific vocal behaviors. It can be adapted for use with a variety of emotions and vocal symptoms.

Task Sequence: Interpersonal Behavior–Vocal Behavior

A . *General Awareness*

1. I can identify feelings people have.

   anger   fear
   frustration   guilt
   joy   anxiety
   boredom   embarrassment
   sadness

2. I can describe how people express these feelings.

   facial expressions   words
   gestures and actions   postures
   voice

3. I can describe how feelings can be hidden.

   withdrawal   lies
   pretense   defiance/boasting
   aggressive/destructiveness   distractions
   humor

B. *Specific Awareness*

1. I can identify negative behaviors exhibited by others when they are in different moods.

   angry
   frustrated
   happy
   embarrassed

2. I can identify positive behaviors exhibited by others when they are in different moods.

   angry
   frustrated
   happy
   embarrassed

3. I can suggest some reasons why people act/react in different ways.

   self-image
   role (e.g., power or authority)
   peer pressure
   fear of consequences

4. I can suggest some ways others can avoid or change inappropriate behaviors.

voice
posture
actions
words

5. I can describe how feelings can be expressed by changes in people's voices.

    pitch level   loudness level
    pitch inflection   loudness changes
    pauses/rate   tension/hard attacks on words
    breathing   amount of talking/silence

6. I can describe how other people use their voices incorrectly in certain emotional states.

    angry   excited or satisfied
    anxious   dissatisfied
    frightened   disappointed

7. I can describe how listeners react to some of these vocal characteristics.

    feel uncomfortable
    withdraw/don't listen
    become aggressive
    cooperate
    feel sympathetic/friendly/put down

8. I can describe the specific behaviors associated with incorrect vocal use.

    talking too loudly/too softly
    not using enough variety
    using a strained/tense/unpleasant voice
    using a hard sound to get started
    not taking in enough air to get started
    not pausing enough to replenish air supply
    talking too fast/too slow
    not responding to listener's feedback
    talking only about self

9. I can describe alternative behaviors people could use in certain emotional states.

    angry   dissatisfied
    anxious   excited
    afraid   disappointed
    satisfied

10. I can describe ways to use the voice correctly.

    take in enough air to begin talking
    pause enough to refill air supply
    use an easy sound to get started
    use an easy/relaxed voice

use an appropriate loudness level
share talking time
use more variety
use gestures, questions, etc.

C. *Production*

1. I can demonstrate alternative nonvocal behaviors to use in certain emotional states.
   angry
   frightened
   satisfied
   anxious
   excited
   dissatisfied
   disappointed

2. I can demonstrate how to use my voice correctly in role-playing certain emotional states.
   angry
   frightened
   satisfied
   anxious
   excited
   dissatisfied
   disappointed

3. I can evaluate the effects of my vocal behavior during role-playing.
   on my body
   on my feelings
   on achieving what I want
   on others' reactions to me

D. *Carryover*

1. I can describe the times in my everyday life when it is hardest for me to use/maintain appropriate vocal behavior.

   emotional state   background noise
   size of group   physical state
   type of activity   specific person spoken to
   time of day   purpose of interaction
   location of the talking

2. I can develop strategies for correct behavior in my difficult emotional states/situations.
   alternative vocal strategies
   alternative nonvocal strategies

3. I can use correct vocal/nonvocal behaviors in difficult emotional states and situations I have preplanned.
   sometimes

most of the time
all of the time

4. I can evaluate the results of my preplanned vocal/nonvocal behaviors.
   on myself
   on others
   on achieving my goal

5. I can use correct vocal/nonvocal strategies in difficult emotional states/situations spontaneously.
   some of the time
   most of the time
   all of the time

In the treatment plan just discussed, extensive use was made of self-regulating speech. The various interpretations of some of the situations were modeled first by the clinician and gradually were picked up and used spontaneously by the boys as new examples were analyzed. It became clear that the boys' expectations concerning the intent of others' actions were frequently that the action was purposeful rather than accidental. The clinician noted this and included more frequent examples of aggressive reactions to "accidental" happenings so that the boys could see that accidents frequently occur. The use of discussion of situations and analyses of events concerning other children proved extremely helpful. The boys delighted in identifying what others did wrong and competed with one another in the group to be the first to find better solutions. The group interaction was stimulating. Nevertheless, the clinician found it necessary to establish and enforce certain ground rules:

1. No two people talk at once—take turns.
2. No solutions can involve lying, physical abuse, or the hurting of another's feeling or property.
3. Talk at a moderate level or forfeit your turn.

The clinician praised the boys liberally when they obeyed the rules and awarded points for appropriate participation in activities. The group kept, and reviewed weekly, a running total of points, and rewards were given each month for the highest number of points. The boys' self-esteem was bolstered by the way the clinician praised their participation (e.g., "Howie is always good at thinking of this kind of solution—I bet he'll know what the boy could try," or, "Now, Joe had trouble with interrupting too much last week, but I can tell he's got that under control today"). The boys responded well to the clinician's reiteration of his confidence in their ability to control their impulses and seek creative solutions to their problems. Their expectations that they could handle tough situations in acceptable (and more profitable) ways seemed to increase as a result of the way the clinician reflected his positive view of their abilities.

One of the most important insights that the boys developed was the need to analyze the purpose of an interaction before discussing alternative strategies. For example, once they clarified that their purpose was to make the listener understand their point of view, rather than react angrily to them, they then could see the advantages of adopting a quieter, more reasonable vocal style, as opposed to a loud, defiant, or belligerent tone of voice.

In this approach the clinician plays an important role in helping the child understand his or her goal in each interaction. The clinician's questioning and prompting during discussions helps children strip away the emotional components in an interaction in order to focus on what they wish to achieve (e.g., to explain their position, to defend their actions, to persuade another to change).

Richard and Dodge (1982) suggest that the generation of many solutions to hypothetical persuasive tasks does significantly increase the number of actual persuasive attempts made by children in behavioral situations. The number of solutions generated does not necessarily predict the competence or success of those attempts. They say that clinicians who wish to train these skills must remember that generating many solutions and generating competent solutions to hypothetical persuasive tasks, are independent cognitive skills.

Bibliography

Adler, S. (1979). *Poverty children and their language*. New York: Grune & Stratton.

Allport, G. W. (1954). *The nature of prejudice*. Cambridge, MA: Addison-Wesley.

American Speech and Hearing Association. (1964). The speech clinician's role in the public schools: A statement by the American Speech and Hearing Association. *Asha, 6*, 189–191.

American Speech and Hearing Association. (1974). Prevention of communication problems. *Asha, 16*, 141–142.

Anderson, V. A., & Newby, H. A. (1973). *Improving the child's speech* (2d Ed.). New York: Oxford University Press.

Andrews, M. L. (1973). Voice therapy with a group of language-delayed children. *Journal of Speech and Hearing Disorders, 38*, 510–513.

Andrews, M. L. (1975). Communication problems encountered in voice therapy with children. *Language, Speech and Hearing Services in Schools, 6*, 183–187.

Andrews, M. L. & Huffman, C. (1984). A comparison of two methods of eliciting basal pitch levels. Unpublished study, Indiana University.

Andrews, M. L., & Madiera, S. (1977). The assessment of pitch discrimination ability in young children. *Journal of Speech and Hearing Disorders, 42*, 279–286.

Andrews, M. L., Tardy, S. J., & Pasternak, L. G. (1984). The modification of hypernasality in young children: A programming approach. *Language, Speech and Hearing Services in Schools, 15*, 37–39.

Arnold, G. E. (1962). Vocal nodules and polyps: Laryngeal tissue reaction to habitual hyperkinetic dysphonia. *Journal of Speech and Hearing Disorders, 27*, 205–216.

Arnold, G. E. (1963). Vocal nodules. In J. F. Daly (Moderator), Voice problems and laryngeal pathology. *N. Y. State Journal of Medicine, 63*, 3096–3110.

Aronson, A. (1973). *Psychogenic voice disorders: An interdisciplinary approach to detection, diagnosis and therapy.* Philadelphia: Saunders.

Aronson, A. E. (1980). *Clinical voice disorders.* New York: Brian C. Decker Division, Thieme-Stratton.

Asher, S. R., & Hymel, S. (1981). Children's social competence in peer relations: Sociometric and behavioral assessment. In J. D. Wine & M. D. Smye (Eds.), *Social competence.* New York: Guilford Press.

Aslin, R. N., Pisoni, D. B., & Jusczek, P. W. Auditory development and speech perception in infancy. In P. Mussen (Ed.), *Carmichael's Manual of Child Psychology (4th ed.): Vol. II Infancy and the Biology of Development* (by M. M. Haith and J. J. Campos, Eds.). New York: Wiley, 1983, pp. 573–687.

Austin, M. D., & Leeper, H. A., Jr. (1975). Basal pitch and frequency level variation in male and female children: A preliminary investigation. *Journal of Communicative Disorders, 8*, 307–315.

Baken, R. J. (1977). Estimation of lung volume change from torso hemi-circumferences. *Journal of Speech and Hearing Research, 20*, 808–812.

Baken, R. J. (1979, June). Respiratory mechanisms: Introduction and overview. *Transcripts of the 8th Symposium: Care of the Professional Voice, 2*, 9–13.

Baken, R. J., & Cavallo, S. A. (1981). Prephonatory chest wall posturing. *Folia Phoniatrica, 33*, 193–203.

Baken, R. J., Cavallo, S. A., & Weissman, K. L. (1979b). Chest wall movements prior to phonation. *Journal of Speech and Hearing Research, 22*, 862–872.

Baranak, C., Potsic, W. P., Miller-Bauer, L., & Marsh, R. R. (1983, December). Changes in sleep patterns with adenotonsillectomy. Paper presented at the annual meeting of SENTAC, San Diego, CA.

Baynes, R. A. (1966). An incidence study of chronic hoarseness among children. *Journal of Speech and Hearing Disorders, 31*, 172–176.

Baynes, R. A. (1967). Voice therapy with children—a global approach. *Journal of the Michigan Speech & Hearing Association, 3*, 11–14.

Bennett, S. (1983). A three-year longitudinal study of school-aged children's fundamental frequencies. *Journal of Speech and Hearing Research, 26*, 137–141.

Bennett, S., & Weinberg, B. (1979). Acoustic correlates of perceived sexual identity in preadolescent children's voices. *Journal of the Acoustical Society of America, 66*, 989–1000.

Bierswich, M. (1967). Some semantic universals of German adjectives. *Foundations of Language, 3*, 1–36.

Bless, D. M., & Abbs, J. H. (Eds.). (1983). *Vocal Fold Physiology*. San Diego, CA: College-Hill Press.

Blonigen, J. A. (1978). Management of vocal hoarseness caused by abuse: An approach. *Language, Speech and Hearing Services in Schools, 9*, 142–150.

Bloom, B. S. (Ed.). (1956). *Taxonomy of educational objectives: Cognitive domain*. New York: David McKay.

Boone, D. R. (1966). Modification of the voices of deaf children. *Volta Review, 67*, 686–692.

Boone, D. R. (1977). *The voice and voice therapy* (2d Ed.). Englewood Cliffs, NJ: Prentice-Hall.

Boone, D. R. (1983). *The voice and voice therapy* (3d Ed.). Englewood Cliffs, NJ: Prentice-Hall.

Broad, D. J. (1973). Phonation. In F. Minifie, T. Hixon, & F. Williams (Eds.), *Normal aspects of Speech, Hearing and Language*. Englewood Cliffs, NJ: Prentice-Hall.

Brodnitz, F. S. (1971). *Vocal Rehabilitation* (4th Ed.). Rochester, NY: American Academy of Ophthalmology and Otolaryngology.

Brown, B. L. (1976). A cross-cultural study of social status markers in speech. *Canadian Journal of Behavioral Science, 8*, 39–55.

Burk, K. W. (1971). Concepts of clinical management with children presenting voice disturbances. *Journal of the Kansas Speech & Hearing Association, 11*, 60–66.

Burk, K. W. (1977). Paper presented at the Indiana Speech & Hearing Association Convention, Nashville, Indiana.

Buss, A. H., & Plomin, R. A. (1975). *A temperament theory of personality development*. London: Wiley.

Bzoch, K. R. (Ed.). (1972). *Communicative disorders related to cleft lip and palate*. Boston, MA: Little, Brown & Co.

Calvert, D. R., & Silverman, S. R. (1975). *Speech and Deafness*. Washington, DC: Alexander Graham Bell Association for the Deaf.

Camp, B. (1977). Verbal mediation in young aggressive boys. *Journal of Abnormal Psychology, 86*, 145–153.

Campbell, D. T. (1967). Stereotypes and the perception of group differences. *American Psychologist, 22*, 817–829.

Carrow, E. A. (1974). A test using elicited imitations in assessing grammatical structure in children. *Journal of Speech and Hearing Disorders, 39*, 437–444.

Champley, E. (1977). A comparison of four methods of eliciting vocal responses from preschool children. Unpublished master's thesis, Indiana University, Bloomington, IN.

Chandler, M. J. (1973). Egocentrism and anti-social behavior: The assessment and training of social perspective-taking skills. *Developmental Psychology, 9*, 326–333.

Clark, H. H. (1969a). Linguistic processes in deductive reasoning. *Psychological Review, 76*, 387–404.

Clark, H. H. (1969b). The influence of language in solving three-term series problems. *Journal of Experimental Psychology, 82*, 205–215.

Coie, J. D., Dodge, K. A., & Coppotelli, H. (1982). Dimensions and types of social status: A cross age perspective. *Developmental Psychology, 18*, 557–570.

Colton, R. H., & Cooker, H. S. (1968). Perceived nasality in the speech of the deaf. *Journal of Speech and Hearing Research, 11*, 553–559.

Cook, J. V., Palaski, D. J., Hanson, W. R. (1979). A vocal hygiene program for school age children. *Language, Speech and Hearing Services in Schools, 10*, 21–26.

Cooper, M. (1973). *Modern techniques of vocal rehabilitation.* Springfield, IL: Charles C Thomas.

Cooper, M., & Yanagihara, N. (1971). A study of the basal pitch level variations in the normal speaking voices of males and females. *Journal of Communication Disorders, 3*, 261–266.

Corsaro, W. A. (1981). Friendship in the nursery school: Social organization in a peer environment. In S. R. Asher & J. M. Gottman (Eds.), *The development of children's friendships.* Cambridge, England: Cambridge University Press.

Courtright, J. A., & Courtright, I. C. (1983). The perception of nonverbal cues of emotional meaning by language-disordered and normal children. *Journal of Speech and Hearing Research, 26*, 412–417.

Curry, E. (1940). The pitch characteristics of the adolescent male voice. *Speech Monographs, 7*, 48–62.

Curry, E. T. (1949). Hoarseness and voice change in male adolescents. *Journal of Speech and Hearing Disorders, 16*, 23–24.

Daniloff, R. G., Schuckers, G. H., & Feth, L. (1980). *The science of speech and hearing.* Englewood Cliffs, NJ: Prentice-Hall.

Darley, F. L. (1965). *Diagnosis and appraisal of communication disorders.* Englewood Cliffs, NJ: Prentice-Hall.

Darwin, C. (1872). *The expression of emotions in man and animals.* London: Murray.

Davitz, Joel, R. (Ed.). (1964). *The communication of emotional meaning.* New York: McGraw Hill.

Deal, R. E., McClain, B., & Sudderth, J. F. (1976). Identification, evaluation therapy and follow-up for children with vocal nodules in a public school setting. *Journal of Speech and Hearing Disorders*, *41*, 390–397.

Dehejia, H. (1981). *The allergy book*. London: Van Nostrand Reinhold.

DeVito, J. A. (1980). *The interpersonal communication book* (2d Ed.). New York: Harper & Row.

DeWeese, D. D., & Saunders, W. H. (1973). *Textbook of otolaryngology* (4th Ed.). St. Louis, MO: C. V. Mosby.

Diehl, C. F., & Stinnett, C. D. (1959). Efficiency of teacher referrals in a school speech testing program. *Journal of Speech and Hearing Disorders*, *24*, 34–36.

Dodge, K. A. (1980). Social cognition and children's aggressive behavior. *Child Development*, 1980, *51*, 162–170.

Dodge, K. A. (1981, April). Attributional bias in aggressive children. Paper presented at the biennial meeting of the Society for Research in Child Development, Boston, MA.

Dodge, K. A. (1981, May). Social competencies and aggressive behavior in children. Paper presented to the Midwestern Psychological Association, Detroit, MI.

Dodge, K. A. (1981c). Behavioral antecedents of peer social rejection and isolation. Presented as part of a symposium on methodological and substantive issues in the observation of peer interaction at the biennial meeting of the Society for Research in Child Development, Boston, MA.

Dodge, K. A., Coie, J. D., & Brakke, N. P. (1982). Behavior patterns of socially rejected and neglected preadolescents: The roles of social approach and aggression. *Journal of Abnormal Child Psychology*, *10*, 389–409.

Dodge, K. A., Schlundt, D. G., Delagach, J. S., & Schocken, I. (1982, November). Multivariate information theory analysis of children's peer group entry behavior. Paper delivered at the annual meeting of the Association for the Advancement of Behavior Therapy, Los Angeles, CA.

Drudge, M. K., & Phillips, B. J. (1976). Shaping behavior in voice therapy. *Journal of Speech and Hearing Disorders*, *41*, 398–411.

Duffy, R. (1970). Fundamental frequency characteristics of adolescent females. *Language and Speech*, *13*, 14–24.

Eckel, F., & Boone, D. (1981). The s/z ratio as an indication of laryngeal pathology. *Journal of Speech and Hearing Disorders*, *46*, 147–149.

Egolf, D. B., & Chester, S. L. (1973). Nonverbal communication and the disorders of speech and language. *Asha*, *15*, 511–518.

Eguchi, S., & Hirsh, I. (1969). Development of speech sound in children. *Acta Otolaryngologica*, 257 (suppl.).

Ekman, P., & Oster, H. (1979). Facial expression of emotion. *Annual Review of Physchology, 30,* 527–554.

Evard, B. L., & Sabers, D. L. (1979). Speech and language testing with distinct ethnic racial groups: A survey of procedures for improving validity. *Journal of Speech and Hearing Disorders, 44,* 271–281.

Fairbanks, G. (1960). *Voice and articulation drillbook.* New York: Harper & Row.

Fairbanks, G., Herbert, E., & Hammond, J. (1949). An acoustical study of vocal pitch in seven- and eight-year-old girls. *Child Development,* 1949, *20,* 71–78.

Fairbanks, G., Wiley, J., & Lassman, F. (1949). An acoustical study of vocal pitch in seven- and eight-year-old boys. *Child Development, 20,* 63–69.

Feshback, S. (1970). Aggression. In P. Mussen (Ed.), *Carmichael's manual of child psychology.* New York: Wiley.

Feshback, S. (1982). When you permit children to play aggressively. In C. Tavris, *Anger, the misunderstood emotion.* New York: Simon & Schuster.

Fisher, H. B. (1975). *Improving voice and articulation* (2d Ed.). Boston, MA: Houghton Mifflin.

Fixsin, D., Phillips, E. L., Baron, R., Coughlin, D., Daly, D., & Daly, P. (1978). The Boys Town revolution. *Human Nature, 1*(11), 54–61.

Flapan, D. (1968). *Children's understanding of social interaction.* New York: Teachers College Press.

Fletcher, S. G., & Daly, D. A. (1976). Nasalance in utterances of hearing impaired speakers. *Journal of Communication Disorders, 9,* 63–73.

Flynn, P. T. (1983). Speech-language pathologists and primary prevention: From ideas to action. *LSHSS, 2,* 99–104.

Fonagy, I. (1981). Emotions, voice and music. In *Research aspects on singing.* Published by the Royal Swedish Academy of Music, No. 33.

Forner, L. L., & Hixon, T. J. (1977). Respiratory kinematics in profoundly hearing-impaired speakers. *Journal of Speech and Hearing Research, 20,* 373–408.

Fox, D. R., & Johns, D. (1970). Predicting velopharyngeal closure with a modified tongue anchor technique. *Journal of Speech and Hearing Disorders, 35,* 248–251.

Frances, S. J. (1979). Sex-differences in nonverbal behavior. *Sex Roles, 5,* 519–535.

Frazier, Claude A. (1978). *Parent's guide to allergy in children.* New York: Grosset & Dunlap.

Freeman, S. R., & Garstecki, D. C. (1973). Child directed therapy for a nonorganic voice disorder: A case study. *Language, Speech and Hearing Services in Schools, 4,* 8–12.

Frey, M. (1978). The prolongation of /s/ and /z/ by pre-school children. Unpublished master's thesis, Indiana University.

Frick, James F. (1960). The incidence of voice defects among school age speech defective children. *Pennsylvania Speech Annual, ·17*, 61–62.

Frisch, R. E. (1978). Critical weights, a critical body composition, menarche and the maintenance of menstrual cycles. In *Biosocial interrelation in population adaptation.* The Hague: Mouton.

Frisch, R. E., & Revelle, R. (1971). Height and weight at menarche and a hypothesis of menarche. *Archives of Diseases in Childhood, 46,* 249.

Fuller, C. W. (1970). Differential diagnosis. In F. S. Berg & S. G. Fletcher (Eds.), *The hard of hearing child: Clinical and educational management* (pp. 203–215). New York: Grune & Stratton.

Gay, T., Hirose, H., Strome, M., & Sawashima, M. (1972). Electromyography of the intrinsic laryngeal muscles during phonation. *Annals of Otology, Rhinology and Laryngology, 81,* 401–409.

Geis, F. L., Carter, M. R., & Butler, D. (1982). *Seeing and evaluating people.* Newark, DE: Office of Women's Affairs, University of Delaware.

Goldfarb, W. (1961). *Childhood schizophrenia.* Cambridge, MA: Harvard University Press.

Goldfarb, W., Braunstein, P., & Lorge, I. (1976). A study of speech patterns in a group of schizophrenic children. *American Journal of Orthopsychiatry, 56,* 544–555.

Goldstein, M. N., & Abramson, A. L. (1983, December). Airway obstruction in the lung due to allergy: Uncommon pediatric problem. Paper presented at the annual meeting of SENTAC, San Diego, CA.

Gottman, J. M., Gonso, J., & Rasmussen, B. (1975). Social interaction, social competence and friendship in children. *Child Development, 46,* 709–718.

Gottman, J. M., & Parkhurst, J. T. (1981). A developmental theory of friendship and acquaintanceship processes. In A. Collins (Ed.), *Minnesota symposia on child psychology* (Vol. 13). Hillsdale, NJ: Erlbaum.

Greenberg, J. H. (1966). *Language universals.* The Hague: Mouton.

Greene, M. C. L. (1972). *The voice and its disorders* (3d Ed.). New York: Pitman.

Grey, P. (1973). Microlaryngastroboscopy and "singer's nodes." *Journal of the Otolaryngology Society of Australia, 3,* 525–527.

Hall, G. S. (1899). A study of anger. *American Journal of Psychology, 10,* 516–591.

Hanley, T. D., & Thurman, W. L., (1970). *Developing vocal skills* (2d Ed.). New York: Holt, Rinehart and Winston.

Hansel, French K. (1975). *Allergy and immunity in otolaryngology* (3d Ed.).

Rochester, MN: American Academy of Ophthalmology and Otolaryngology.

Harris, P. L., Olthof, T., & Terwogt, M. (1981). Children's knowledge of emotion. *Child Psychology and Psychiatry, 22*(3), 247–261.

Hartup, W. W., Glazer, J. A., & Charlesworth, R. (1967). Peer reinforcement and sociometric status. *Child Development, 38*, 1017–1024.

Hasek, C., Singh, S., & Murry, T. (1980). Acoustic attributes of preadolescent voices. *Journal of the Acoustical Society of America, 68*, 1262–1265.

Hengerer, A. S., & DiTirro, F. (1983, December). Acute epiglottitis: Evolution and management in the community hospital. Paper presented at the annual meeting of the Society for Ear, Nose & Throat Advances in Children, San Diego, CA.

Henry, D. P., Pashley, N. R. T., & Fan, L. (1983, December). Anticipation of laryngeal injury incurred by an endotracheal tube in children. Paper presented at the annual meeting of SENTAC, San Diego, CA.

Hirano, M. (1981). Structure of the vocal fold in normal and disease states: anatomical and physical studies. In C. L. Ludlow & M. O. C. Hart (Eds.), *Proceedings of the conference on the assessment of vocal pathology: Report II.* Rockville, MD: American Speech and Hearing Association.

Hixon, T. (1970). Clinical implications of recent advances in speech breathing mechanics. Paper presented at the American Speech and Hearing Association convention, New York.

Hixon, T. J., Mead, J., & Goldman, M. D. (1976). Dynamics of the chest wall during speech production: Function of the thorax, rib cage, diaphragm and abdomen. *Journal of Speech and Hearing Research, 19*, 297–356.

Hokanson, J. E., & Burgess, M. (1961). The effects of three types of aggression on vascular processes. *Journal of Abnormal and Social Psychology, 63*(2), 446–449.

Hokanson, J. E., Willers, K. R., & Korapsak, E. (1968). The modification of automatic responses during aggressive interchange. *Journal of Personality, 36*, 386–404.

Holinger, P. H., & Brown, W. T. Congenital webs, cysts, laryngoceles and other anomalies of the larynx. *Annals of Otolaryngolgoy, Rhinology and Laryngology, 76*, 1967.

Hollien, H. (1983). Vocal frequency control mechanisms. In D. M. Bless & J. M. Abbs (Eds.), *Vocal fold physiology.* San Diego, CA: College-Hill Press.

Hollien, H., & Malcik, E. (1967). Evaluation of cross sectional studies of adolescent voice change in males. *Speech Monographs, 34*, 80–84.

Hollien, H., Malcik, E., & Hollien, B. (1965). Adolescent voice change in southern white males. *Speech Monographs, 32*, 87–90.

Hood, L., & Bloom, L. (1979). What, when, and how about why: A longitudinal study of early expressions of causality. *Monographs of the Society for Research in Child Development*, 44 (6, Serial No. 181).

Horii, Y. (1983a). An accelometric measure as a physical correlate of perceived hypernasality in speech. *Journal of Speech and Hearing Research*, *3*, 476–480.

Horii, Y., & Monroe, N. (1983b, September). Auditory and visual feedback of nasalization using a modified accelometric method. *Journal of Speech and Hearing Research*, *3*, 472–475.

Inhelder, B., & Piaget, J. (1964). *Early growth of logic in the child: Classification and seriation*. New York: Harper & Row.

Isshiki, N. (1964). Regulatory mechanism of voice intensity variation. *Journal of Speech and Hearing Research*, *7*, 17–29.

Itoh, M., Horii, Y., Daniloff, R. G., & Binnie, C. A. (1982). Selected aerodynamic characteristics of deaf individuals during various speech and nonspeech tasks. *Folia Phoniatrica*, *34*, 191–209.

Jeffrey, W. E. (1958, December). Variables in early discrimination learning: 11. Mode of response and stimulus difference in the discrimination of tonal frequencies. *Child Development*, *29*(4), 531–538.

Kahane, J. (1975). The developmental anatomy of the human prepubertal and pubertal larynx. Doctoral dissertation, University of Pittsburgh.

Katz, S., McDonald, J. L., & Stuckey, G. K. (1972). *Preventive dentistry in action*. Upper Montclair, NJ: D. C. P. Publishing.

Kelly, H. D. B., & Craik, J. E. (1952). Laryngeal nodes and the so-called amyloid tumour of the cords. *Journal of Laryngology and Otolaryngology*, *66*, 339–358.

Kent, R. (1976). Anatomic and neuromuscular maturation of the speech mechanism: Evidence from acoustic studies. *Journal of Speech and Hearing Research*, *19*, 421–447.

Kero, P., Puhakka, H., Erkinjuntti, M., Iisalo, E., & Vilkki, P. (1983). Foreign body in the airways of children. *International Journal of Pediatric Otorhinolaryngology*, *6*, 51–59.

King, R. G., & Dimichael, E. M. (1978). *Articulation and voice: Improving oral communication*. New York: Macmillan.

Klock, L. (1968). The growth and development of the human larynx from birth to adolescence. Medical thesis, University of Washington, School of Medicine.

Kolbenschlag, M. (1981). *Kiss Sleeping Beauty goodbye*. New York: Bantam.

Kolvin, I., & Fundudis, T. (1981, July). Elective mute children: Psychological development and background factors. *Journal of Child Psychology and Psychiatry*, *22*(3), 219–232.

Konno, K., & Mead, J. (1967). Measurement of the separate volume changes of rib cage and abdomen during breathing. *Journal of Applied Physiology*, *22*, 407–422.

Langer, E., Blank, A., & Chanowitz, B. (1978). The mindlessness of ostensibly thoughtful action: The role of "placebic" information in interpersonal interaction. *Journal of Personality and Social Psychology*, *36*, 635–642.

Launer, P. G. (1971). Maximum phonation time in children. Unpublished master's thesis, State University of New York at Buffalo.

Laupus, W. E., & Pastora, P. N. (1967). The larynx. In E. L. Kendig, Jr. (Ed.), *Disorders of the respiratory tract in children* (pp. 204–212). Philadelphia, PA: W. B. Saunders Co.

Lazarus, R. (1975). The self-regulation of emotions. In L. Levi (Ed.), *Emotions—their parameters and measurement*. New York: Raven Press.

Lazarus, R. S. (1968). Emotions and adaptation: Conceptual and empirical relations. In W. J. Arnold (Ed.), *Nebraska symposium on motivation*. Lincoln, NE: University of Nebraska.

Lieberman, P. (1975). Intonation, perception and language. *Research Monograph*, No. 38 (3d Ed.). Cambridge, MA: MIT Press.

Lieberman, P. (1977). *Speech physiology and acoustic phonetics*. New York: Macmillan.

Ling, D. (1975). Amplification for speech. In D. R. Calvert & S. R. Silverman (Eds.), *Speech and Deafness* (pp. 64–88). Washington, DC: Alexander Graham Bell Association for the Deaf.

Ling, D. (1976). *Speech and the hearing-impaired child: Theory and practice*. Washington, DC: Alexander Graham Bell Association for the Deaf.

Luchsinger, R. (1965). Physiology and pathology of respiration and phonation. In R. Lucksinger & G. E. Arnold (Eds.), *Voice-speech-language. Clinical communicology: Its physiology and pathology*. Belmont, CA: Wadsworth.

Luchsinger, R., & Arnold, G. E. (1965). *Voice-speech-language. Clinical communicology: Its physiology and pathology*. Belmont, CA: Wadsworth.

Lyons, J. (1963). *Structural semantics*. Oxford, England: Blackwell.

McDonald, T., & Chance, B. (1964). *Cerebral Palsy*. Englewood Cliffs, NJ: Prentice-Hall.

McFall, R. M., & Dodge, K. A. (1982). Self-management and interpersonal skills learning. In P. Karoly & F. H. Kanfer (Eds.), *Self-management and behavior change*. Elmsford, N.Y.: Pergamon.

McGuire, J. M. (1973). Aggression and sociometric status with preschool children. *Sociometry, 36*, 542–549.

McMahon, O. (1961, May). Exploring music with children. *Australian Pre-school Quarterly, 1*(4), 10–15.

Madiera, S. (1975). Children's use of relational terms "high" and "low": Some implications for therapy. Unpublished master's thesis, Indiana University.

Mallick, S. K., & McCandless, B. R. (1966). A study of catharsis aggression. *Journal of Personality and Social Psychology, 4*, 591–596.

Michel, J. F., & Tait, N. (1977, November). Maximum duration of sustained /s/ and /z/. Paper presented at annual convention of the American Speech and Hearing Association, Chicago, IL.

Miller, G. A., Galanter, E., & Pribram, K. H. (1960). *Plans and the structure of behavior.* New York: Holt, Rinehart & Winston.

Miller, S. Q., & Madison, C. L. (1984a, January). Public school voice clinics, Part I: A working model. *Language, Speech and Hearing Services in Schools, 15*(1), 51–55.

Miller, S. Q., & Madison, C. L. (1984b, January). Public school voice clinics, Part II: Diagnosis and recommendations—a 10 year review. *Language, Speech and Hearing Services in Schools, 15*(1), 58–63.

Minifie, F. D., Hixon, T. J., & Williams, F. (1973). *Normal aspects of speech, hearing and language.* Englewood Cliffs, NJ: Prentice-Hall.

Moncur, J. P., & Brackett, I. P. (1974). *Modifying vocal behavior.* New York: Harper & Row.

Monson, R. B., Engelbretson, A. M., & Vernula, N. R. (1979). Some effects of degrees on the generation of voice. *Journal of the Acoustical Society of America, 66*, 1680–1690.

Montague, J. C., & Hollien, H. (1973). Perceived voice quality disorders in Down's syndrome children. *Journal of Communication Disorders, 6*, 76–87.

Moore, G. P. (1971). Voice disorders organically based. In L. E. Travis (Ed.), *Handbook of speech pathology and audiology* (pp. 535–570). New York: Appleton-Century-Crofts.

Moore, G. P. (1971). *Organic voice disorders.* Englewood Cliffs, NJ: Prentice-Hall.

Mowrer, D. (1978). Speech problems: What you should and shouldn't do. *Learning, 6*, 34–37.

Mysak, E. D. (1971). Cerebral palsy speech syndromes. In L. E. Travis (Ed.), *Handbook of speech pathology and audiology* (pp. 673–695). New York: Appleton-Century-Crofts.

Mysak, E. D. (1980). *Neurospeech therapy for the cerebral palsied: A neuroevolutional approach* (3d Ed.) New York: Teachers College Press.

Neubauer, P. (Ed.). (1965). *Concepts of development in early childhood education.* Springfield, IL: Charles C Thomas.

Nilson, H., & Schneiderman, C. R. (1983). Classroom program for the prevention of vocal abuse and hoarseness in elementary school children. *Language, Speech and Hearing Services in Schools, 14*(2), 121–127.

Novak, A. (1972). The voice of children with Down's syndrome. *Folia Phoniatrica, 24*, 182–194.

Noyce, P. W. (1983, December). The shape of the infant sub-glottis. Paper presented at the annual meeting of SENTAC, San Diego, CA.

Oden, S., & Asher, S. R. (1977). Coaching children in social skills for friendship making. *Child Development, 48*, 495–506.

Pannbacker, M. (1984). Classification systems of voice disorders: A review of the literature. *Language, Speech and Hearing Services in Schools, 15(3),* 169–174.

Parisier, S. C., & Henneford, G. E. (1969). Surgical correction of acquired vocal cord webs. *Archives of Otolaryngology, 90*, 103–107.

Pashley, N. R. T., Henry, D., & Fan, L. (1983). Selections of the child with early subglottal injury for treatment by anterior cricoidotomy. Paper presented at the annual meeting of SENTAC, San Diego, CA.

Pasquariello, P. S., Potsic, W. P., Miller, L, & Corso, C. (1983). Nutrition in adenotonsillar hyperplasia. Paper presented at the annual meeting of SENTAC, San Diego, CA.

Pellegrini, A. D. (1982). Applying a self-regulating private speech model to classroom settings. *Language, Speech and Hearing Services in Schools, 13*, 129–133.

Phillips, E. L., Shenker, S., & Revitz, P. (1951). The assimilation of the new child into the group. *Psychiatry, 14*, 319–325.

Physicians' Desk Reference, (Charles E. Baker, Jr., publisher). Medical Economics Co., a Litton division at Oradell, NJ 07649. Edition 38, 1984.

Piaget, J. (1926). *The language and thought of the child.* New York: Harcourt Brace Jovanovich.

Piaget, J. (1928). *Judgment and reasoning in the child.* New York: Harcourt Brace Jovanovich.

Piaget, J. (1929). *The child's conception of the world.* New York: Harcourt Brace Jovanovich.

Piaget, J. (1930). *The child's conception of physical causality.* London: Kegan Paul.

Piliavin, J. A., & Martin, R. R. (1978). Effects of sex composition in groups on style and social interaction. *Sex Roles, 4*, 281–296.

Pletcher, B. P., Locks, N. A., Reynolds, D. F., & Sesson, B. G. (1978). *A guide to assessment instruments for limited English speaking students*. New York: Santillana.

Pronovost, W. (1939). *An experimental study of the habitual and natural pitch levels of superior speakers*. Unpublished doctoral dissertation, State University of Iowa.

Prutting, C. A., & Connolly, J. E. (1976). Imitation: A closer look. *Journal of Speech and Hearing Disorders, 41*, 412–422.

Punt, N. A. (1967). *The singer's and actor's throat* (2d Ed.). Oxford, England: Alden Press.

Putallaz, M., & Gottman, J. M. (1981a). Social skills and group acceptance. In S. R. Asher & J. M. Gottman (Eds.), *The development of children's friendships: Description and intervention*. New York: Cambridge University Press.

Putallaz, M., & Gottman, J. M. (1981b). An interactional model of children's entry into peer groups. *Child Development, 52*, 986–994.

Randolf, T. G., & Moss, R. W. (1980). *An alternative approach to allergies*. New York: Lippincott & Crowell.

Rastatter, M. P., & Hyman, M. (1984, January). Effects of selected rhinologic disorders on the perception of nasal resonance in children. *Language, Speech and Hearing Services in Schools, 15*(1), 44–50.

Reese, H. W. (1970). Imagery in children's learning: A symposium. *Psychological Bulletin, 73*, 404–414.

Richard, B. A., & Dodge, K. A. (1982a). Children's compentence at persuasion: The relation between cognitive skills and behavioral performance. Paper presented at the annual meeting of the Association for the Advancement of Behavior Therapy, Los Angeles, CA.

Richard, B. A., & Dodge, K. A. (1982b). Social maladjustment and problem solving in school-aged children. *Journal of Consulting and Clinical Psychology, 50*(2), 226–233.

Rosen, B., & Jerdee, T. H. (1974). Influence of sex-role stereotypes on personal decisions. *Journal of Applied Psychology, 59*, 9–14.

Rosenthal, R. (1974). *On the social psychology of the self-fulfilling prophecy: Further evidence for pygmalion effects and their mediating mechanisms* (Module No. 53). New York: MSS Modular Publications.

Ryan, R. E. (1968). *The nose in health and disease*. Lincoln, NE: Dorsey Laboratories.

Sapir, E. (1944). Grading: A study in semantics. *Philosophy of Science, 11*, 93–116.

Schachter, S. (1975). Cognition and peripheralist—centralist controversies in motivation and emotion. In M. S. Gazzaniga & C. Blakemore (Eds.), *Handbook of psychobiology*. New York: Academic Press.

Schiffman, H. R. (1976). *Sensation and Perception*. New York: Wiley.

Schoen, P., Gill, G., & Wallace, K. (1983, December). Tracheostomized school children. Paper presented at the annual meeting of SENTAC, San Diego, CA.

Senturia, B. H., & Wilson, F. B. (1968). Otorhinolaryngic findings in children with voice deviations. *Annals of Otology, Rhinology and Laryngology, 77*, 1027–1042.

Shanty, C. U. (1975). The development of social cognition. In E. M. Hetherington (Ed.), *Review of child development research* (Vol. 5). Chicago, IL: University of Chicago Press.

Shearer, W. H. (1972). Diagnosis and treatment of voice disorders in school children. *Journal of Speech and Hearing Disorders, 37*, 215–221.

Sherif, M., Harrecy, O. J., White, B. J., Hood, W. R., & Sherif, C. W. (1961). *Inter-group conflict and co-operation: The Robbers Cave experiment*. Norman, OK: Institute of Group Relations.

Shipp, T., & McGlone, R. E. (1971). Laryngeal dynamics associated with voice frequency change. *Journal of Speech and Hearing Research, 14*, 761–768.

Silverman, E. M., & Zimmer, C. H. (1975). Incidence of chronic hoarseness among school-aged children. *Journal of Speech and Hearing Disorders, 40*, 211–215.

Simon, B., & Handler, S. D. (1981). The speech pathologist and management of children with tracheostomies. *Journal of Otolaryngology, 10*, 440–448.

Simon, B. M., Fowler, S. M., & Handler, S. D. (1983). Communication development in young children with long-term tracheostomies: Preliminary report. *International Journal of Pediatric Oto Rhino Laryngology, 6*(1), 37–50.

Skinner, B. F. (1971). *Beyond freedom and dignity*. New York: Knopf.

Snyder, M., Berscheid, E., & Tanke, E. D. (1977). Social perception and interpersonal behavior: On the self-fulfilling nature of social stereotypes. *Journal of Personality and Social Psychology, 35*, 656–666.

Spivack, G., & Shure, M. B. (1974). *Social adjustment of young children: A cognitive approach to solving real-life problems*. Washington, DC: Jossey-Bass.

Staub, E. (1975). *The development of prosocial behavior in children*. Morristown, NJ: General Learning Press.

Strodtbeck, F. L., & Mann, R. D. (1956). Sex role differentiation in jury deliberation. *Sociometry, 19*, 3–11.

Tait, N. A., Michel, J. F., & Carpenter, M. A. (1980). Maximum duration of /s/ and /z/ in children. *Journal of Speech and Hearing Disorders*, *45*(239).

Tanner, J. (1969). Growth and endocrinology of the adolescent. In L. Gardner (Ed.), *Endocrine and genetic diseases for childhood*. Philadelphia: Saunders.

Tavris, C. (1982). *Anger, the misunderstood emotion*. New York: Simon & Schuster.

Titze, I. R. (1976). On the mechanics of vocal-fold vibration. *Journal of the Acoustical Society of America*, *60*, 1366–1380.

Titze, I. R. (1980, September). Comments on the myoelastic-aerodynamic theory of phonation. *Journal of Speech and Hearing Research*, *23*(3), 495–510.

Titze, I. R. (1981). Biomechanics and distributed-mass models of vocal fold vibration. In M. Hirano & K. N. Stevens (Eds.), *Vocal fold physiology*. Tokyo, Japan: University of Tokyo Press.

Vandell, D. L., & George, L. B. (1981). Social interaction in hearing and deaf preschoolers: Successes and failures in initiations. *Child Development*, *51*, 627–635.

Van Riper, C. (1972). *Speech correction: Principles and methods* (5th Ed.). Englewood Cliffs, NJ: Prentice-Hall.

Van Riper, C., & Irwin, J. V. (1958). *Voice and articulation*. Englewood Cliffs, NJ: Prentice-Hall.

Vendler, Z. (1968). *Adjectives and nominalizations*. The Hague: Mouton.

Vuorenkoski, V., Lenko, H., Tjernlund, P., Vuorenkoski, L., & Perheentupa, J. (1978). Fundamental voice frequency during normal and abnormal growth, and after androgen treatment. *Archives of Disease in Childhood*, *53*, 201–209.

Warr-Leeper, Y. A., McShea, R. S., & Leeper, H. A. (1979). The incidence of voice and speech deviations in a middle school population. *Language, Speech and Hearing Services in Schools*, *10*, 14–20.

Weinberg, B., & Bennett, D. (1971). Speaker sex recognition of 5- and 6-year-old children's voices. *Journal of the Acoustical Society of America*, *50*, 1210–1213.

Weinberg, B., & Zlatin, M. (1970). Speaking fundamental frequency characteristics of five- and six-year-old children with mongolism. *Journal of Speech and Hearing Research*, *13*, 418–425.

Welch, R. C., & Harvin, V. R. (1976). Strategies for developing concepts in elementary school mathematics. *Viewpoints*, Bulletin School of Education, Indiana University, *52*(1), 13–26.

Werner, H., & Kaplan, B. (1963). *Symbol formation*. New York: Wiley.

Westlake, H., & Rutherford, D. (1961). Speech therapy for the cerebral palsied. Chicago, IL: National Society for Crippled Children and Ádults.

Wiener, F. D., Lewnau, L. E., & Erway, E. (1983). Measuring language competency in speakers of black American English. *Journal of Speech and Hearing Disorders, 48*, 76–84.

Wilder, C. N., & Baken, R. J., (1974). Respiratory patterns in infant cry. *Human Communication, 3*, 18–34.

Wilson, D. Kenneth (1972). *Voice problems of children.* Baltimore, MD: Williams & Wilkins.

Wilson, D. Kenneth (1979). *Voice problems of children* (2d Ed.). Baltimore, MD: Williams & Wilkins.

Wilson, F. B. (1971). The voice disordered child: A descriptive approach. *Language, Speech and Hearing Services in Schools, 4*, 14–22.

Wirz, S. L., Subtelny, J. D., & Whitehead, R. L. (1981). Perceptual and spectrographic study of tense voice in normal hearing and deaf subjects. *Folia Phoniatrica, 33*, 23–36.

Withers, B. T. (1961). Vocal nodules. *Eye, Ear, Nose, Throat Monograph, 40*, 35–38.

Word, C. O., Zanna, M. P., & Cooper, J. (1974). The nonverbal mediation of self-fulfilling prophecies in interracial interaction. *Journal of Experimental Social Psychology, 10*, 109–120.

Wyke, Barry (1974). Laryngeal reflex mechanisms in phonation. Paper presented at the Sixteenth Internationl Congress on Logopedics and Phoniatrics, Interlaken, Switzerland, 528–537.

Zemlin, W. R. (1981). *Speech and hearing science.* Englewood Cliffs, NJ: Prentice-Hall.

Sample
Worksheets

Voice Pictures (pitch changes)

Name_____

Grade_____

1. We can make word pictures by making our voice sound like a picture in our minds. We can make a word sound high or low. A squeak is high and a grunt is _____. Color the high words red and the low words blue, and then read the words aloud.

roof	deep	father	thunder	sky
basement	twinkle	baby	piglet	dark
tunnel	tweet	mice	kite	moose
air	moo	elephants	anchor	pin

2. Sometimes we slide our voices up or down. Pretend you are sliding down a slide. Move your finger down the picture of the slide as your voice goes down on "ah." Slide your voice as you say these words:

   dropped ↓

   soared ↗

   kites fly up ↗

   arrows shoot up ↗

   leaves fall down ↓

   elevators go up ↗ and down ↓

   helicopters lift off ↗ and land ↓

   rockets zoom ↗ and crash ↓

   dive down ↓ and pop up ↗

3. When we ask a question, the end of the sentence goes up. Let's make questions from these words and sentences.

Who?	Me?	You?
Now?	Today?	He can play?
Are you coming?	Whose is it?	

Let's take turns saying the same words. You say it like a question and I'll say it like an answer. Then we'll switch.

Yours?	Yours!	Tomorrow?	Tomorrow!
Chocolate?	Chocolate!	Um?	Um!
OK?	OK!	No?	No!
Maybe?	Maybe!	Bedtime?	Bedtime!

4. When we are feeling good, our voices show it. Our voices can smile and make happy voice pictures, or our voices can frown.

   Draw a happy face or a frowning face beside the words as I say them. Then you read the words to me. (Did you match your voice to the face you drew?)

No way	recess	swimming
I won't do it	Christmas	angry
It's my birthday	It's broken	scared
He's a bully	ice cream	movies

5. Find some words and phrases in your reading book that make good voice pictures. Write them on this sheet and then practice saying them either high or low.

Voice Pictures
(loudness changes)

Name_____

Grade_____

1. One way to make words interesting is to make pictures of the words with our voices. This makes an important word sound different from the others near it. Sometimes we make a word loud so that people will really notice it. Underline words you think should be said louder than the other words in these sentences.

   The gun went bang.
   She hit the water with a splash.
   The boy yelled at me.
   The plane crashed.
   "Stop," he said.

2. Most people know about making words loud, but that is not the only way to make people take notice of a special word. Sometimes, if a word is soft, it really gets noticed even more.

   Think about the words that are underlined and how a soft voice might make the best pictures.

The story made me <u>shiver</u>.	The dog's ears are <u>silky</u>.
It was <u>dead</u> as could be.	I know a <u>secret</u>.
I <u>hate</u> it.	A <u>gentle</u> animal.
It's <u>delicious</u>.	A <u>slimy</u> snake.
<u>Warm</u> cocoa.	A <u>ghost</u> lives here.

3. Feelings show through our voices. The way we use our voices affects how other people feel when they hear us, too. Finish the sentences below.

   a. When people yell loudly at me, I feel

   _____.

   b. My mom makes me feel good when she talks to me in a

   _____ voice.

   c. When people are tense, their voices sound

   _____.

d. Some people get a headache if the voices around them are

_____.

e. If I want to frighten someone, I sometimes use a

_____.

f. If I want to comfort or calm someone, I try to use a

_____ voice.

4. A voice that is always loud or a voice that is always soft is boring to listen to. We need to vary our voices if we want people to listen to what we are saying. Practice saying the sentences that follow in different ways. At least two words in each sentence are picture words. Circle them first and then think how you'll say them.

a. It was quiet, and then came the thunder.

b. The scream made him scared.

c. The ship exploded and sank.

d. The dog crouched, then attacked.

e. The siren got louder and louder.

f. The door banged, and the tap dripped.

Voice Pictures (duration changes)

Name_____

Grade_____

1. When we talk slowly or quickly all the time, our words all sound the same. We can make different word pictures if we have a change of pace. Read this sentence in six different ways.

   The man went down the road. (He was walking fast; he was on crutches; he stopped after every second step; he was running; he walked jerkily; he drove smoothly in a big car.)

2. Sometimes it is fun to make pictures by changing the rate of different groups of words. Some words can be made long and others can be made short to make special pictures. What words in the paragraph below would you make long or short? Say them aloud, and then fill in the columns

   The Indian trod carefully through the forest. A twig snapped. He quickened his pace and began running. He ran faster and faster and then stopped. A slow smile crossed his face.

Long	**Short**
carefully	quickened

   Now read the passage aloud, varying the rate of each sentence.

3. When we stop talking, we give our listeners time to think about what we have said. We use pauses to make our meaning clear and to take in air. Periods and commas tell us to stop, but we have to choose other places to pause also. In the following paragraph, mark places where you would pause. Then read it aloud.

   The boy who was wearing a red shirt and blue pants was walking faster than the girl who was trailing behind him. He suddenly came to a halt and turned to her and called "Come on or we'll miss the bus."

4. Sometimes we stop before or after important words so that they stand out from the others. In the following sentences try to think of as many different places to pause as you can. Then discuss how pausing alters the meaning. For example,

I .... hate you.
I *hate* .... you.
I hate *you* .....

a. Give it to the most deserving person.
b. Peanut butter sticks to the roof of your mouth.
c. Cigarettes have been proved to cause lung cancer.
d. Give me time to answer the question please.

Producing Mouth Sounds in Isolation

Name_____

Grade_____

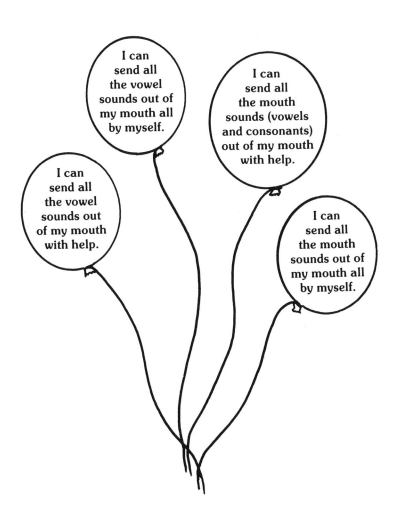

I can send all the vowel sounds out of my mouth all by myself.

I can send all the mouth sounds (vowels and consonants) out of my mouth with help.

I can send all the vowel sounds out of my mouth with help.

I can send all the mouth sounds out of my mouth all by myself.

Producing Mouth Sounds in Monosyllabic Words

Name_____

Grade_____

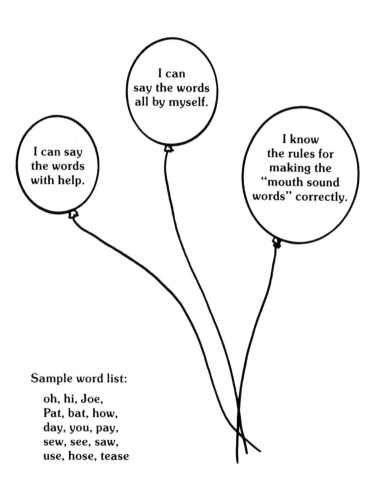

I can
say the words
all by myself.

I can say
the words
with help.

I know
the rules for
making the
"mouth sound
words" correctly.

Sample word list:

oh, hi, Joe,
Pat, bat, how,
day, you, pay,
sew, see, saw,
use, hose, tease

Producing Mouth Sounds in Sentences

Name_____

Grade_____

Sample sentences:

Oh, hello.
Hi, Joe.
Bill is a boy.
How are you?
I love to eat.
Show it to her.
Give her a cookie.
Yes, please, Ted.
Ray is sick.
Go away, Liz.

Star speaker
of mouth
sounds in
sentences.

I can say sentences
(all mouth
sounds) all
by myself.

I can say
sentences (all
mouth sounds)
with help.

Evaluation of Anticipatory and Retroactive Nasality

Name_____

Grade_____

1. Listed below are a list of syllables and a list of words using the syllables. Practice saying these words and syllables into a tape recorder and then listen to how you sound.

Syllables		Words	
nar	arng	mar	arm
nor	orng	nor	horn
noo	oong	new	tune
ner	erng	nerve	burn
nee	eeng	meat	teen

2. Now make up some sentences using these words and syllables. Write them down and then say them into the tape recorder.

_____

_____

_____

_____

_____

_____

I can tell when I open the door

a. too soon ———————— in syllables
              in words
              in sentences

b. too late ———————— in syllables
              in words
              in sentences

WORKSHEET 8
Evaluation of Production

Name_____

Grade_____

I made the mouth sounds well because

_____ 1. I opened my mouth wide.
_____ 2. I talked slowly.
_____ 3. I lengthened the vowels.
_____ 4. I thought about closing the door.
_____ 5. I marked the hard words on the page before I started to read.
_____ 6. I kept my tongue down/relaxed.
_____ 7. I used my lips well.
_____ 8. I used a low pitch.
_____ 9. I dropped my jaw.
_____ 10. I took a deep breath.
_____ 11. I said it loudly.

I can make the mouth sounds well in

_____ 1. Syllables
_____ 2. Words
_____ 3. Carrier phrases
_____ 4. Reading sentences
_____ 5. Sentence completions
_____ 6. Conversation

Timing of the Evaluation

Name_____

Grade_____

Fill in the blanks below by inserting words that rhyme with **clown**. Think about the vowel sound. See if you can prevent opening the trap door too soon. Then listen to the tape recording of the sentences as we play them back, and judge them!

a. Smile, don't _____.

b. My shoes are _____.

c. Another name for a city is a _____.

d. A naming word is a _____.

e. A dress can be called a _____.

f. Not up, but _____.

I knew it was correct--incorrect

_____ a. after I said it.
_____ b. while I was saying it.
_____ c. when I was getting ready to say it.

Resonance Self-Evaluation Checklist

Name_____

Grade_____

    _____ 1. I can identify mouth and nose sound.

    _____ 2. I can tell when the door is open or closed.

    _____ 3. I can say all vowels with the door closed.

    _____ 4. I can tell when a vowel sound comes out of my nose and I can change it.

    _____ 5. I can describe all of the rules.

    _____ 6. I can say words with all mouth sounds.

    _____ 7. I can say sentences with all mouth sounds.

    _____ 8. I can say both mouth and nose sounds in one word.

    _____ 9. I can say sentences containing both nose and mouth sounds.

    _____ 10. I know when I make a mistake with nose and mouth sounds in words.

    _____ 11. I can think of a "trick" to correct any mistake I've made.

    _____ 12. I can use a "trick" to prevent making mistakes.

WORKSHEET 11
Maximizing Resonance
(sound carriers)

Name_____

Grade_____

1. In the following wordlist circle all the "sound carrying" consonants. Some are short sounds that are exploded and are over quickly. Some continue longer, and we can hang on to the vibrations.

ham	find	zip	bell	Vi
melt	zonk	lemon	than	melon

Now list all the voiced plosives and all the voiced continuants.

Voiced Plosives
(short sounds)

1. _____   4. _____

2. _____   5. _____

3. _____   6. _____

Voiced Continuants
(long sounds)

1. _____   4. _____

2. _____   5. _____

3. _____   6. _____

2. Vowels are good "sound carriers" too. Write down all the different vowels in the words above.

1. _____   6. _____

2. _____   7. _____

3. _____   8. _____

4. _____   9. _____

5. _____   10. _____

3. Listen to some vowels and consonants together in small words. When I say the words, put a check beside the ones where I make the most of the "soundcarrying" consonants.

am	zee	no	ill	my	Ev
I'm	vee	all	owl	lie	in

4. Some people say the vowel too fast and don't give it time to vibrate well. Remember that the vowel is the heart of the word—if I say the vowel too quickly, the word is "scrunched up" and has no heart. Draw a heart over the words where I "open up" and vibrate the vowel sound well. Draw an X through the ones I don't say well.

hat   boy   down   moon   sell

fail   go   ways   trees   pies

5. Some hints for making our voices carry are these:

   a. Open the mouth well.
   b. Make sure the vowel vibrates on the bones of the face.
   c. "Vibrate" the soundcarrying consonants on the front of the face.
   d. "Hang on to" the consonants that can be continued.
   e. Use lips and tongue well to explode the consonants that are short.
   f. Linger on the vowel—it is the heart or center of the word.

6. While I say these words, you tell me what I can do to improve them

   me   oil   Lyn   need
   bees   nob   I've   them

7. Now *you* say the words, and I'll tell you which of the hints you remembered and which you forgot. Before you begin, tell me again what the hints are. I'll put an X beside each hint every time you forget it.

Hints	Trials
mouth opening	
vibrations on face	
use of lips and tongue	
"hang on to" the continuants	

8. Some people like gym a lot because you exercise your whole body. When we "work out" on words, using the muscles of our lips and tongue and throwing vibrations to the front of our face, it is sometimes called "mouth gym." Do some "mouth gym" on the following words. After each try, mark the columns.

Words practiced	Felt like a good workout	Could be better	Lots of vibrations	Could be more vibrations
1. maybe				
2. lady				
3. Daddy				
4. Danny				
5. baby				
6. navy				
7. thieves				
8. shoes				
9. coming				
10. angle				

Maximizing Resonance (projected speech)

Name_____

Grade_____

1. Write down as many suggestions as you can think of to help people improve the way their voices carry.

2. Imagine you are playing outdoors and you want someone to hear you. Show me how you would throw your voice across the distance as you say the following:

   "I'm coming."
   "No, I don't want any."
   "The ball wasn't in."
   "Throw it to me."

3. Show me how you would mark the following passage if you were practicing it to speak in a large hall at a school.

   Ladies and gentlemen. You all know that our principal is leaving our school. On behalf of all of the children I would like to present him with this present.

   Now stand up and pretend you are speaking the words in the large, noisy hall.

4. Record the following sentences or fragments using the best tone focus and richest voice you can. Then listen while they are replayed and mark the sentences with a + or a − to show the ones you think need more practice.

   _____ 1. Rising and soaring, the birds flew away.
   _____ 2. Boys and girls running to school
   _____ 3. No one knows the trouble I've seen.
   _____ 4. I'm never able to buy pies and peas.
   _____ 5. These plains belonged to the Indians.
   _____ 6. I've got spurs that jingle and jangle.
   _____ 7. *Fee, fi, fo, fum*, I smell an Englishman.
   _____ 8. Yo, ho, ho and a barrel of rum
   _____ 9. The pirates of Penzance sang of their treasure with pleasure.

5. Prepare five questions that you would ask me in an interview on television. Write them down for homework. Practice them aloud. When you ask me the questions, pretend you are a professional speaker in front of a large studio audience.

WORKSHEET 13
Describing Angry Feelings

Name_____

Grade_____

1. Circle the things that you believe make most people feel angry with others:

being called names

being put down

being treated unfairly

not being given an equal

   share (treats, time,

   attention, etc.)

being physically hurt

having others touch their

   property

having others take their

   property

having others destroy their

   property

feeling they are not

   respected (liked, loved,

   believed, listened to)

2. Add any other things (or situations) that you can think of.

3. Circle the things that you believe make most people angry with themselves:

when they do something

   dumb

when they break something

when they don't do as well as

   they'd hoped (in school, in

   sports, in handling a tough

   situation, etc.)

when they lie or cheat

when they don't do

   something to correct an

   unfair situation

when they lose control

when they feel bad inside

4. Add any other things (or situations) that you can think of.

5. Everyone gets angry. Some people get more angry at some things than at others. Can you think of some examples? For example, what is something your mom gets angry about that you don't (e.g., mud on the kitchen floor)? Your teacher (e.g., too much noise in the room)? Why do you think people react differently?

6. Anger can be expressed lots of different ways. We often *choose* the way we want to express it. How we choose to express it depends on

   a. the situation. What if your sister makes a face at you in church?
   b. the person we are angry with. Compare your reaction to someone spilling your soft drink—an infant, your worst enemy, etc.
   c. what we know (or suspect) about a person's intentions. Think about someone who "forgets" to give you an important message.
   d. the possible penalty. If you are angry with your teacher or your brother would you express it the same way?
   e. how badly you feel.

7. Getting angry is ok as long as we do not let our anger keep spoiling our chances of getting what we want. Think of all of the different ways anger can be expressed. We make different choices at different times. Some ways we can choose to express our anger follow:

   a. using our voice (list some ways)
   b. using our body
   c. confronting the cause head-on
   d. redirecting or transforming the feelings
   e. putting off expressing the feelings until later

8. List some situations where you saw other people get angry. Describe the choices they made in expressing their anger.

9. Complete these sentences:

   a. When my mom is angry, her voice sounds

      _____.

   b. I know my teacher is angry when _____.

   c. If I want to make my friend angry, I

      _____.

   d. When I'm a parent, I'll get angry if my kids

      _____.

   e. When people get angry, they should

      _____.

Handling Our Angry Feelings

Name_____

Grade_____

1. List some things that always make *you* angry.

2. Describe the last time you were really angry at someone.

3. Describe the last time you were really angry at yourself.

4. How did you handle your anger? Did your choice work well for you? What benefits or penalties did you receive?

5. Describe the things you do most often when you are angry:

   a. With your voice.

   b. With your body.

   c. To make yourself feel better.

   d. What do you think you most want to achieve when you express your anger?

6. What are some ways you know to express your feelings of anger without hurting yourself (your own feelings, your own body, etc.); without hurting others (their feelings, their body, their things); without hurting your voice; without damaging your relationships?

Describing Anxious Feelings

Name_____

Grade_____

1. Underline the things that you believe make most people anxious:

When the doctor wants to give a shot.

When someone wants a fight.

When someone is mad with them.

When they are alone in the dark.

When they don't feel cared for (loved, understood).

When something is their fault.

When they've told a lie.

When they are in a strange place.

When they don't have any friends.

When they don't know what to expect.

When they think they'll fail or be punished.

Can you think of some other things?

2. Everyone feels scared and anxious sometimes. List some situations that you know cause some of your friends to be anxious or worried.

3. What are some signs that a person is anxious or worried?

    a. in their voice?

    b. in their body?

    c. in things they do?

4. Think about some of the ways different people try to deal with their feelings of anxiety.

   a. Admitting that they are anxious sometimes helps.
   b. Identifying the cause of the problem may be useful.
   c. Talking about it sometimes makes them feel better.
   d. Asking questions about what is happening can help too.
   e. Yelling and screaming sometimes makes people feel worse.
   f. Strained, tense talking is hard on their throat if they do it too much.
   g. Trying to relax can sometimes ease pain.
   h. Some people talk too loudly or too much when they are frightened.

5. Complete these sentences:

   a. It's hard for me to _____.

   b. I feel silly when _____.

   c. Sometimes I'm afraid of _____.

   d. I hate it when _____.

   e. I am afraid to _____.

   f. I would hate to lose my _____.

   g. I was really scared once when _____.

   h. When I am scared, my voice sounds _____.

   i. When I am frightened, I cover it up by _____.

   j. After I cry, I _____.

Handling Our Anxious Feelings

Name_____

Grade_____

1. List some things that always make you anxious.

2. Describe the last time you were really anxious about something.

3. How did you handle your anxiety? Did you feel better because of what you did to deal with your feelings?

4. Suggest some ways you could deal with your anxiety (without straining your voice) in the following situations:

   a. when someone is mean or teases you

   b. when you want to act as if you are not scared

   c. when someone blames you for something you didn't do

   d. when someone tries to pick a fight with you

5. Sometimes, the way we talk to ourselves (inside our heads) helps us to feel better when we are frightened or anxious. Check the things you sometimes say to yourself:

_____ It will be over soon.
_____ It's not that bad, really.
_____ Just pretend you feel fine.
_____ Please, God, help me through this.
_____ I can do it.
_____ Even grown-ups feel scared sometimes.

What are some other things you say to yourself?

Words to Practice Easy Onset of Phonation

Name_____

Grade_____

and	extra	ashen
add	amateur	Ellen
ouch	amiable	Eleanor
all	Edgar	American
ant	elephant	oozing
art	eggplant	underground
eat	animosity	uncle
ate	expert	unaware
old	appetite	ostrich
ache	anxious	onion
Andy	alternate	office
Alfie	eccentric	oddity
ill	excruciating	autumn
Eve	outsize	evenings
our	outhouse	ancient
every	instinct	undecided
own	Asia	ostentatious
each	Africa	unrolled
ice	Australia	awesome
out	Iceland	oatmeal
I'd	outer	ocean
eyes	igloo	Oxford
is	inland	Ottawa
easy	irrigate	oxygen
able	Easter Islands	outpost

Index